Kenneth S. Rhee
and
Stephanie L. Rhee

Doing
Exemplary
Research

To our children
Paul, Caitlin, and Maeve; Brigid and Kerry

Doing Exemplary Research

Edited by
Peter J. Frost
Ralph E. Stablein

SAGE PUBLICATIONS
The International Professional Publishers
Newbury Park London New Delhi

The cover art *In Search of Creativity #1* is copyrighted by the artist Carla Weaver. For permission to use copyrighted material, acknowledgment is made on pages 19, 49, 79, 113, 143, 179, 207, 240. On page 16, the panel, "Stairway to Heaven" which is part of the Ngata screen included in Mau Mahara—Our Stories in Craft, is used by permission of the Crafts Council of New Zealand, Inc., and by permission of Henare K. Ngata (the artist's son). The drawing on page 293 is by Johannes Richter.

For information address:

SAGE Publications, Inc.
2455 Teller Road
Newbury Park, California 91320

SAGE Publications Ltd.
6 Bonhill Street
London EC2A 4PU
United Kingdom

SAGE Publications India Pvt. Ltd.
M-32 Market
Greater Kailash I
New Delhi 110 048 India

Printed in the United States of America

Library of Congress Cataloging-in-Publication Data

Main entry under title:

Doing exemplary research / edited by Peter Frost, Ralph Stablein.
    p. cm.
    Includes bibliographical references.
    ISBN 0-8039-3908-6. — ISBN 0-8039-3909-4 (pbk.)
    1. Social sciences—Research—Case studies. 2. Organizational
sociology—Research—Case studies. 3. Organizational behavior—
Research—Case studies. I. Frost, Peter J. II. Stablein, Ralph E.
H62.D617 1992
300'.72—dc20   91-37216

92 93 94 95 10 9 8 7 6 5 4 3 2 1

Sage Production Editor: Astrid Virding

Contents

Part II. Lessons from the Journeys

Foreword

Absorbing. Instructive. These are at least two of the words that best describe this book for me. It is absorbing in the sense that any good book of short stories draws readers in and holds their interest tightly from one chapter to the next—virtually a "can't put it down until I've finished" volume. It is, then, thoroughly engrossing in a charmingly engaging manner. However, the book is also much more than that— much more than the proverbial "good read." This is because it is also highly instructive in the way in which it makes you think and ponder while you are perusing it. No one, rookie or veteran, can come away from this collection of commentaries and observations without having learned something at a deeper level about the research process. This volume illuminates and teaches as well as entertains. For this, we in the field of organizational studies—researchers, teachers, and students—owe the originators/editors, Drs. Frost and Stablein, a debt of gratitude for providing this kind of innovative input and assistance to our mutual endeavors.

The book presents an intriguing combination of excerpts from seven "exemplary" articles, retrospective views on those articles by their respective authors, and commentaries by knowledgeable scholars in the field who are able to provide unique insights on the research process behind a given article and/or its particular contributions to expanding our knowledge of organizational phenomena. In this observer's view, it is not just the individual elements by themselves that make this volume so valuable; rather, it is the blending of those elements into a coherent whole that makes the sum greater than the parts. To put it another way: This book is more than a simple collection of related pieces of work; it is, instead, a carefully constructed intellectual product. The value of this product is also expanded considerably by the analytical overviews of themes and implications of the sampled exemplary research provided by the editors in the final two essays in the book.

It is important to emphasize that this book focuses primarily on the process, as opposed to the content, of good research in our field. As such, it provides a much-needed redress to our habitual tendency to devote most of our attention to looking at results rather than also considering the kinds of efforts that were involved in obtaining those results. With its concentration on the research process, this book tells us something about the current state of our field and its relative degree of maturity. It is doubtful that such a volume could have been put together with this much depth and degree of perspective as recently as 10 years ago. We have had a great expansion, not only in the amount of research in the organizational field in the past decade or so, but, even more consequentially, in the types, methods, and approaches to doing research. It is this development that makes this book both possible and, especially, timely. It is also why, when one reflects on the contents of this book, there are substantial grounds for optimism about the future of our field.

As the editors point out in their introduction, they wisely avoided attempting to select the "best" articles of the 1980s. Rather, they chose "seven very good articles that may serve as templates or models for other good research," that is, seven exemplary articles. In so doing, and together with their elicitation, they have produced an exemplary book.

Lyman W. Porter
Professor, Graduate School of Management
University of California, Irvine

Preface

This book is about the science, art, and craft of research. It reports the journeys taken on seven different investigations by researchers who were interested in understanding phenomena relevant to organizational life. In some cases investigators traveled alone; in others they proceeded in the company of others. The reader will quickly discover that none of these endeavors was truly solitary. All the research described here involved collaboration of one kind or another. Investigators drew on and were offered information, advice, critique, and support along the way. The stories they tell as they reflect on the work they report here are stories of passion, persistence, immersion in ideas and data, and a measure of good fortune. We think that established researchers as well as those who are beginning to learn their craft will find much in the stories that will intrigue them.

While the research field in this book is organizational analysis, broadly defined, the emphasis is on the process of doing empirical research, rather than on any particular topic or theme or on the use of any particular method. We present ideas and information through examination of the recollections of investigators and the observations of commentators about what might make this process exemplary.

We hope that what the reader finds here will help to demystify what goes on in research. We are particularly interested in providing those in various professions who are new to the research craft with ideas about how good work gets done. We encourage readers to compare what they read with other sources on research and with their own experiences of the process. The research act as depicted in many research texts seems to us to be somewhat idealized, abstract, and mechanical. When we look at the research product in journals it resembles a rather stylized and even sterile product. There is rarely much more than a hint to the reader in texts and in published articles of what went on behind the scenes when the research was being done, of the human face of research. Drawing on the research exemplars in this book, we have learned that doing research is a much messier and more imperfect endeavor than most official sources of information about the process recognize or admit. It is also more personal. People doing research become intrigued, excited, frustrated, and depressed along the investigation trail. They experience despair and exhilaration. They are often puzzled and surprised by what they find. Along the way to completing their studies, the researchers who write about their experiences in this book appear to have acquired a mixture of humility and wisdom.

It is not possible, nor would we argue, that the self-reported experiences associated with seven empirical studies tell the whole story of so complex an enterprise as research. However, we think the candor of the reporters in this volume will ring true for many who have been engaged extensively in their own research. It is our fond hope that those who read this book will find insights and ideas that will inform and inspire them in their own work. We encourage readers to compare their own experiences of the research process with those presented here and to challenge and expand the frontiers of what we know about this important process. We think it deserves a wider and more open discourse than we perceive exists at present.

In the Introduction, we describe the origins of the project, outline its aims, and explain the selection of exemplars. We describe the studies in the set. Part I then provides the reader with seven case reports, one for each of the studies. Each report includes a recollective piece by the investigator or investigators. Each recollection describes, in the words of the researcher(s), the origins, experiences, and outcomes of the study. Each report also includes two commentaries by scholars who are familiar with the study and who have expertise in the topic. Each report is accompanied by excerpts that illustrate the formal research output of the study being discussed.

Part II of the book comprises two essays. In the first, we describe and discuss several themes and issues about the research process that emerge from an analysis of the seven reports. In the second, we identify several metathemes and issues that we believe are relevant to debates and discussions aimed at enhancing the research process and developing the potential of apprentice researchers.

We have been equal partners on this journey. It has taken us jointly to Vancouver, Canada, to San Francisco and to Los Angeles in the United States, and to Dunedin in New Zealand. We have traversed some fascinating intellectual territory as we have worked with the stories that constitute the bulk of the book. Like the authors of these reports, we have received much help along the way. We are most grateful to the investigators whose work is discussed here. They have had the courage to share their experiences candidly with us and with you, the reader. Thank you to Stephen R. Barley, James N. Baron, Frank R. Dobbin, Cathy A. Enz, Miriam Erez, Debra C. Gash, Connie J. G. Gersick, P. Devereaux Jennings, John M. Jermier, Gary P. Latham, Edwin A. Locke, Alan D. Meyer, Gordon W. Meyer, Anat Rafaeli, and Robert I. Sutton. Our thanks go also to the commentators who took the time and the care to give us their assessments of the research on which the reports were based: Janice M. Beyer, John P. Campbell, Larry L. Cummings, P. Christopher Earley, J. Richard Hackman, Joanne Martin, Richard T. Mowday, Walter W. Powell, Linda L. Putnam, Linda Smircich, Barry M. Staw, Pamela S. Tolbert, Karl E. Weick, and Mayer N. Zald. John Van Maanen gave us some wise and pointed feedback when we were starting out on this project. We may not have taken all his advice, but John forced us to be clear about our intentions and to be wary about developing an unmanageable product. We are grateful to the nominators for taking our call seriously and thus giving us the base from which to build the set of exemplars: Stephen Barley, Janice Beyer, William Barnett, Terry Connolly, L. L. Cummings, Dennis Gioia, Robert Guion, Michael Harris, David Hickson, Nancy Langton, Thomas A. Mahoney, Joanne Martin, Richard Mowday, Walter Nord, Jeffrey Pfeffer, Craig Pinder, Linda Putnam, Linda Smircich, John Van Maanen, and Karl Weick.

We also received many helpful comments and criticisms from participants at seminars we gave at the universities of Alberta, British Columbia, California, Irvine, and Otago. Thank you Bob Hinings, Ann Tsui, Larry Shetzer, and John Selsky for inviting us to your seminars. Our special thanks to Ken MacCrimmon, who read the nearly complete manuscript and tested portions in the classroom. We are grateful to the universities of British Columbia and Otago for partially funding this project. Bill Hicks of Jossey-Bass Publishers and Ann West of Sage Publications gave generously of their time and expertise when we were getting started. Ann West has been our patient champion throughout the journey. Our thanks also to Sarah Gaze who has patiently and skillfully managed the production of the working draft of this book. Thanks, too, to Sonya Foley and Valerie Thompson for their production support. We wish to acknowledge the contribution of artist Carla Weaver of Vancouver, B.C., who created the painting *In Search of Creativity #1*, used as the cover for this book. Finally, we appreciate the work done by all the Sage personnel. We accept responsibility for any errors and omissions in this manuscript.

Introduction

Genesis of the Book

For several months, I had been having this recurring thought that it might be interesting to write a book about the way research is conducted in our field. I have an abiding interest in process, in trying to reveal and understand processes underlying organized action. I had worked with Larry Cummings on a project that focused on journal publication, which had been published as *Publishing in the Organizational Sciences* (Cummings & Frost, 1985). I had learned a great deal about the publishing game from that exercise. I also recalled how much energy and time we had invested in that project, and I was reluctant to put myself through that experience again. So I kept pushing the thought away. However, I have come to recognize in myself over time that some ideas that start somewhere in my psyche simply will not go away when told to do so. They seem to develop lives of their own. They start showing up in my dreams and even seem to trigger waking periods that start reliably at 3:30 in the morning. Eventually, I find myself having to give these ideas voice in some way.

This was one such idea. At this stage it was a half-formed notion, more of an intuition that some shape could be given to an investigation of the research process that would be informative and interesting to me. Like *Publishing in the Organizational Sciences*, it might serve to make accessible to readers the sometimes daunting and mysterious craft and tools of our profession. Research methodology is not an area I claim to be expert in, so I needed to team up with someone who could compensate where I lacked expertise. I also wanted such a joint venture to be a creative undertaking and to be intellectually stimulating. I wanted the journey to be personally enjoyable. I did not have to reflect for very long on who might bring qualities and energy to the project that would help me meet these objectives. One likely colleague worked right next door to me at UBC . . . (P. J. Frost)

Ring, ring . . .

In the midst of my final days of packing for the big move to New Zealand, I had a call from Peter, my UBC colleague. We were next-door neighbors in the Commerce office building on UBC's well-tended campus. Four and a half years earlier, I had applied for my first position at UBC (they had not advertised), in part because of a perceived commonality of outlook with Peter. We often talked and always had intended to collaborate on something, but never had. Now I was moving on, having decided tenure was unattainable due to a combination of paralysis under the always kind but constant evaluation of the department, unbalanced time management that favored teaching and maintaining general command of the organizational literature, and my personal life choices in meeting, marrying, and having a child with my partner.

To me, Peter's suggestion sounded like an exciting and intellectually rewarding project. I knew that I would enjoy working with Peter and knew that I would learn a lot from, and with, him.

I didn't want to write about how to do research. I had rejected this approach in my teaching practice. On the whole it reduced the problem to one of method and technique, the application of rules. Instead, I designed my research seminar around building students' decision-making capacities by examining the philosophical, historical, and sociological context of research. A variety of methodological choices in organizational studies were illustrated by looking at, and discussing, good examples from the organizational literature. Over the next several months these and other ideas bubbled on the back burner as I looked for housing, designed and taught new courses, cared for a new baby, and so on. (R. E. Stablein)

1

The Project Begins to Take Shape

We were able to get together at the Academy of Management meetings in Anaheim, California, in 1988, to share the results of our independent musings. We were pleasantly surprised to discover that our ideas had developed in similar directions. Fruitful brainstorming and piggybacking ensued, reinforcing our shared excitement and hope for the project. From this point our perspective on the project has been sufficiently shared to make us comfortable with the use of the collective first-person pronoun throughout.

We began the book project talking about the need to provide an effective primer on the new methods in the field. We wrote a book plan that we eventually sent to two publishers. Our original book plan claimed:

> The approach of this book is to provide an aid to doing research that utilizes "new" (at least to organization studies) techniques or methods. The book is particularly timely because many of these new techniques are now established enough to be worthy of examination. They are no longer purely of curiosity or novelty value. On the other hand, they are not well-understood, well-used tools in the researchers' kitbag. To date, expertise in these methods has been limited to relatively small groups, usually advocates of a particular theoretical position (e.g., organizational culture and symbolism, critical perspectives, transaction costs) that has been buttressed by research using these new methods. The persistence of these new schools of thought in organization studies and their growing acceptance and effect on the mainstream of the field requires that all serious scholars begin to develop an independent capacity for the evaluation and practice of these methods.

This excerpt from our book plan reveals the implicit assumptions with which we began the project. We implicitly defined research as the application of techniques, tools, and methods. These methods can, we presumed, be separated from the context and content of their use. They can be learned and appropriated by any serious scholar. We claimed as our book's contribution the further rationalization of organizational research by making these new methods for expanding knowledge widely understood and available. This contribution will increase objectivity by reducing the implicit potential for abuse of the field by the elite subgroups who now control knowledge of these research weapons. The allocation of resources to this effort is justified in efficiency terms: the benefits of acquisition now balancing the costs in effort expenditure. *The Principles of Scientific Research Management* would have been a thoroughly appropriate title to capture the essence of this approach.

As our discussions proceeded, we found ourselves talking about the actual process of getting research done: the excitement of generating ideas, the myriad small and large decisions along the way, the adaptation to surprises and to resource constraints, the acceptance of uncertainty and uninterpretable results, the making sense of it all and grinding it down into a sensible-seeming presentation. Among others, Becker (1986), Daft (1983), Mills (1959), and Wildavsky (1989) have discussed these sorts of research craft issues. We explicitly rejected the conception of research embedded in that book plan. Instead, we clearly identified the uncovering of "good" research processes as the phenomenon to be investigated.

But where to look for direction in "good" process? We inevitably turned to products, to acknowledged good pieces of research. We proceeded on the assumption that good research process is often linked to good research outcome. We did not have a prior conception of the generalizability of good process. Rather, we believed that reflection on the specific experiences of scholars doing exemplary research could provide a basis for individual researchers to explore, and possibly experiment with, their own process.

From this point, two features defined the nature of the emerging book concept. First, our interest broadened from research methodology to include the entire process. Second, we committed ourselves to grounding our discussion in cases of actual research. Thus we focused on identifying "exemplars" and engaging the authors of the exemplars to share their stories of how research was created and produced.

We tested our ideas in separate discussions with Bill Hicks of Jossey-Bass Publishers and Ann West of Sage Publications. They encouraged us and made substantive contributions to our evolving plan. By the end of the meeting, we had concocted a proposal for a curious mixture of original book, edited volume, and book of readings. We would write a few chapters laying out the foundation and context of organizational research. This would be followed by reprints of exemplary research works representing a variety of methods. Each exemplar would be discussed by the author(s) and several independent commentators. A series of bibliographic essays leading the reader to key references for each method would top it off. Publishers were interested, but unanimous in suggesting that we were proposing too much for one book.

Our respect for their opinions and the results of our preliminary drafts of the book plan convinced us that they were right. We came to focus on the exemplars with accompanying commentaries as the key contribution of such a book. We adopt Kuhn's (1970) use of the term *exemplar*:

> By it [exemplar] I mean, initially, the concrete problem-solutions that students encounter from the start of their scientific education, whether in laboratories, on examinations, or at the ends of chapters in science texts. To these shared examples should, however, be added at least some of the technical problem-solutions found in the periodical literature that scientists encounter during their post-education research careers and that also show them by example how their job is to be done. (p. 187)

We focus on "technical problem-solutions found in the periodical literature." Certain studies serve as models to be emulated by others in the same discipline. As such, exemplars are not necessarily the most extraordinary pieces of research, but they are good studies that can serve to define the standards for research practice.

In addition, we chose to limit the domain of the book in several ways. First, we limited our selection of exemplars to the field of organizational studies. This is the area of our training and job experience. Originally, we saw organizational researchers as our audience. Now, we suspect that much of the description and discussion of research process in this book could be beneficial to a variety of audiences. We know that we have benefited from the efforts of researchers in other disciplines, for example, *Sociologists at Work* (Hammond, 1964), which takes an approach similar to ours. We hope those in other business and social science disciplines may learn from the experiences and reflections of organizational scholars.

Second, only empirical work was to be included. Conceptual work was excluded not because it is unimportant or secondary, but because we see conceptual or theoretical research contributions as reasonably distinct from empirical research.

Third, we chose to limit the domain to research published in the 1980s, rather than going back to older classic studies. This decision was motivated by a desire to limit the scope of the task and a presumption that more recent publications would be more relevant, theoretically and methodologically. Also, we felt that the good recent work would partially subsume the lessons of the classics.

Fourth, we chose to limit the domain to journal articles. This decision was initially motivated by the concept of the book, that is, that each exemplar would be reproduced in the book. This decision was strongly challenged by John Van Maanen. In a letter to us, he stated:

> The problem becomes amplified when I try to think of good ethnographic (or, even more broadly, qualitative work) articles. Such studies don't neatly fit journal requirements—at least the organizational ones (Human Orgs and Journal of Contemporary Ethnography, Symbolic Interactionism and Qualitative Sociology being exceptions). Monographs might be more suitable in this category—Moral Mazes, America's Working Man, Bitter Choices, One of the Boys, etc. come to mind here but fall outside the mandate.

Could not these be exemplary? Our domain definition would not allow it. His point led us to a lot of reflection and reconsideration of the decision. Ultimately, and with difficulty, we chose to stick to this domain limitation. We acknowledge the validity of John's point. There are no ethnographies in this book. But that is not because we judge that there are no exemplary organizational ethnographies.

Fifth, constraints on book length dictated that the selection of articles to serve as exemplars would be small. We managed to expand the number slightly by giving up our original conception of reprinting the articles in toto. Instead, we provide excerpts from the original articles that we hope communicate the flavor of the pieces. The articles should be easily available to most readers. We hope they will be consulted in full.

Even with excerpting, we have included only seven exemplars. Many exemplary studies within the domain of the book could not be included. Necessarily many areas of organizational research and several important methodologies are not represented in this selection.

Selection of Exemplars

Once we had decided to focus on journal articles in the decade of the 1980s, we initiated a process of selecting exemplary studies. We created a sample panel of nominators that comprised 40 scholars in the field of organizational studies. We included current and former editors of major relevant journals: *Administrative Science Quarterly, Academy of Management Journal, Academy of Management Review, Organization Science, Organization Studies, Journal of Applied Psychology, Organizational Behavior and Human Decision Processes, Personnel Psychology,* and the *Canadian Journal of Administrative Sciences.* We also drew for our panel from among scholars familiar with qualitative research, with specific research techniques such as LISREL, with approaches to research such as laboratory and field studies, and with particular organizing frameworks such as institutional theory and critical perspectives on organization. We included some of the younger scholars in the field whose judgment on research quality we respected.

To each panel member we sent a brief description of the research project and a questionnaire that simply asked the nominator to identify one or more articles and journals during the 1980s that were examples of outstanding research method and design in the field of organizational studies. We asked nominators to give us a brief rationale for the selection(s) they made and to identify a contact person for the article.

We received replies from 20 nominators, yielding 53 journal articles as exemplars. Some of these exemplars were nominated by two or more members in the sample. All the articles used in the final selection were nominated by more than one individual. Many nominations were single cases of exemplary studies. The sheer number and diversity of nominated studies speaks to how many articles published in journals during the 1980s are considered exemplary. It also signals the range of opinions and judgments in the field about what constitutes excellent published research in journals. The list of nominated articles is presented in the Appendix of this book.

We read all of the comments of the nominators as well as the articles themselves, and then began to make some decisions about which studies we would include for further investigation. We used a number of criteria for inclusion of articles. We must be candid and say that the criteria, the blend of criteria, and the path to our final choices relied on our individual and joint senses of what made for interesting, important, and instructive exemplary research. In the process of our reading and assessment of the papers, we became convinced of the validity of our earlier hunch that it was not possible to separate the research question, the discussion of theory, and the realities of the particular research context from the specific techniques and methods employed. That is, we became less concerned with identifying the best field study, the best LISREL analysis, the most outstanding laboratory experiment, and became instead more interested in the way good research was conducted. From a reading of the papers and a reflection on what we wanted to know about research, we decided to shift from the level of specific technique to a more general level of research as the work of asking questions, of identifying and solving problems.

We strove to identify a selection of papers that, taken together, would represent the diversity that is organizational studies. We conceptualized that diversity along several dimensions. We knew we would not be able to represent any dimensions comprehensively, let alone construct a factorial sampling strategy. However, we consciously examined the following characteristics to help ensure some broadness in our selections and to get some range of representation on the criteria we chose to make explicit.

(1) *Organization of the study.* Was the research tight or messy? That is, were the conditions and propositions underlying the study clearly specified in advance, or did the investigator(s) by intention or through encounter with the phenomena cast around in various ways for information, insight, and understanding? Did the research as reported unfold in an orderly or in an unexpected, serendipitous manner?

(2) *Methodology.* Was the methodology of the study quantitative? Qualitative? A mix of these methodologies? Field or lab? Archival?

(3) *Status of researchers.* Were the investigators senior people in the field with high visibility based on their research records, or were they newcomers in the field?

(4) *Intention.* Was the study planned or opportunistic? A mix of planning and opportunism?

(5) *Relationship to theory.* Was the study one that tested theory? Did it generate theory? Did it describe theory?

(6) *Gender.*

(7) *Single versus multiple authorship.*

We employed one criterion in our selection on which we did not seek variety, and that was the quality of writing. We quickly discovered in our canvassing that the well-written papers stood out. In Journey 3 in this volume, Alan D. Meyer reports learning from Bill Starbuck that "the best insight was that clear writing is not just an adornment laid on at the end to show off research results in their best light." We heartily agree. Some of the characteristics of the investigators whose work was chosen are listed in Table 1.

To clarify what we mean by *exemplary*, it may be worth noting what we did *not* do in our selection process. We did not develop a unitary or multidimensional index of "exemplariness," rank the articles on it, and pick the top seven. Our seven selections are not the best seven articles published in the 1980s. We do not believe that a valid judgment of this sort could be made. They are seven very good articles that may serve as templates or models for other good research. There are other

TABLE 1 Research Exemplars: Some Characteristics of Investigators

Professional Status	
Graduate student (N = 6)	Dobbin, Gash, Gersick, Jennings, A. Meyer, G. Meyer
Assistant professor (N = 3)	Barley, Rafaeli, Sutton
Associate or full professor (N = 5)	Baron, Erez, Jermier, Latham, Locke
Gender	
Females	4
Males	10
Research Institutions	University of California, Berkeley; Cornell University; University of South Florida; Stanford University; University of Washington; Yale University

NOTE: Status and research institution characteristics reflect the situations when the studies were being conducted.

articles that could serve as well. Our selection of these seven was a necessary first step in our strategy for examining the process of doing good research. The value of this book lies in bringing to the reader the opportunity to interact with descriptions of the process that generate exemplars and a discussion of what is exemplary about them.

The Research Exemplars

Based on these criteria we selected seven articles to form the basis of our data for the book. The research questions asked, the methods used, and the specific journeys of investigators as reported in the articles are different across the seven studies. The studies are listed in Table 2.

Three of the studies included in this book won awards of excellence from their profession, based on peer evaluations of the high quality of their work. Sutton and Rafaeli won the *Academy of Management Journal* best article of the year award for 1988. Gersick received the 1988 award for "outstanding contribution to organizational behavior" from the Organizational Behavior Division of the Academy of Management; Latham, Erez, and Locke won this same award in 1989.

The focus of each of the seven studies is as follows:

TABLE 2 The Research Exemplars

Barley, Stephen R., Meyer, Gordon W., & Gash, Debra C. (1988). Cultures of culture: Academics, practitioners and the pragmatics of normative control. *Administrative Science Quarterly, 33,* 24-60.

Baron, James N., Dobbin, Frank R., & Jennings, P. Devereaux. (1986). War and peace: The evolution of modern personnel administration in U.S. industry. *American Journal of Sociology, 92,* 350-383.

Gersick, Connie J. G. (1988). Time and transition in work teams: Toward a new model of group development. *Academy of Management Journal, 31,* 9-41.

Jermier, John M. (1985). "When the sleeper wakes": A short story extending themes in radical organization theory. *Journal of Management, 11,* 67-80.

Latham, Gary P., Erez, Miriam, & Locke, Edwin A. (1988). Resolving scientific disputes by the joint design of crucial experiments by the antagonists: Application to the Erez-Latham dispute regarding participation in goal setting. *Journal of Applied Psychology, 73,* 753-772.

Meyer, Alan D. (1982). Adapting to environmental jolts. *Administrative Science Quarterly, 27,* 515-537.

Sutton, Robert I., & Rafaeli, Anat. (1988). Untangling the relationship between displayed emotions and organizational sales: The case of convenience stores. *Academy of Management Journal, 31,* 461-487.

NOTE: This list is in alphabetical order according to authors' names. Discussion of the exemplars in this volume does not follow this order.

- Barley, Meyer, and Gash, "Cultures of Culture: Academics, Practitioners and the Pragmatics of Normative Control": This article presents a linguistic analysis of the published academic and practitioner literature on organizational culture. The authors coded and content analyzed all the 192 papers written on organizational culture between 1975 and 1984. They examined them for evidence of acculturation. Specifically, the authors wanted to see whether academics and practitioners writing on organizational culture had in this time period influenced each others' points of view on the nature and use of the organizational culture concept.
- Gersick, "Time and Transition in Work Teams: Toward a New Model of Group Development": This is an exploratory, hypothesis-generating field study of group process. The author studied the complete life spans of eight naturally occurring teams. Analysis of transcripts of her detailed observations of team meetings provided the basis of the model she developed for understanding and predicting group development and performance.

- Meyer, "Adapting to Environmental Jolts": This paper reports a field study of administrative practices in hospitals that was interrupted by a physicians' strike over a hike in malpractice insurance rates. The author conducted a case study of responses of three hospital administrations to this unexpected action by medical practitioners. He developed a model for understanding and predicting organizations' responses to crises emanating from the environment.

- Sutton and Rafaeli, "Untangling the Relationship Between Displayed Emotions and Organizational Sales: The Case of Convenience Stores": The authors started out with a theory of emotion in relation to work behavior and designed a study to analyze the relationship between smiles of cashiers and company performance in convenience stores. The original data consisted of a very comprehensive set of observations of more than 11,000 customer service transactions in a national random sample of 585 stores. Puzzling and disconfirming results led the researchers to conduct a follow-up field study involving participant observation to make sense of the data and to develop a model for understanding and predicting emotional reactions in the workplace.

- Latham, Erez, and Locke, "Resolving Scientific Disputes by the Joint Design of Crucial Experiments by the Antagonists: Application to the Erez-Latham Dispute Regarding Participation in Goal Setting": The authors designed a series of four crucial experiments to try to resolve marked differences in earlier findings by Latham and by Erez on the effect of participation on goal commitment and performance. Locke served as a third-party mediator between the two researchers. Latham in his previous research had found no significant relationship between participation and goal commitment and performance. Erez, in her research, had found a positive relationship between participation and goal commitment. She had also reported significant relations between goal commitment and performance. The study provides a report on both the design of laboratory experiments and a process for mediating disputed research findings.

- Baron, Dobbin, and Jennings, "War and Peace: The Evolution of Modern Personnel Administration in U.S. Industry": This article presents a study of the evolution and transformation of the employment relationship in several industries in the United States using archival resources. The authors analyzed survey data on employment practices from National Conference Board studies in 1927, 1935, 1939, and 1946 to understand the emergence and diffusion of professional personnel practices. They also examined historical data, including federal documents and corporate histories. The authors worked back and forth between the archival survey data and the historical information to develop their ideas about forces that shaped the evolution of the modern workplace.

• Jermier, "When the Sleeper Wakes": A Short Story Extending Themes in Radical Organization Theory": In this article, the author uses the literary method to present field data. He drew on data from a field study of a phosphate plant to write a short story illustrating a theory of consciousness. The story served as data and was used as the basis for a description and discussion of three conceptions of the worker in organizations: traditional organization theory, critical theory, and dialectical Marxist theory.

Author Commentaries

A major intent of this book is to provide an array of ideas and insights about how research takes place that leads to exemplary outcomes. Reports from authors were expected to tell us some useful things about how they believed the research was really done. We added a third perspective on the research, that of commentators, invited by us to read the articles and to tell us and the reader what they liked about the work and to state what impact they felt it made on the field.

We were interested in exploring the research process in each study and the experiences and lessons of the investigators as they engaged in this process. To this end, we wrote to the authors of each article and explained the project to them, told them of the nomination and election of their articles as exemplars for study, and invited them to reconstruct and reflect on the origins, processes, and outcomes of the work that culminated in the article we had identified as exemplary.

All the authors agreed to participate in the project. We sent each of them a letter in which we asked a series of questions intended to elicit their recollections and interpretations of the processes that contributed to the research. These questions were organized around a chronological framework (genesis, process, production of research output, and aftermath) and a set of key issues (activities, relationships, feelings, and resources). In this letter, we attempted to stimulate but not shape the authors' thoughts about their research practice. Embedded in the categories and questions were a variety of metaphors and emphases to stimulate author responses. The questions we posed in the letter to authors are presented in Table 3.

TABLE 3 Excerpt from Letter to Authors of Exemplary Research

As a guide to the kinds of issues of concern, we share with you the framework we are using to guide our discussion of the research process. Basically it is a four-by-four matrix of research issues. On one axis is the chronology of a research project: genesis, process, production of the research output, and aftermath. On the other axis are four key aspects of the process at each stage: events/activities, relationships, feelings, and resources. We do not expect you to work through the sixteen resulting boxes. Perhaps one row or one column is of special interest, or perhaps another structure that does not fit this framework will work for reporting your particular experience.

In any case, some of the questions we think will stimulate interesting answers can be listed in the following outline:

Genesis of the research project
  —How? Why? When?
  —What did you expect/intend at the beginning? Anything special or different about this project? Relation to other projects?
  —Feelings: Excitement? Motivation? Commitment?
  —Relationships with coauthors, colleagues, mentors, students?
  —Resources: Was availability of time, money, access, labor, etc. an issue?

Process of the project
  —What did you do first? Level, distribution, and type of work over the life cycle of the project?
  —Problems and solutions along the way?
  —Any surprises? Changes in intentions/expectations?
  —Relationship issues: Shifts in involvement? Research site and participant issues?
  —Feelings: Frustration? Boredom? Satisfactions?
  —Resources: Strategies for gaining, retaining, and utilizing?

Production of the research outcome: shaping the process into a product
  —Deciding what to include/not include?
  —First "public" appearance of the work: Working paper? Seminar? Conference?
  —Length of time from genesis to product?
  —Role of early feedback?
  —Decision on publication outlet? Did the first choice work?
  —Your experience of the submission, review, and editing process?
  —Did you specifically attend to the quality of writing itself? If so, what did you do?
  —Relationships: Questions of authorship credit?
  —Feelings: Reactions to reviews?
  —Resource issues at this stage?

Aftermath and Reflection
  —What kind of feedback have you received?
  —In one paragraph, what is the contribution of this piece of research?
  —Has it changed your view of the field, your position on an issue of substance, your knowledge of organizations?
  —Has it changed how you do research? How?
  —Would you do it again? Why? What would you do differently?
  —Relationships: Any effects on working relationships, friendships, etc.?
  —Feelings: Satisfaction? Regrets?
  —If some resource constraints could have been removed, what would you have done differently?

You will likely want to sample from these questions. Further, as we require brief commentaries, we encourage you to be creative and experimental in your approach.

What is the value of these author commentaries? Do they provide us with insight into the production of exemplary research? The reports are subject to retrospective reconstruction. The pressure for self-presentation in a positive light to colleagues in the potential audience is high. The authors are in a position to censor, consciously and unconsciously, many aspects of their "real" experiences. However, these reasons do not lead us to dismiss these accounts, although they do limit the validity of the accounts. We must interpret the meaning of the reports in the light of these criticisms.

We must also consider the reasons to accept the accounts. The authors have been given a legitimate opportunity to reflect on the process aspects of their research activities. The writers are members of a profession that involves a heavy socialization in the values of honesty and growth of knowledge. These are the bases for positive self-presentation. Thus, for example, Meyer fears writing an "essay on the research as I idealized it, not as I did it," and Meyer, Barley, and Gash warn that "while we have tried to be truthful, the truth is less solid, less consistent, and less amenable to verbal expression than our prose suggests." Some aspects of each report refer to public behavior that is not easily censored. Finally, it is our belief that the authors share a genuine concern for the development of research scholars and scholarship in organization studies.

The authors have shared with us their imperfect accounts. We, as readers, must accept the burden of interpretation and action. Our research is embedded in a matrix of experience, colleagues, and resources that differs from that of the authors of these exemplars. To make our own interpretations of these accounts, we may test their experiences against our own. We may experiment creatively in our research practice based on ideas generated from our reflection on these accounts. We may do neither. The choice is ours.

Choosing Commentators

In addition to the authors' accounts, we invited independent commentators to provide their perspectives on the exemplary research. Most of the commentators were chosen for their ability to highlight the contributions of the exemplary articles to the field of organization studies. Our selection of commentators was based on their familiarity with the research area, with the particular article itself, and/or the author(s) involved in the research. In three cases, commentators were chosen because they were in unique positions to provide insight on an aspect of the research process. Two had been editors involved with the review and revision stages of the article. Jan Beyer, former editor of *AMJ*, was asked to comment on the Connie Gersick article. Rick Mowday, another former editor of *AMJ*, was invited to comment on the Bob Sutton and Anat Rafaeli article. In one case we invited commentary from a scholar who had served as a dissertation adviser on work that subsequently resulted in an exemplary journal article: Richard Hackman was Connie Gersick's dissertation adviser, and he comments on her *AMJ* article.

We invited a constructive, positive appraisal of each work rather than either an unabashed praising of the research or a detailed critique of its weaknesses. Our expectation was that other readers of the work, including those who read this book, would singly or collectively make their own assessments of strengths and weaknesses, based on ideological stance, paradigmatic preference, and level of sophistication with empirical research techniques and methodologies. In the current climate of discussion of research in the field of organizational research, the bias, in our opinion, is toward the search for fatal flaws, and for reasons to discount research. Often this is done while holding some ideal condition of research in mind that has been borrowed from the physical sciences. This is not necessarily an erroneous strategy for evaluating studies of psychological, social, and organizational phenomena. We think it can be misleading and even destructive, however, when carried out without attention to the possible positive contributions of any piece of carefully executed research completed in the context of constraints facing the investigators. Hence our charge to commentators was to tell us what the strong points and useful contributions of these studies might be.

We turn our attention now to the exemplars themselves and the author and expert commentaries on them.

Maori Journey Tapestry. In Maori mythology, this panel represents the trials on the journey of Tane up to the heavens to obtain the three baskets of knowledge—good, evil, and ritual—and his return with them to the people.

PART I

Doing Exemplary Research: Seven Journeys

Cultures of Culture: Academics, Practitioners and the Pragmatics of Normative Control

Stephen R. Barley
Cornell University
Gordon W. Meyer
Bucknell University
Debra C. Gash
Michigan State University

This paper presents a method for assessing whether members of two subcultures, in this case academics and practitioners, have influenced each other's interpretations. Conceptual and symbolic influence are seen as special instances of acculturation, and their occurrence can be studied by specifying changes in the language that members of different subcultures use to frame a topic or issue. Models of academic- and practitioner-oriented discourse on organizational culture were derived from early papers on the topic. The texts of 192 articles on organizational culture written between June 1975 and December 1984 were then examined for evidence of acculturation. The data strongly suggest that those who wrote for practitioners and academics initially conceptualized organizational culture differently. Over time, however, academics appear to have moved toward the practitioners' point of view, while the latter appear to have been little influenced by the former. Besides showing that it is possible to study acculturation by investigating language use, the analysis raises important questions about the links between theory and practice in organizational behavior.•

Perhaps because they have always worked at the margin between basic and applied social science, organizational theorists have long contemplated how the academic community and the managerial community influence each other (Thompson, 1956). Over the years, two competing views of the relationship have evolved. The dominant perspective frames the relation in terms of the diffusion and utilization of knowledge (Cherns, 1972; Duncan, 1974; Beyer, 1982). The terms are borrowed from the physical and life sciences where they denote the process by which basic research inspires practical advances in technical fields such as computers and medicine. From this vantage point, academics are seen as impartial sources of empirical principles that are taught to practitioners who, in turn, put the knowledge to worldly use (Beyer and Trice, 1982). Since diffusion theorists presume that knowledge flows from the academy to the field, their primary concern has been to disseminate information and stimulate applications of new knowledge (Corwin and Louis, 1982; Dunbar, 1983).

The second view, which we dub the political perspective, stands in sharp contrast to the notion of knowledge diffusion. Whereas diffusion theorists assume that academics frame problems for practitioners, political theorists contend that scholarly endeavors are ultimately defined by the interests of those who dominate society and by whose largess academics retain the privilege of pursuing research (Wassenberg, 1977; Salaman, 1979; Clegg and Dunkerley, 1980; Watson, 1980). The interests of the powerful are said to shape research more significantly than the curiosity of the researcher, primarily because the former control the latter's access to critical resources.

Unsurprisingly, both perspectives offer competing interpretations of the process by which new schools of thought arise. Numerous texts have recounted organizational theory's rise from its early beginnings in scientific management, through its human relations period, to the birth of contingency theo-

© 1988 by Cornell University.
0001-8392/88/3301-0024/$1.00.

•

Earlier versions of this paper were delivered at the Standing Conference on Organizational Culture, Montreal, June 1986, and at the Academy of Management Meetings, New Orleans, August 1987. At one time or another our thinking has been honed by the insights and criticisms of friends and colleagues: Mitch Abolafia, Gibb Dyer, Tove Hammer, Mike Hannan, George Jakubson, Dave Krackhardt, Gideon Kunda, Ed Schein, Bob Stern, and John Van Maanen. We are particularly grateful to Peter Frost, who helped us identify those papers that were delivered at what may have been the first conference on organizational culture, held at Champaign-Urbana in 1979, and which later appeared among the papers in the collection, *Organizational Symbolism*.

Introductory Remarks:
Journey 1

"Cultures of Culture: Academics, Practitioners and the Pragmatics of Normative Control," by Stephen R. Barley, Gordon W. Meyer, and Debra C. Gash. Published in *Administrative Science Quarterly*, 33 (1988), 24-60. Copyright 1988 by Cornell University. Excerpts from this article are reprinted in this volume by permission.

Our intent has been to open an important topic for further debate but also to provide an empirical approach for bringing data to bear on the issue. (Barley, Meyer, & Gash, 1988, p. 55)

So Barley, Meyer, and Gash end their report of an impressive piece of scholarship. The "important topic" is the nature of the relationship between the ivory towers of academe and the glass towers of practicing managers. Do managers and business academics listen to each other? Are they affected by what they hear? The authors pose the question as an issue of acculturation. Do academics influence the "worldview" of managers or vice versa? In this report, they narrow the broad question to an examination of how each community's understanding of the concept of corporate culture has developed.

As Mayer Zald points out in his commentary on "Cultures of Culture," "There are several ways one could study such questions." The "empirical approach" developed by the authors is to look for evidence of acculturation in the artifacts of the academic and practitioner groups. Barley, Meyer, and Gash identify an aspect of each community—communications, their journals—as appropriate artifacts for examination. Traditional methods of content analysis are not sufficient. The authors must develop a method that is sensitive to the way each group discusses corporate culture. Their solution is rooted in the linguistic subdiscipline of "pragmatics", the study of "how the meaning of a word or phrase is shaped by its surrounding context" (p. 28).

First, they identify the journals that constitute the academic discourse and the practitioner discourse, respectively. Next, they identify two sets of "contextual markers" that represent the academic and practitioner discussions of corporate culture, respectively. Operational indicators of these contextual markers are identified. Finally, they code the value of the 22 indicators for each paragraph of every journal article on corporate culture from 1975 to 1985—a total of 192 articles.

The exercise results in a sophisticated content analysis that allows the authors to assess the change over time in the pragmatics of the discourse about corporate culture within the two communities. Because the two communities differ in the contextual treatment of culture in the earlier 1975-1982 period, the authors are also able to look at the dynamic relationship between the two streams of discourse. They are able to demonstrate that the academic discourse shifts over time to match the model of the practitioner community.

In Journey 1, Meyer, Barley, and Gash share with us individual and collective reflections on their experiences in producing this study. It is a story of "whole" people, people with complex combinations of personal, professional, and intellectual motivations. We get a sense of the reality of the long hours, the dogged determination, and the playful comic relief necessary to produce the methodological rigor so evident in the article.

The commentators broaden our appreciation of this work by focusing on its relevance for social science. Mayer Zald concentrates on the contribution of Barley, Meyer, and Gash with respect to their methodology at a time when "the walls of positivism are crumbling in all the social sciences." He sees their work as indicative of the directions in which the analysis of meaning in organizational life must develop. Cathy Enz explores the implications of the studies of findings, especially the shift of academic writing on culture to a more functionalist paradigmatic perspective.

Our first impression on reading this study was an appreciation of the clear, reasoned line of argument that the authors develop. A closer reading reveals that this is accomplished by very careful, economical prose. Every sentence makes an essential contribution to the whole. Tony Athos once suggested that a useful tactic for learning academic writing skills is to copy good examples in longhand. We would suggest that this exemplar could serve that purpose well.

The second feature of "Cultures of Culture" that impressed us was its rigor. It is the epitome of thorough, methodological "tightness" in an empirical study. One might even say the article is "too" good. Certainly, the authors did more than is normally required for publication in a top journal. Barley, Meyer, and Gash studied the universe rather than a sample of culture articles. They launched a separate study to classify the journals as academic or practitioner. They coded every paragraph, rather than a sample of paragraphs from each article, on 19 indicators.

A third feature of the study that influenced our decision to include it was its reflexive method. The authors used the methods of cultural analysis to research the nature of research on culture. Gouldner (1970) claims that the future of social science depends on the development of reflexivity in our research. Perhaps his claim is extreme, but, with Campbell, we could claim that "our research enterprise is an institution worthy of study using the same models, procedures, and accumulated literature that we use on 'them' " (see Campbell's commentary in this volume). This study provides one of the few models of reflexive research available in the organizational literature.

A final feature of the study deserves comment in a volume explicitly devoted to the development of better researchers and research in organizational studies, and that is the authors' concern that as an academic community, we appear to be unwilling to discuss the most important research issue of all: what to research. We hope that inclusion of this study in this volume will motivate relevant individual reflection and a collective conversation.

Obsession and Naïveté in Upstate New York: A Tale of Research

Gordon W. Meyer

Stephen R. Barley

Debra C. Gash

How can three coauthors jointly tell a tale of collaborative research without sacrificing each individual person's perspective? The issue is one of style, of point of view. After experimenting with variations on the first-person plural, which created an unrealistically unanimous voice, we settled on telling our story from the point of view of an omniscient observer. The deceit enabled us to relate both our common and our idiosyncratic stories in a readerly fashion, but not without cost. Specifically, the third person imparts to the telling an undeserved aura of facticity. The tenor of our experience was neither as clear nor as brittle as our prose makes it seem. Moreover, the text creates the subtle impression of more coherence than our experiences and actions warrant. In this regard, the telling has much in common with the literary fictions found in the methods sections of most research papers. Fragile memories and the objective voice are the stuff from which rational reconstructions arise. Thus we warn the reader from the start: While we have tried to be truthful, the truth is less solid, less consistent, and less amenable to verbal expression than our prose suggests.

The Project's Genesis

THE BIRTH OF AN OBSESSION

The intellectual seeds from which "Cultures of Culture" grew were sown at MIT in the late 1970s and early 1980s. During this period Barley, Gibb Dyer, Deborah Dougherty, Gideon Kunda, and several other graduate students joined with Edgar Schein and John Van Maanen to hold seminars, pursue research, and write papers on the cultural aspects of organizational and occupational life. The group's primary interest was to explore the utility of anthropological concepts and methods for the analysis of organizations. The relevance of anthropological studies was hardly a new idea at MIT. Van Maanen had long championed ethnographies of work in the tradition of E. C. Hughes, Howard Becker, and other "Chicago school" sociologists. Schein was also a longtime advocate of field research. However, it was during the late 1970s that members of the Organization Studies Group first turned systematically to anthropology rather than sociology for theoretical inspiration and began to speak explicitly of "organizational and occupational cultures."

The developments at MIT dovetailed with the work of other scholars, such as Peter Frost, Joanne Martin, Meryl Louis, and Alan Wilkins, who were beginning to examine the symbolic and cultural aspects of organizations at roughly the same time. In fact, Wilkins and Martin made trips to MIT during this period to exchange ideas, and Louis spent a semester with the Organization Studies Group as a visiting scholar. As papers from the period clearly indicate, most members of this loose network thought that anthropologically oriented studies of organizations would lead to better-grounded theories and a more realistic understanding of organizational life. Some even thought that an anthropologist's eye might challenge and therefore lead researchers to question the unreflective position that then dominated the field. The rapid success and increasing frequency of symposia and conferences on organizational culture during the early 1980s sparked hope that an anthropological agenda might even gain legitimacy in organization studies.

At approximately the same period of time, however, several trade books that utilized the concept of organizational (or "corporate") culture were released to instantaneous acclaim (Deal & Kennedy, 1982; Ouchi, 1981; Peters & Waterman, 1982).[1] These publications subsequently unleashed a flood of articles on corporate culture in the business and popular press. For Van Maanen, Kunda, and Barley, in

Cultures of Culture

Figure 2. Papers published annually on organizational culture, 1975–1985.*

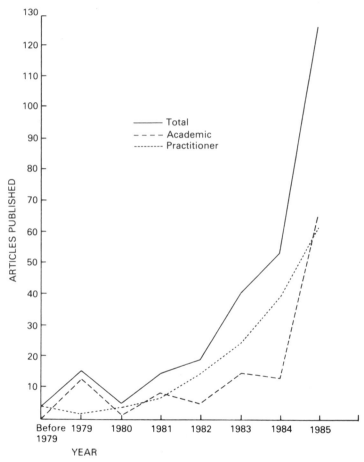

*Data are based on a search of six bibliographic data bases.

(Barley, Meyer, & Gash, 1988, p. 33)

particular, disconcerting motifs seemed to enter discussions of organizational culture almost immediately, especially at the meetings of the Academy of Management. More often than not, such discussions seemed to incorporate, if not actually cater to, management's concerns with such issues as competing with the Japanese, improving productivity, and, most ominously, gaining greater control over the work force.[2]

For Barley, the managerial tone of the popular and, increasingly, the academic literature on corporate culture raised issues central to the sociology of knowledge. Might the metamorphosis of the rationale for studying culture reflect a fundamental problem plaguing the development of knowledge in an applied social science such as organizational behavior? Could environmental and political pressures on organizational behavior be so great that any attempt to pursue research primarily for the sake of better understanding a phenomenon risk being rapidly redirected toward practical issues or, worse, toward subservience to a managerial agenda (Baritz, 1960; Goldman & Van Houten, 1977)?

Barley brought these questions and concerns with him when he moved to Cornell as an assistant professor in 1984. By then he perceived that the literature on organizational culture offered an opportunity for examining why theory and knowledge in organizational behavior might fail to develop the sophistication and depth characteristic of a less applied discipline. Although the uneasy, and perhaps dialectical, relationship between theory and practice in organization studies had generated some discussion (see Baritz, 1960; Wassenberg, 1977), no research had addressed the issue rigorously.

Moreover, if there had, in fact, been a shift in the meaning of "organizational culture" since the late 1970s, then such a shift would itself constitute a *cultural* phenomenon insofar as cultures consist of socially available frameworks for interpretation. Following the tenets of linguistic anthropology, any shift in the concept's meaning should be embedded in the language that people use when writing and talking about culture. Consequently, it should be possible to use linguistic and textual analysis to verify or refute the occurrence of the shift while simultaneously demonstrating the possibility of analyzing textual materials rigorously for evidence of cultural change.

> **❝** A more open view of the relation between academics and practitioners would begin by positing two worlds that exist as separate but interdependent social systems characterized by different traditions, languages, interests, and norms. Under such conditions, the direction and degree of influence might vary from issue to issue. On any issue about which the opinions of academics and practitioners initially differ, one of four patterns of influence would be plausible: (1) practitioners and academics might exert no influence on each other, (2) academics might exert greater influence on practitioners, (3) practitioners might exert greater influence on academics, or (4) each might exert significant influence on the other. The first pattern would be consistent with a thesis of segregated social worlds; the second with diffusion theory; the third with political theory; while the fourth would imply the need for a more complex, and potentially

dialectical, theory of mutual adjustment. To determine empirically which pattern more accurately describes relations between academics and practitioners requires (1) a notion of the paths by which the two communities can influence each other, (2) a technique for identifying the incidence of influence, and (3) an examination of specific issues that would allow one to observe influence in the making.   **99**

(Barley, Meyer, & Gash, 1988, p. 25)

Thus the impetus for the project lay in Barley's commitment to an anthropological vision and his discomfort with the "reconstruction" or redirection of that perspective toward managerial interests. Coupled with this was Barley's obsession with subjecting his ideas about the development of knowledge in organization behavior to empirical test. Barley recognized that his intuitions might be no more than idiosyncratic interpretations or, worse, the ruminations of a disgruntled deviant. He therefore wanted to do more than simply offer an ideological critique that he could easily formulate but that others could just as easily dismiss. However, the task of verifying shifts in discourse on organizational culture would require developing precise linguistic indicators as well as compiling a longitudinal data base on the linguistic attributes of the culture literature—a daunting task even if one were to examine only articles published after 1975. Not only could Barley not hope to complete such a project on his own, he had no financial resources to support such a study.

ENTER MEYER AND GASH

Gordon Meyer and Debra Gash were among the more senior graduate students in organizational behavior at the School of Industrial and Labor Relations when Barley arrived as a junior faculty member. Their graduate careers were in a period of limbo: Neither had well-defined dissertations but both had completed their formal course work and were without obligations to other faculty. They were also at or near the statute of limitations with respect to financial support from the university, so neither could hope to obtain assistantships by working with other faculty members. Meyer and Gash had met Barley while he was still a student at MIT, and the three had established a peer relationship reinforced by the closeness of their ages and the recency of their graduate school experiences.[3] Both Meyer and Gash had read and discussed Barley's papers on semiotics in a seminar at Cornell and had concluded that Barley was into intriguing and "exotic" topics.

In the winter of 1984, Barley invited Meyer and Gash to discuss the possibility of doing the research jointly. After that meeting two matters seemed clear to Meyer and Gash. First, Barley was passionately committed to the project and was absolutely convinced of its feasibility. Second, because developing the coding scheme and compiling the data base would be tasks of considerable scope and complexity, Barley fully expected to share the authorship of any publications. In fact, he had expressed a desire for collegial cooperation and signaled that hierarchically based deferential behavior would be intolerable. Co-authorship was not to be viewed as a replacement for the financial remuneration that Meyer and Gash could not receive; rather, it was offered with the understanding that Meyer's and Gash's efforts would be crucial for the study's completion.[4]

Meyer and Gash had several reactions to Barley's proposal. Both thought that his commitment to joint authorship and collegial relations with graduate students was unusual and refreshing; neither had ever been invited to join a project at its inception. Meyer was engaged intellectually by the project's thesis, since he also had been concerned for some time with ideological biases in the organizational literature. Here, finally, was a project with which he could identify at a time when he was admittedly drifting as a scholar. Meyer's interest and willingness to pursue the project were further fortified by his perception that Barley had a knack for successfully accomplishing the unconventional.

Gash's reactions were more circumspect and utilitarian. She was incredulous that Barley would propose to study so exhaustively such a large and expanding literature. She had some doubts about the project's feasibility and was concerned with how it might affect her progress as a student. On the other hand, she was keenly aware of the increasing pressure placed on Ph.D. candidates to publish while in graduate school, and the possibility of obtaining this elusive goal seemed strengthened by Barley's track record. Although she did not share Barley's and Meyer's ideological commitments to the project, in the end she was "swept along" by their enthusiasm for the question and the act of uncovering the data. In retrospect, however, all three can now see that they underestimated the arduousness of the task in which they were about to engage.

The Process

From the start, the work was driven by an obsessive concern for completeness and objectivity. However, the motive was not simply (or even primarily) that of achieving "scientific objectivity." Barley was adamant that to be accepted for publication and to stimulate the sort of dialogue he desired about the nature of the field, the research would need to be as impervious to methodological criticism as possible. If the data proved to be consistent with the thesis, readers should not be allowed the opportunity to deny easily or to overlook the study's substantive message on methodological grounds. Such a stance led the researchers to question their methods continually and to adopt a norm of thoroughness that swallowed time in a vortex of work.

For example, Barley's fixation with incontrovertibility, which ultimately infected Meyer and Gash, led the authors to examine the entire universe of papers written on organizational culture between 1975 and 1985 rather than work with a random sample of papers. Similarly, rather than leave themselves open to the criticism that their findings were an artifact of their own idiosyncratic classification scheme, the researchers surveyed academic opinion on the nature of specific journals and then allocated papers to academic and practitioner camps on the basis of an empirically demonstrable consensus. Finally, after much deliberation, Barley, Meyer, and Gash chose to assign codes to each paragraph in every article rather than to rely on abstracts, which were not only less common in the practitioner literature but could conceivably have been written by someone other than the paper's author. It is difficult to assess, post hoc, how much extra time and effort these measures exacted. The decisions largely emerged once the participants had become committed to the project and to doing a tight piece of research; hence the extra demands were generally not questioned.

In February 1985, Meyer searched six on-line data bases for articles written on organizational culture and compiled a list of the outlets in which they had been published. A survey soliciting the opinions of academics regarding each outlet's typical audience was then developed and sent to a randomly selected sample of members of several divisions of the Academy of Management as well as a sample of culture researchers. By March 1985, with the survey in the mail, the authors began the initial phase of what would ultimately become a grueling two years of reading and coding approximately 200 articles.

In a meeting in Barley's office, the three reached consensus on 20 articles that they thought were representative of the universe's diversity. The researchers read the papers and began a series of meetings designed to hammer out the indices that would ultimately be used to code the entire data base. Barley's original conception of the project only vaguely articulated the contextual markers or indicators that might be useful for assessing the pragmatics of academic and practitioner discourse on organizational culture. Hence the researchers had to formulate and operationalize linguistic models before the coding could proceed in earnest. The authors initially searched the literature on content and textual analysis for assistance in working out their coding scheme. However, they were unable to find suitable exemplars. As a result, they decided to develop their own coding scheme, based largely on the conviction that they could ultimately develop clear textual indicators of ideas they wished to measure.

Norms for the tenor of the group's meetings were established early. In a memorandum summarizing the first meeting that was held to "devise and perfect the coding scheme," Barley wrote that the work would be an iterative process, "marked by frequent arguments, endless clarification, and constant negotiation and renegotiation." And so it was. Gash quickly emerged as a champion of precision and clarity. Her discomfort with Meyer and Barley's willingness to wallow for eternity in a mire of impressionistic attributions drove her to write, after several weeks of hermeneutic digressions, a memorandum systematically discussing the conceptual distinctions between indicators of "gaining or losing control over and through culture." The memorandum represented a quantum advance over the working definitions of only a few days before and ultimately became a template for the types of codes that were ultimately sought. Gash's memo forced the coauthors to recognize the utility of indicators defined in terms of explicit semantic sets and syntactical rules.

> **66** Most early papers on culture counted unity, cohesion, loyalty, and commitment among the positive consequences of having a "strong" organizational culture. In fact, most authors of early practitioner-oriented texts argued that culture's promise hung on the following pseudosyllogism: culture enhances social integration; social integration increases performance and productivity; therefore, if one can enhance social integration by manipulating culture, then, substantial increments in performance and productivity should ensue. . . .
>
> Two lexical indicators measured culture's association with social integration:
>
> *System integration (Sys):* The percentage of a paper's paragraphs that contained references to systemic integration. Lexical cues for systemic integration included "social glue," "cohesion," "family feeling," and "structural integration."
>
> *Individual integration (Ind):* The percentage of a paper's paragraphs that contained references to the integration of the individual and the organization. Lexical cues for individual integration included "loyalty," "commitment," "trust," etc. **99**

(Barley, Meyer, & Gash, 1988, p. 43)

> **66** Social inte- Sys   "Managers call it a company
>   gration   philosophy or religion, the social
>   glue holding the company together."
>   (Baker, 1980)
>   Ind   "Its well-entrenched culture . . . has
>   brought it tremendous loyalty from
>   its staff." (*Business Week*, 1980) **99**
>
> (Barley, Meyer, & Gash, 1988, p. 60)

In addition to its substantive contribution, however, Gash's memo also triggered a form of interaction that was rapidly legitimated and thereafter typified the collaborators' work style over the course of the project: the importance of "razzing." Meyer and Barley quickly labeled Gash the team's "psychologist," which, roughly translated, meant that of the three she was the most concerned with parsimony and that she was less willing to conceptualize phenomena as social structural in nature. The label (hotly contested by Gash) became a leitmotif that stood in good currency for two years. For instance, it was ultimately at Gash's instigation that the authors split a variable measuring social integration into two separate indicators: one measuring references to individual integration into the organization and the other integration at the level of the social system. The move required that all previously coded papers be recoded. Afterward, Barley and Meyer continually prodded Gash to adopt a "sociologist simulation rule" to counteract her tendency to overlook linguistic indicators of systemic integration.

No one, including Barley, was spared the pain of verbal digs and epithets. Gash often had occasion to remind Barley that he was once again "foaming at the mouth" and that he was far too stubborn for his own good. Meyer was repeatedly told that he was in danger of becoming even "more of an ideologue than Barley." Such playful teasing was a backhanded way of acknowledging each author's unique and (usually) valued contributions. For instance, without Gash's insistent emphasis on the techniques that won her the label of "psychologist," Barley and Meyer may have succumbed to a "true believer" syndrome, which might have resulted in findings more open to criticism. Moreover, aggression seemed to release tension and cement the relationship among the three authors.[5]

By the summer of 1985 the coding scheme was well defined and inscribed in a manual that the authors kept prominently on their desks for the next 18 months. Every two weeks, the authors would read and code a set of 20 articles individually. Gash would calculate interrater reliabilities, and the three would then meet for three to five hours on one or two evenings to discuss variables on which agreement was low.

The meetings, which rarely began until Barley and Meyer had put their kids to bed and Gash had returned from her nightly dance class, typically ran late and were both physically and emotionally draining. Because all of the authors are reasonably stubborn and because all assumed that they had been extremely careful and thoughtful in their initial coding, the meetings generated heated intellectual debates and, occasionally, interpersonal conflict.

> 66 The coding progressed in seven rounds during which the three researchers examined and coded sets of twenty to thirty articles individually. After individual codings were completed, we calculated interrater reliabilities and met to discuss those indicators whose reliability coefficients were less than .70. During these discussions, the coding rules were refined and articles about which we had seriously disagreed were recoded in light of refinements. By the end of the third round, the coding rules stabilized. At that point, we recorded articles examined in previous rounds to ensure consistency of rule use over time. Cronbach's alphas calculated for all the papers in the data set suggest a high level of agreement among the three coders. All 22 indicators used in the study yielded alpha coefficients greater than .80. These coefficients suggest that one can, in fact, reliably observe the indicators described in the following discussion of academic- and practitioner-oriented discourse. 99

(Barley, Meyer, & Gash, 1988, p. 39)

The norms guiding the process were that each person's reasoning deserved consideration and that, in return, one was expected to provide compelling support for his or her judgments. As a result, Meyer, Barley, and Gash spent considerable time and energy debating what outsiders might have considered minutiae. There was little loafing during these meetings, because each member held the others to standards of high performance and involvement that implicitly stipulated consensual agreement. Conceding an argument early was taken as a sign that it was time to "call it an evening," since abdication generally occurred only when someone was tired.

The tension between being thorough and "getting the job done" was constant. Because consensual decision making was the rule, every issue over the proper assignment of a code was "wrestled to the ground." Barley frequently felt as if he had to "bite his tongue" in order not to pull rank, impose a decision, and move on to the next code. He resisted, in part, because of his acute awareness of the need to have unassailable evidence. But more important, he realized that he could not afford to alienate his partners, since the project depended as much on Meyer and Gash's continued involvement as on his. Meyer and

Gash often suffered similar feelings of tedium. Gash later described this period of intensive coding and seemingly endless debate aptly as "a burden . . . like doing your laundry. There was work to do every week . . . it was a never-ending thing."

Although Barley worked hard to resist reinforcing the latent hierarchy, he readily acted as taskmaster when needed. For example, several months before initial results were to be presented at the Standing Conference on Organizational Symbolism, held in Montreal in June 1986, Barley wrote a memo to Gash and Meyer titled "Putting Nose to Grindstone." The memo included statements such as "Gordon, you have to bite the bullet and finish coding by this Sunday. . . . On Sunday, I expect us to divide these tasks and set *ambitious* and *firm* deadlines for each" (emphasis in the original). It is noteworthy that such urgings (still collegial) were not necessary until Meyer had assumed a full-time teaching position at a college 90 miles from Cornell and Gash had begun to spend considerable time gathering field data for her dissertation.

Producing the Product

By the summer of 1986, the initial data set had been compiled and the process of analyzing the data and producing the first of several drafts of a paper had begun. With these tasks, Meyer and Gash's identification with the project and its products began to change dramatically, with unanticipated consequences. Gash was now engaged full-time in her dissertation research. Given that all of the coding originally envisioned was complete, it made sense to everyone that Gash allow her involvement in the project to wane so that she could focus her energy more or less completely on her dissertation.[6] She did so, but nevertheless experienced periodic feelings of guilt about her withdrawal. At the beginning of the summer, Meyer moved from Ithaca to be closer to his teaching job, but continued to try to balance the beginning phase of his dissertation's field research with the completion of the culture project.

As Meyer and Gash became less involved, issues of the production of articles for presentation and publication became salient. During the spring, all three coauthors had conducted statistical analyses and had written analytic memos pertaining to information that would be vital for various sections of a research monograph. However, at least privately, Meyer and Gash acknowledged that they could not imagine writing a complete draft of an article that would be acceptable to Barley. They had, for some time, been fond of teasing him by claiming that in order to read and understand his papers they had to work in isolation, with dictionaries by their sides.

As early as the summer of 1985, when the theory behind the research was first presented at the Academy of Management, Barley had taken the lead in outlining the presentation. This division of labor continued throughout the preparation of subsequent products, including two later conference presentations and two versions of the article that were reviewed prior to its acceptance for publication. Thus it was without explicit discussion of the responsibilities of authorship that Barley began working on the article in the summer of 1986. Barley sent copies to Meyer and Gash for their suggestions each time the paper was revised, and shared with them reviewers' comments. In turn, Gash and Meyer responded with suggestions for revision. Nevertheless, Meyer and Gash have always perceived the article to be more Barley's contribution than their own. Since the article's publication, they have routinely acknowledged comments from others in ways that urge the commentator not to give them more credit for the paper than they believe they are due.

Although Barley admits that he wrote the paper largely by himself, he is acutely aware that he could have neither done the research nor formulated the ideas as clearly without Meyer and Gash's collaboration. He therefore feels vaguely guilty about Meyer and Gash's tendency to distance themselves from the article and fears that they might thereby suffer even more sharply than usual from the field's elitist tendency to discount a graduate student's contribution to papers coauthored with a faculty member.[7] Meyer and Gash, however, are comfortable with their degree of identification for several reasons. First, the paper's style is such that anyone familiar with Barley's other work will immediately recognize that it was written by him. Second, Meyer and Gash believe that Barley's writing showcases their thinking in a much more favorable light than either of them could have achieved on their own. Finally, Meyer and Gash know from personal experience that Barley has always acknowledged their contributions as essential to the process that led to the paper. Among the coauthors there is strong mutual understanding and immense regard for the importance of the contributions that each made to the research. Ultimately that may be all that really counts.

The Aftermath

As previously mentioned, Barley, Meyer, and Gash had hoped that the article would stimulate debate on the social forces that impinge on the field of organizational behavior. However, as of the winter of 1990, response to the article has been disappointing. Although there have been occasional requests for reprints, and although Meyer and Gash have both been invited to review manuscripts that they would otherwise not likely have received, with Frost and Stablein's choice to include the paper in this volume, few efforts have been made to engage the authors in a substantive dialogue regarding the study's findings or the authors' concerns for the field. While it is probably too early to expect such discourse to appear in print, the authors regret the absence of debate in less formal contexts. Exchanges that follow the publication of research typically take one of three forms. Authors receive brief verbal congratulations, requests for reprints, or citations in later publications. Unfortunately, each form of feedback is devoid of interaction and fails to engage the field directly in a substantive exchange regarding a work's content or its implications for the field.

The authors are collectively left posing again a number of the questions that stimulated the research. Can the field of organizational behavior sustain a serious stream of basic research over an extended period of time without being influenced by the social forces that seem to have affected discourse on organizational culture? If not, why not? Are students of organizations simply unwilling to think critically about why they do research or about the uses to which their research is put? What social forces influence the topics that researchers pursue and the directions in which the research develops? Which forces are external to the research community and which do we, wittingly or unwittingly, create for ourselves? Finally, there is a normative question: Should we allow the patterns of influence documented in "Cultures of Culture" to occur and, if so, under what conditions?

Notes

1. Meyer recalls being a participant in a course at Cornell during the fall of 1982 to which Karl Weick brought a prepublication copy of *In Search of Excellence* and spoke favorably of its challenge to rationalistic perspectives.

2. These concerns eventually gave rise to a set of papers that explore the relation between the mania over organizational culture and managerial ideologies of control. The genesis of our paper can therefore perhaps be best understood when viewed as a member of this set. Schein (1981) almost immediately published an attack on manage-

rially oriented portrayals of "strong cultures" as an antidote to Japanese competition. Kunda (1991) undertook for his dissertation an ethnography of the culture of an engineering firm known for its explicit interest in cultural indoctrination—a research project designed to examine the questionable aspects of "engineering culture." Van Maanen and Kunda (1989) coauthored a critical examination of how the desire to create "strong" cultures represented an attempt to control emotional expression. More recently, Kunda and Barley (1988) have attempted to situate the sudden popularity of cultural rhetorics within the trajectory of twentieth-century managerial ideology.

3. Moreover, Meyer and Barley were neighbors, had become fathers within five weeks of each other, and had almost immediately begun to exchange baby-sitting services.

4. The subtle tension between hierarchical and collegial relationships that tinged the authors' interaction was clearly rooted in the fact that Barley chose to work with graduate students rather than other faculty. Moreover, the tension was probably heightened by the fact that the authors had known each other as peers prior to Barley's acceptance of a faculty position at Cornell. Had Barley been at a later stage of his career and had the coauthors not been previously his peers, the collaboration might have more easily slipped into the hierarchical pattern typical of faculty-student relations, thereby eliminating the tension altogether. One might ask why Barley chose to work with students rather than other faculty, since such a choice might have eliminated the tension in favor of an unambiguous collegial relationship. The answer is simple: Few academics (junior or senior) are likely to be excited by the idea of dropping their own work to pursue a collaborative project that might consume the majority of their time for a two-year period and yield but a single coauthored paper. In short, the reward system for academic publication and advancement appears to work against faculty collaboration on projects of such intensity.

5. As Simmel noted long ago, triads are inherently unstable social structures, in that two members of a triad typically align more frequently with each other than they do with the third. The triadic dynamic appears to have influenced the authors' interactions. Even though each of the authors took his or her share of abuse, the most frequent alignment was clearly Barley and Meyer against Gash. From time to time, Meyer and Barley discussed their regret at "ganging up" on Gash. At some level, the alignment probably reflected the fact that Gash was a "solo" on a number of dimensions. In contrast to Meyer and Barley, Gash was single, female, more interested in psychology, and less ideologically committed. Although the triadic dynamic did not seriously disrupt the authors' collaboration, and although Gash claims that she was not conscious of being unduly persecuted, such dynamics may be inherently troublesome when research teams are composed of three persons.

6. After the SCOS conference in Montreal, Meyer and Barley ran a second search of the on-line data bases referenced in "Cultures of Culture" to see whether they had missed any papers that were added to the data bases after their initial search nearly a year before. The search yielded approximately 80 additional articles for coding. Meyer and Barley coded these articles during the late summer and early fall of 1986 and then reanalyzed the data before submitting a draft of the paper to *ASQ*.

7. In all likelihood, an untold number of published research papers actually ride on the work and ideas of students. Too often students are not even acknowledged in footnotes. To claim that unacknowledged students only ran the data is to pretend that statistical analysis involves no substantive decisions about how to treat the data and how to decipher their meaning. We suspect that very few full-time academics would accept such treatment from their colleagues.

Commentary

The Culture of
Social Science Research

Cathy A. Enz

No social science can ever be "neutral" or simply "factual," indeed not "objective" in the traditional meaning of these terms. (Myrdal, 1969)

Stephen Barley, Gordon Meyer, and Debra Gash's "Cultures of Culture: Academics, Practitioners and the Pragmatics of Normative Control" is a rich and suggestive paper in which they attempt, among other things, to explore the influences of academics and practitioners on each other's portrayals of a new issue, namely, organizational culture. They do so by employing textual analysis of a carefully selected set of theory and practice articles on organizational culture to determine whether or not one perspective has acculturated or changed the other. The results indicate that over time the discourse of academics has become more like that of practitioners. Academics have been acculturated, increasingly defining their discussions of culture according to the interests and issues of practitioners. In contrast, practitioners were not influenced by the conceptual and symbolic language of early academics. An equally intriguing finding is that the early academic writers who continued to write on the subject altered their later writing to reflect the practitioner orientation and the traditional functionalist framework of "mainstream" academic writers.

> 66 Perhaps because they have always worked at the margin between basic and applied social science, organizational theorists have long contemplated how the academic community and the managerial community influence each other (Thompson, 1956). Over the years, two competing views of the relationship have evolved. The dominant perspective frames the relation in terms of the diffusion and utilization of knowledge (Cherns,

1972; Duncan, 1974; Beyer, 1982). The terms are borrowed from the physical and life sciences where they denote the process by which basic research inspires practical advances in technical fields such as computers and medicine. From this vantage point, academics are seen as impartial sources of empirical principles that are taught to practitioners who, in turn, put the knowledge to worldly use (Beyer and Trice, 1982). Since diffusion theorists presume that knowledge flows from the academy to the field, their primary concern has been to disseminate information and stimulate applications of new knowledge (Corwin and Louis, 1982; Dunbar, 1983).

The second view, which we dub the political perspective, stands in sharp contrast to the notion of knowledge diffusion. Whereas diffusion theorists assume that academics frame problems for practitioners, political theorists contend that scholarly endeavors are ultimately defined by the interests of those who dominate society and by whose largess academics retain the privilege of pursuing research (Wassenberg, 1977; Salaman, 1979; Clegg and Dunkerley, 1980; Watson, 1980). The interests of the powerful are said to shape research more significantly than the curiosity of the researcher, primarily because the former control the latter's access to critical resources.

The problem with both perspectives is that each offers an oversimplified and essentially ideological account of what is likely to be a complex process (Pettigrew, 1985). Both explanations presume that relations between academics and practitioners are hierarchically structured: that one world awaits direction from the other. The two simply reverse the role of leader and follower. Moreover, both assume from the outset that the two worlds have similar interests: in the first case, more accurate and useful knowledge; in the second, maintenance of a system of dominance. Consequently, neither allows for the possibility that managerial and academic worlds might conflict or that reciprocal influence might occur. Most critical, however, is the fact that neither perspective has subjected its claims to empirical tests, largely because each takes the direction of influence for granted.   99

(Barley, Meyer, & Gash, 1988, pp. 24-25)

This paper is valuable to any social scientist, whether he or she studies culture or not, because it empirically investigates the extremely important question of the linkage of theory and practice. Barley, Meyer, and Gash are deserving of considerable praise for their effort to take the question beyond the realm of ideological positions, into the domain of testing patterns of change and influence. They employed an innovative methodology to compare the pragmatics (connotative meanings) of language usage in academics' and practitioners' articles. However valuable this methodology might be for subsequent research, I will concentrate on the results themselves, and use them as an opportunity to reflect on how organizational researchers do social science.

For me the major contribution of "Cultures of Culture" is not its use of an intriguing methodology or its presentation of data in a studied, objective, and rule-guided form. I like a paper that grounds its questions in previous work and can place some tension between two perspectives, but this alone is not what I found fascinating. I applaud the authors for their deliberate and precise refutation of possible criticisms of method and analysis. It is always delightful to raise a question while reading, only to have the authors raise and answer it in the next sentence; this is good practice of the craft, but not what I find exemplary about this paper. What captures my interest and draws me back again to this paper is what it does not explain, what it cannot say, and what it might suggest for all of us making a living as social scientists. I like this paper because it forces me to examine the way I do research, the sources of my thinking, and the ways in which language shapes our research agenda.

The Data Are Silent

Barley and his colleagues accurately note that the data are silent on why academic outlets adopted or accommodated practitioners' issues. The data are mute on why academic discourse shifted toward the language evident in early practitioner texts, while practitioner texts remained the same over time. We do not know why the same academics who wrote before 1982 changed their perspectives after that time. These are the puzzles of Barley, Meyer, and Gash's study.

Sorting through the distinctions among early academic, later academic, and practitioner texts is part of the challenge in understanding the culture literature. Close examination of the academic speech community's model shows that early academic texts introduced culture as an alternative paradigm to the functionalist models for studying organizations. These texts were varied in their own frames, making them more difficult to categorize, but shared an emphasis on departing from traditional organization theory. In contrast, the practitioner writings had a consistent discursive model that stressed causality and embodied functionalist references to bureaucracy, structural differentiation, and rational control. Emphasis was placed on how management could control people and things in the face of environmental volatility.

Barley, Meyer, and Gash demonstrate that the shift from early to later academic writing is not just a move from interpretive to functionalist research traditions, but their analysis does reveal the close linkages between the practitioner and traditional functionalist academic texts.

In fact, both are incorporated into the practitioner model of discourse. The use of pragmatics in this study highlights the "radical" nature of early academic writing and offers some intriguing possibilities for speculation about acculturation in the organizational sciences.

> 66 It is possible to argue that the change in academic discourse offers testimony to nothing more than functionalism's resilience. As previously stated, many early academic authors viewed organizational culture as an opportunity to build a phenomenologically attuned, if not a fully interpretive, theory of organizational life (Van Maanen, 1979a; Louis, 1983). As Smircich (1983:347) put it, interpretive theorists viewed culture as something that organizations "are," not as something they "have." In making such a distinction, the interpretive theorists rebelled against the dominant tenets of a functionalist paradigm (Parsons, 1951; Kroeber and Parsons, 1958; Jaeger and Selznick, 1964). If the interpretive rebellion was quickly cooled by a resurgence of functionalism, then one would expect academics' and practitioners' rhetorical styles to have converged, not because academics adopted a managerial perspective but because practitioners never abandoned a functionalist ontology. The results might therefore reflect little more than the fact that academics gradually reappropriated functionalist language. To counter such an argument would necessitate showing that recent academic rhetoric is as indicative of managerialism as it is of functionalism.
>
> As an intellectual doctrine, functionalism is a variant of systems theory: it concerns dynamics that exist beyond (and in spite of) actors' volitions (Boudon, 1979). A functionalist theory of culture should therefore posit impersonal forces of control for whose operation the intentions of the powerful are irrelevant. To the degree that academic discourse began to sanction an intent to control, one could argue that its authors moved beyond the rhetorical requirements of functionalism to adopt a more managerial stance. Individual regressions of the four indicators that measure a purely systemic view of control on year of publication showed that only $CthrO^+$ and $CthrO^-$ became more common in academic texts. The two other indicators ($CthrC^+$, $CthrC^-$) remained constant over time. There is, then, some support for the claim that academic rhetoric became more functionalist. However, there is also evidence that the rhetoric became more managerial. Eight indicators implied an actor's ability or desire to control and, hence, were indicative of more than the mere restraints of an impersonal system ($Covo^+$, $Covo^-$, $CthrOA^+$, $CthrOA^-$, $Covc^+$, $Covc^-$, $CthrCA^+$, $CthrCA^-$). Separate regressions of these indicators on year of publication revealed that six of the eight became more common in academic discourse by the end of 1984. Thus, it seems fair to argue that the convergence between academic- and practitioner-oriented discourse cannot be explained by a resurgence of functionalism alone. 99

(Barley, Meyer, & Gash, 1988, p. 53)

Why did the pragmatics of early academic texts change? Would the change have occurred if the early texts had not challenged the traditional academic community? Is it possible that the findings of this study on organizational culture are unique because the early writers departed from the ontological and epistemological assumptions of doing research within the organization studies discipline? Could the shift from academic to practitioner concerns reflect pressures to sustain legitimacy in the academic community at large, to address practitioner relevance, and to survive in the academic enterprise? The lack of answers to these questions makes Barley, Meyer, and Gash's study all the more intriguing as a context for commentary and reflection on doing social science research.

Since the early academic work relied on an interpretive orientation to culture that challenges the fundamental assumptions and methods of functionalist research, it is not surprising that this research was not sustained. Herein lies an intriguing opportunity for speculation that emerges from the Barley et al. study. The findings raise disturbing questions about the culture of academia in the organizational sciences. Can alternate paradigms be sustained after being introduced when they challenge the traditional, taught, and presumably fundamental assumptions and ways of setting up the problem? The evidence of this study suggests not. To understand how a scientific community functions as a producer and validator of sound knowledge, we must ultimately understand the unique set of shared standards and values for doing research that serve to control the production of scholarship. We must further consider our roles as teachers of the practitioners of tomorrow, for they will likely solve the problems of tomorrow with the solutions and theories we provide today. The practitioners' interest in normative cultural control may be an extension of what they were taught about formal control in organizations. The able practitioner, like the bright student, may model a new problem on another previously encountered and solved. In addition, the shifting of academic discourse may suggest a rubber band approach to theorizing in which new ideas may stretch or challenge conventional thinking, but ultimately bounce back to traditional or popular thinking.

Framing a Research Agenda

I believe that Barley, Meyer, and Gash's study suggests that we are what we read, learn, and take for granted. Biases permeate theoretical and practical approaches to social problems, and we must be aware and apprehensive as we proceed in the offering of solutions. I cannot help but wonder how many of the newcomers to the culture literature were doctoral students moved simultaneously by the practitioner books and the early cultural writings within an interpretive framework. Figuring larger than life between the notable contrasts of these different writings were dissertation advisers who wanted to see "sound positivist empiricism" and the subsequent "marketability" of the work to recruiters and journals in the field. As the student of organizational culture struggled for clarity, a host of academic subcultures diverged and possibly muddied their thinking.

66 Similarly, one cannot decide from the data whether the convergence is to be welcomed or lamented. Such an evaluation rests ultimately on one's sense of the rightful relationship between organizational theory and practice. It may be appropriate for organizational theory, as an applied discipline, to concern itself with issues that trouble organizations during specific eras. To the degree that the data suggest this has occurred, they may indicate the field's responsiveness rather than the ease by which it is co-opted. Alternately, if applied social sciences require basic social research as a fount of knowledge (as is generally assumed to be true of the hard sciences), then the results should give us pause, for the data suggest that there may exist a set of social dynamics strong enough to compromise, in less than a decade, a stream of research that is apparently without immediate practical relevance. Since it is clear that no one gains when knowledge is pushed to relevance before its time, it would behoove organizational theorists to identify the social pressures that might contribute to such a rapid convergence of aim and to determine whether these dynamics are harmful. 99

(Barley, Meyer, & Gash, 1988, p. 55)

"Cultures of Culture" has reinforced my belief that social science research is not and cannot be objective, and that systematic biases are present because of the assumptions and value premises we employ, many of which are grounded in our education as academics (or MBAs) and reinforced by what is written in journals, newspapers, and magazines. The findings that (a) academics are influenced by how practitioners frame the problem of organizational culture and (b) early academic texts changed to fit practitioner and mainstream academic texts are intriguing but troubling. The message I have chosen to draw from this study is that it is the responsibility of every researcher and practitioner to identify the sources of their assumptions and to articulate their value premises carefully. Theory and practice are both grounded in beliefs and opinions that require specification if we are to understand the lens through which the social world is viewed.

Myrdal (1969, p. 40) contends that "facts kick," by which he means that social research will eventually correct itself so long as the researcher avoids seeking what is not there. I, like Myrdal, believe in the power of self-healing that can be obtained through diligent empiricism. Exemplary research in my opinion begins with an intriguing idea, such as the one in the Barley et al. study, but is not a single study. In fact, research is exemplary when many researchers amass observations and analysis to find what they had not expected. It is my hope that the "facts" of this empirical paper "kick" other researchers into attempting further empirical examination of discipline-based influences and assumptions in the field of organization studies. We have yet to understand fully either our roles as theorists and applied scientists or the subcultures that shape our thinking.

Commentary

Comment on
"Cultures of Culture"

Mayer N. Zald

It is very clear that postmodernism has breached the walls of the positivist empire. The analysis of narrative form and the devices of rhetoric, semiotics, and deconstructionist renditions of social texts and behavior are entering realms previously off-limits. The walls of positivism are crumbling in all of the social sciences, though at different rates (see Zald, 1988, 1989).

What has been less clear is the direction that would be taken by the transformed disciplines. Are the social sciences to become adjuncts to the humanities, merely convenient groupings of scholars reading societal structures and objects as texts? Are the social sciences to be seen as interpretive disciplines, giving up the logic of hypothesis testing and systematic explanatory models? Or, on the other hand, are we to find ways of retaining positivist goals while finding new modes of systematically studying texts and discourse? Can we tame the analysis of the symbolic order, so that we study meaning-in-use in a systematic and coherent mode? At the most general level, what are the modes of combining the humanities and the social sciences? What are the costs and benefits of different ways of reordering the intellectual agenda (at the boundaries of disciplines)?

It has been clear for some time that Stephen Barley has had a conception of one way to go on these issues. He has taken for his agenda the systematic study of the symbolic realm. In particular, he has seen that certain methods of semiotic and linguistic analysis can profitably be used to explore topics of interest to social scientists, but inaccessible in the older kit bag of content analysis. The result is a hypothesis testing and explanatory approach to meaning, to the complex utilization of symbols and signs.

Barley, Meyer, and Gash set out to test hypotheses about the transformation of the conceptual world of practitioners and academicians. The question is, as the term *culture* came to be employed by practitioners and academicians, who influenced whom? Did practitioners borrow from academics? Did academics merely jump onto the practitioners' bandwagon?

I presume that there are several ways one could study such questions. An investigator could do an interview study, for instance, in which he or she asked scholars and practitioners how they had developed their conceptions of culture, who they had read, and so on. Or citation patterns in journal articles could be examined. One could look to see if practicing managers claimed to be influenced by academics or vice versa. Barley, Meyer, and Gash do none of these. Instead, they examine the pragmatics of linguistic usage. They employ systematic coding techniques and relatively high-powered quantitative statistics to test hypotheses.

> 66 Determining precisely which patterns of change had occurred required regressing, separately for each speech community, the three factors on the year of a paper's publication. Since the regressions were now confined to a single community, if the coefficient for year of publication was significant, its sign would indicate whether a theme had become more or less prevalent in a given stream of discourse. As was explained in the discussion of Figure 1, by comparing the coefficients for each pair of regressions, it was possible to specify the direction of influence among academics and practitioners.
>
> Results for the paired regressions are displayed in Table 7. For both "the economic value of controlling culture" and "rational control and differentiation," the beta weights for academic texts were positive and statistically significant. In contrast, the coefficients for practitioner-oriented texts were insignificant. This pattern of coefficients is consistent with the type of convergence portrayed in panel C of Figure 1. The third pair of regressions indicates that neither speech community changed its position on the "integrative value of culture" since the coefficients for both equations were insignificant (yielding a configuration similar to that of Figure 1, A). These results strongly suggest that the rubric of practitioners' discourse remained stable over time, while the pragmatics of academics' discourse changed. Specifically, those who wrote for academics gradually placed more emphasis on the economic value of controlling culture and on rational control and differentiation. In this regard, the pragmatics of academic discourse came to resemble more closely that of the practitioners' subculture.   99

TABLE 7 Trends in the Pragmatics of Organizational Culture in Academic- and Practitioner-Oriented Texts, January 1975 to December 1984

Factor score	Academic texts			Practitioner texts		
	Inter	Year	R^2	Inter	Year	R^2
Economic value of controlling culture	−1.77*	.23*	.20*	.17	.05	.03
Rational control and differentiation	−1.65*	.27*	.27*	.62*	−.09	.03
Integrative value of culture	.39	−.06	.02	.49	−.10	.04

*$p > .01$.

(Barley, Meyer, & Gash, 1988, pp. 51-52)

It appears to me that "Cultures of Culture" is not part of a larger program in the sociology of the professions or the sociology of science; although the authors studied academics' relationships to practitioners, they were more interested in the method than in the particular substantive hypotheses. If that is the case, the question is, Does this method get us further than we got with older tools?

I would argue that it does. Before we began reaching out to semiotics and linguistics, social scientists were restricted to what Jonathan Reider has called "earnest" analyses of meaning. Either casually or systematically, we were restricted to the announced normal language definitions of the users. The values of a political speech were those announced by the user—no subtext, no means of finding dark spaces, no systematic rendering of ideological complexity. Although the social scientist as interpreter might render complexity, there was little hope of replication or systematic interpretation. In the older mode the systematic analyst might employ content analysis, but that method was relatively limited in its ability to do more than count themes.

Now, however, we will be able to study meaning in complex ways. Most important, the tools of analysis can be taught and studies and findings can be replicated. One thing that distinguishes interpretive from scientific approaches is the desire for replicable results. How do we tell that one interpretation is better than another? How do we tell that the findings are not merely in the eye of the beholder? Positivist approaches separate interpretation from data gathering in order to

make explicit the measurement and observational phase of the knowledge acquisition process. Interpretive modes are not without criteria
of validity, but they tend to downplay observational rigor.

Barley, Meyer, and Gash present a method that can be taught to
others and that can lead to replication. I am not sure that one wants to
replicate this particular study, but I do believe that the study of
meanings and their transmission is aided by their effort. If we reject a
simpleminded behavioristic conceptualization of life in organizations,
we must inevitably include an analysis of the production and transmission of meaning. The next question becomes, then, How are we to
do it? Barley, Meyer, and Gash point the way.

© Academy of Management Journal
1988, Vol. 31, No. 1, 9–41.

TIME AND TRANSITION IN WORK TEAMS: TOWARD A NEW MODEL OF GROUP DEVELOPMENT

CONNIE J. G. GERSICK
University of California, Los Angeles

This study of the complete life-spans of eight naturally-ocurring teams began with the unexpected finding that several project groups, studied for another purpose, did not accomplish their work by progressing gradually through a universal series of stages, as traditional group development models would predict. Instead, teams progressed in a pattern of "punctuated equilibrium," through alternating inertia and revolution in the behaviors and themes through which they approached their work. The findings also suggested that groups' progress was triggered more by members' awareness of time and deadlines than by completion of an absolute amount of work in a specific developmental stage. The paper proposes a new model of group development that encompasses the timing and mechanisms of change as well as groups' dynamic relations with their contexts. Implications for theory, research, and practice are drawn.

Groups are essential management tools. Organizations use teams to put novel combinations of people to work on novel problems and use committees to deal with especially critical decisions; indeed, organizations largely consist of permanent and temporary groups (Huse & Cummings, 1985). Given the importance of group management, there is a curious gap in researchers' use of existing knowledge. For years, researchers studying group development—the path a group takes over its life-span toward the accomplishment of its main tasks—have reported that groups change predictably over time. This information suggests that, to understand what makes groups work effectively, both theorists and managers ought to take change over time into account. However, little group-effectiveness research has done so (McGrath, 1986).

One reason for the gap may lie in what is unknown about group development. Traditional models shed little light on the triggers or mechanisms of change or on the role of a group's environment in its development. Both areas are of key importance to group effectiveness (Gladstein, 1984; Goodstein & Dovico, 1979; McGrath, 1986). This hypothesis-generating study,

I am grateful to Richard Hackman, Kelin Gersick, David Berg, Lee Clarke, Barbara Lawrence, William McKelvey, and several anonymous journal reviewers for their helpful comments on earlier drafts of this work. This research was supported in part by the Organizational Effectiveness Research Program, Office of Naval Research, under contract to Yale University.

Introductory Remarks:
Journey 2

"Time and Transition in Work Teams: Toward a New Model of Group Development," by Connie J. G. Gersick. Published in *Academy of Management Journal*, 31 (1988), 9-41. Copyright 1988 by the *Academy of Management Journal*. Excerpts from this article are reprinted in this volume by permission.

What does a group in an organization do, from the moment it convenes to the end of its life-span, to create the specific product that exists at the conclusion of its last meeting? (Gersick, 1988, p. 11)

With this question, Connie Gersick began her research assistant assignment in a Yale MBA classroom, watching a student case analysis group. The question differed from that of traditional group research in two important respects. First, the groups were work teams. They were charged by an external authority to produce an output for evaluation or use by powerful others. In contrast, the group dynamics tradition focused on groups of self-motivated equals coming together to develop in individual interpersonal maturity. The group decision-making tradition focused on temporary groups in laboratory settings. Second, Gersick was interested in the *content* as well as the process of the groups' interactions and decisions.

To answer the question, Gersick adopted an unorthodox approach. She chose to ignore the normative linear movement from careful literature review, to deduction of hypotheses, to careful operationalization, to design, to inference making. Instead, Gersick temporarily put aside the disciplines of convention in favor of the abandon of enthusiastic curiosity and unconstrained involvement in the organizational world. She watched and recorded, not with the intention to confirm or disconfirm, but rather with the intention to "see."

Her observation of the MBA case group was soon followed by observation of another group, then another and another. For each case, hours of observation required days of transcript analysis and case history development. She came to the conclusion that the processual stages of group development and group decision-making traditions did not apply to these work teams. Rather, a series of chronological phases seemed to underlie otherwise disparate group experiences. In particular, she conceptualized the notion of a "midpoint transition." This transition occurs halfway through the time allotted to a group for its project. At the midpoint, each team reappraised its group process and the content of its work. Based on this reappraisal, the group made decisions that oriented the team's activity for the remainder of its life cycle.

After developing these ideas, Gersick returned to the field to watch again. This time, four diverse groups came under her attentive eyes and ears. No longer a naive observer, she developed more disciplined and rigorous analytic methods to prevent her from selectively discovering evidence for her hypotheses.

Data collection, data analysis, and dissertation behind her, Gersick faced and mastered the task of presenting her qualitative findings in the journal article format. There were few extant exemplars to serve as templates.

In her commentary, Gersick takes us "backstage" (Goffman, 1959) by presenting "some of the conditions that fostered and shaped my work." She emphasizes the requirements of ample time, a supportive environment, and supportive colleagues as crucial to her success. She describes, in detail, the nature of the support and help she received from a variety of sources. In addition, she notes how her lack of investment in the existing literature allowed her to be lucky enough to see the midpoint transition.

Richard Hackman was Connie Gersick's dissertation adviser. In his commentary, he shares with us his unique perspective on Gersick's work and draws what he sees as the lessons of her experience. Hackman stresses the importance of intimate involvement with the phenomenon of interest. That involvement will lead the researcher to develop methods appropriate to the questions generated. Finally, he encourages researchers to trust themselves and not the "marketplace" of employers and gatekeepers when doing exemplary research. As Gersick's work demonstrates, new findings and ideas may be too fragile to stand up to the rigors of premature testing against established understandings and methods. Subsequent laboratory studies have shown that the results of Gersick's exploratory study do stand up to scrutiny using traditional methods and standards (Gersick, 1989).

Janice Beyer is the other commentator on Gersick's article. She, too, has a unique viewpoint on Gersick's work. She shares with us the progress of the manuscript through the editorial process under her guidance as editor of the *Academy of Management Journal*. This description is set in the context of a discussion of the exemplary features of Gersick's research and her own goals for the journal under her editorship.

We have little to add to the commentators' identification of the exemplary qualities of this research. We can add a comment on our decision to include the Gersick study. The decision revolved around the paradigm-making nature of her research. In this article, Gersick announces a new paradigm for the study of work teams. We see her research process as a potential exemplar for those who would set new puzzles.

We note that paradigm making is not a solitary process. Relative to more traditional puzzle solving, such research involves substantial uncertainty. A high level of researcher commitment and an environment rich in support for the researcher's endeavor are required to absorb this uncertainty. We need to consider the availability of research environments conducive to paradigm making. Paradigm making appears to be a task of almost heroic proportions. Should this be the case? Is it best left to idealistic graduate students and rogue researchers?

Finally, we admire Gersick's courage in undertaking this research. Those who fish in the murky waters of "real" phenomena without the security of a nomological net take risks. Having spent much time and energy, they may return empty-handed. When they do return with new insights, they are met by skeptical colleagues who have heard too many fish stories/anecdotes or the uncomprehending stares of those who haven't "been there." Only with the disciples of normal science can the pearl be set in the academic discourse of theory and method. In doing so, Gersick recognized the utility of "punctuated equilibrium" from evolutionary science as a theoretical frame for her work. She overcame all obstacles to provide us with new insight into the workings of work teams in organizations.

Time and Transition in My Work on Teams: Looking Back on a New Model of Group Development

Connie J. G. Gersick

To me, what is most exciting about my research is the phenomenon of group development itself. Though it has been nine years since I started this work, I still find it fascinating that groups fall into patterns so rapidly, stay within them so long, and—most interesting of all—break out of old patterns and into new ones with such predictable timing. So, when asked to reflect on how I produced this piece of research, I have to say that a large part of it was luck. I happen to have focused my attention on a place where something intriguing was going on.

On the other hand, if this were entirely a matter of choosing a lucky research site, then midpoint transitions and punctuated equilibria in group development would have been discovered long ago. People had been studying small groups for 30 years before I started. Luck may be necessary for doing research that turns out interesting, but it is probably not sufficient. In the hopes of conveying something that others may find useful, then, I have tried to identify some of the conditions that fostered and shaped my work. Some of these deal with my research methods; many deal with the help other people gave me.

Making an Interesting Discovery

In a small way, the beginning of my research had something in common with the Hawthorne studies. In both cases, a project was designed to study one question, something unexpected happened, and the researchers turned to explore it. In 1980, my third year of graduate school, I took a job as research assistant to Richard Hackman. My first assignment was to develop a field guide for observing groups that could be used to test Hackman's team effectiveness model. The strategy was to watch some real live groups and develop anchored rating scales based on how they actually got work done. It struck me that people might work differently depending on where they were in their development as a group, so I decided I had to watch a couple of complete group life cycles if I wanted to do a good job. This got me started on project teams—where I could see a product created from beginning to end.

A second decision set the stage for me to find the midpoint transition. In exchange for letting me observe, I promised teams a history of how they made their product. I approached that task by centering on the product itself and trying to identify exactly what the team did, at what times, to make its product come out as it did. This was different from traditional approaches, which commonly disregard the particulars of teams' outputs and actions to concentrate on finding an abstract succession of behaviors or themes that can be categorized and coded.

66 THE MIDPOINT TRANSITION

As each group approached the midpoint between the time it started work and its deadline, it underwent great change. The following excerpts from transitional meetings illustrate the nature and depth of this change. Particular points to notice are members' comments about the time and their behavior toward external supervisors.

Excerpt 5 (E5). The students begin their meeting on the sixth day of an 11-day span.

1. Rajeev: I think, what he said today in class—I have, already, lots of criticism on our outline. What we've done now is OK, but we need a lot more emphasis on organization design than what we—I've been doing up to now.
2. Jack: I think you're right. We've already been talking about [X]. We should be talking more about [Y].
3. Rajeev: We've done it—and it's super—but we need to do other things, too.
4. (Bert agrees.)
5. Jack: After hearing today's discussion—we need to say [X] more directly. And we want to say more explicitly that . . .
6. Rajeev: . . . should we be . . . organized and look at the outline? . . . We should know where we're going.

(The group goes quickly through the outline members had prepared for the meeting, noting changes and additions they want to make.)

7. Rajeev: The problem is, we're very short on time.

The students came to this meeting having just finished the outline of the strategic plan they had set out to do at their opening encounter (see E1). At their midpoint, they stopped barreling along on their first task. They marked the completion of that work, evaluated it, and generated a fresh, significantly revised agenda. The team's change in outlook on its task coincided with a change in stance toward the professor. Revisions were made that were based on "what he said today in class" and "hearing today's discussion." Having reaffirmed the value of their first approach to the case, members reversed their original conviction that it was "not an organizational design problem." This was the first time members allowed their work to be influenced by the professor, and at this point, they accepted his influence enthusiastically.

It is significant that Rajeev's remark, "we've very short on time," was only the second comment about the adequacy of the time the group had for the project, and it marked a switch from Jack's early sentiment that "we've got some more time" (E2, 6). A new sense of urgency marked this meeting.   **99**

(Gersick, 1988, p. 23)

I thought it would be most helpful to the teams to show them the patterns and decisive actions I had observed, picking out quotations from their meeting transcripts to illustrate. I remember explaining to the first team I studied how they had "begun a new era" at a certain meeting, and to the second team how they had "turned a corner" in their work. My notes show that I told both these teams how they had established certain patterns right away, and stuck with them. Had I been trying to abstract teams' behavior into categories at that point, I would have missed these things. The midpoint transitions were one-shot events, kicked off by remarks made in only one or two speaking turns, and the predictive power of first meetings was visible only if one paid attention to the particulars of teams' work.

At the time I had completed two observations, my method had enabled me to "find" the basic elements of my theory, but I did not *see* them. In my initial attempt to make conceptual sense of my observations, I was earnest and enthusiastic, but not very successful. I prepared a report to tell Richard how the project was going, with conclusions about how teams made progress. I even had a series of sketches of products taking shape, which looked a little like a stop-action film of toast popping out of a toaster. Richard's reaction to this was not what I expected. Instead of being captivated by my fledgling theories, he wondered what this had to do with his model. I had gotten so wrapped up in what I was doing that I had forgotten about it!

At this point, it is important to note the fortunate conditions under which I was working. From the start, Richard had treated me as a skilled colleague. Being his research assistant did not mean making photocopies or executing detailed instructions. I had lots of room to find my own way and develop my own ideas. This did take me, temporarily, "off the track" for purposes of his research. However, I had plenty of good data to use for the observational tool (I did eventually come up with something Richard liked), and the independence I had been given allowed me to make some unexpected discoveries. I was also fortunate to have—after a short delay—Richard's support and interest in my ideas. With his encouragement, I decided to pursue my vague findings, study two more teams on my own, and write a technical report on the four observations.

I think it was not until I had studied and presented feedback to four teams that I realized *all* of them had "turned a corner" in the middle of their projects. Even then, I am sure it took one more stimulus to bring the midpoint transition into focus. Dan Levinson's work on adult development (which I had been following avidly for years, for entirely nonacademic reasons) both helped me appreciate important patterns in my own data and showed me ways to understand them. My "midpoint transition" is an explicit analogy to Levinson's (1978) concept of the midlife transition.

Turning My Findings Into a Dissertation

The process of writing the technical report—105 pages of single-spaced typescript—gave me an opportunity to flesh out my findings. I wrote detailed case studies of each of the four teams I'd observed thus far. This helped me to identify several characteristics that showed up in each team's transition, and to think through some other things about how the groups accomplished their work. The Yale Organizational Behavior Program's "design-your-own" qualifying examination was instrumental in this, because it let me justify the months I spent writing this report by fitting it into my doctoral requirements.

Somewhere around the time I was finishing the technical report, I had to select a dissertation topic. It boiled down to a choice between a study of the workplace dynamics that ensue when professional women become pregnant and a follow-up on my groups work. Several people, mostly from outside Yale, warned me against the first possibility ("You'll never get a job"). I gave it up, partly because of the discouragement but also because my very source of interest in the topic (I had two young children) limited my work time and made me uncomfortable undertaking something on which I would have to start from scratch. In contrast, I had a nice head start on the groups topic, and a lot of curiosity about what exactly happened in this midpoint transition. I decided to expand my technical report into a dissertation.

At this juncture, I again departed from traditional practice. In most places, I believe it is normal for doctoral students to start dissertations with lengthy proposals that typically include thorough literature reviews and succinct hypotheses to be tested. My research was half done when I started the dissertation, and though it had been guided by a clear *question*, I had begun without hypotheses. My only review of the literature was a perfunctory duty performed for the technical report, after I had collected and analyzed the data for my first four teams. I must have done a dissertation proposal, because I know Richard (my committee chairman) told me I had to have one, but I do not remember it. I do remember my committee declaring, in response to an idea I cooked up one week when feeling overworked, that I could not simply write "Dissertation" on the technical report and call it quits. Among other things, I had to double my sample.

My next set of challenges was probably typical of any field project. My efforts to get suitable sites got nowhere for a couple of months, despite lots of introductory appointments, letters, and the rental of an answering machine just in case anyone returned my calls. Once I got my four sites, things became easier. My fear that groups would schedule meetings at overlapping times became reality only once (exactly between Labor Day and Christmas—the midpoint for two groups!), and the team I couldn't observe was kind enough to tape that meeting for me. Most of the meetings I observed were interesting; some were funny. A few times, I had the feeling I was watching something truly uncanny. The strongest example of this was the university administrators' seventh meeting, when I was reminded on arriving that it was midterm week, and then saw a "perfect" transition unfold before my eyes.

> 66 Analysis of the second set of groups again began with the construction of a detailed project history for each team, but construction of the second set of histories was more systematic. To help preserve the literal completeness of project histories and to forestall premature closure on the developmental model, I condensed each team's transcripts in three successive steps. Every turn members took to speak was numbered and the content condensed to retain the literal meaning in a streamlined form; for example, "628: Rick role-plays president's reaction to the idea of

> tiering the account." I then condensed these documents by abstracting members' exchanges, a few statements at a time, into a detailed topic-by-topic record of the meeting; for example, "646-656: strategizing how to get soundings from outsiders on whether or not to tier the account." The third condensation produced a concise list of the events—the discussions, decisions, arguments, and questions—of each meeting. The following is a sample item: "Team estimates outsiders' reactions to tiering account. Decides to test the waters before launching full design effort; plans how to probe without losing control over product design." The condensation process reduced transcripts of 50 or more pages to 1-page lists, concise enough to allow an overall view of teams' progress across all meetings, yet documented minutely enough to trace general observations back to the numbered transcripts for concrete substantiation or refutation. **99**

(Gersick, 1988, p. 15)

The most daunting part of my data collection was observing the bankers. They talked so fast, interrupted each other so often, and used such unfamiliar jargon that I couldn't follow their meetings, and could barely understand the tapes. I considered dropping them from the sample. Richard talked me out of that mistake, and, after hours of hard labor transcribing, I finally caught on to what they were doing. (In the end, that team provided some of the easiest to explain examples of punctuated equilibrium dynamics.)

As each team finished its project, I interviewed the members and then prepared feedback—the same kind of analysis of how groups created their products as for the first four groups. I wanted to get literal histories, complete with the unique details, before I started focusing on the special events in which I was now interested. Since I was no longer a naive observer, I felt I had to be particularly methodical about this. I tried to remain open to new discoveries, even while I was looking for evidence to test and flesh out my preliminary hypotheses.

Three years after my first group observation, I was ready to pull all eight case studies together and develop my ideas about the midpoint transition—which I had made the focus of the dissertation. At this stage, meetings with Richard became especially important. He had warned me at the start that he wasn't one who believed "it's only a dissertation, just get it done," and that he had come to expect to clash with students, sooner or later, over how much was "enough." I thought this was fine. I was obsessed with the work, and sufficiently idealistic to assume that my chairman should take it seriously.

Given this combination of perfectionists, my dissertation ended up taking a lot of Richard's time. I would draft a chapter, and we would talk about it. He shared my enthusiasm, asked excellent questions, and was especially good at catching "sloppy thinking." His criticisms and questions almost always looked *right* to me—one reason the work was so much fun despite its difficulty. (I think some students feel they have to struggle with their advisers—I felt my adviser was helping me struggle with the material.) Another reason was that Richard was much more likely to ask questions than to suggest answers. He didn't take over.

One way that he did exert strong influence was in his effort to persuade me to get "conceptual." He would ask me why some group behaved as it had, and I would start describing the specifics of what happened, for example, between Sandra and Bernard at the first meeting. "But you've got to go *beyond* that!" he would say. I didn't know what he was getting at, and he, meanwhile, expressed doubts about pushing me to do something I hadn't automatically chosen myself. After a while, I finally understood, and it was an invaluable lesson in how to build abstract theory—not just interesting stories—from qualitative data.

> 66 In sum, the proposed model described groups' development as a punctuated equilibrium. *Phase 1*, the first half of groups' calendar time, is an initial period of inertial movement whose direction is set by the end of the group's first meeting. At the midpoint of their allotted calendar time, groups undergo a *transition*, which sets a revised direction for *phase 2*, a second period of inertial movement. Within this phase 1-transition-phase 2 pattern, two additional points are of special interest: the first meeting, because it displays the patterns of phase 1; and the last meeting, or completion, because it is a period when groups markedly accelerate and finish off work generated during phase 2. 99
>
> (Gersick, 1988, p. 17)

Taking It Public

The first time I talked to other people about my ideas, outside a few occasions at Yale, was for my job interviews. This began after most of the data collection was finished, but before I wrote the dissertation. It was very helpful to be asked hard questions by people who didn't "just know," the way I did, what was interesting about what I was doing. Happily, my first interview went well enough. People seemed receptive and interested, and I enjoyed the interchange.

In contrast, my second interview was valuable mainly as a foreshadowing of some negative reactions ahead. I was asked to visit a doctoral program because "Hackman says you can walk on water"—not because of my work, which my hosts apparently had not read. A few minutes into my talk, the senior professor who invited me inquired, with some impatience, what I was getting at. A graduate student expressed bafflement and, indeed, indignation, that I had not measured the performance of my eight groups and determined which did best. She did not see the point of doing research without being able to correlate which inputs led to the best outcomes. At lunch after the talk, the senior professor launched a full-scale attack (politely held back during the talk) against my work. I have forgotten the details, but, in general, he was troubled by its qualitative, exploratory nature.

I thought I responded to the assault pretty well as it was happening, but the minute it was over, I started feeling bruised and angry. When I got back to New Haven, I went to see Clay Alderfer. He helped me think about people's reactions to qualitative work, and explained his own convictions that one should not—and need not—ever apologize for it. This put the criticism in perspective, and helped with later presentations and papers.

66 PRESENTATION OF RESULTS

> Qualitative research permits wide exploration but forgoes the great economy and precision with which quantified results can be summarized and tested. This study employed description and excerpts from meetings and interviews to document, in members' words as often as possible, what happened in the teams and how they progressed over time. 99

(Gersick, 1988, p. 15)

I did not begin the real work of making my findings public until after I had settled at UCLA and started carving an article out of the dissertation. The major focus of my first attempt was just condensing it, without developing the ideas so much. Reducing my several hundred pages to journal article size seemed especially challenging, with qualitative data on eight different teams to convey and no statistics to help display the findings, much less prove them. Dan Levinson's work, and some devices I had used in my first feedback session, provided leads. Following Dan's example, I decided to present a few case studies in detail (selected to illustrate important contrasts), and to set them within a summary description of my findings for the whole sample. Following my own feedback technique, I found short, key quotations from every team to "document" (a term Richard suggested) some of the central findings.

❝ FIRST MEETING AND PHASE 1

Almost immediately, in every team studied, members displayed the framework through which they approached their projects for the first half of their calendar time. Excerpts show the scope, variety, and nature of those frameworks.

Excerpt 1 (E1). A team of three graduate management students start their first, five-minute encounter to plan work on a group case assignment, defined by the professor as an organizational design problem. (All names used in this report are pseudonyms.)

1. Jack: We should try to read the (assigned) material.
2. Rajeev: But this isn't an organizational design problem, it's a strategic planning problem.
3. (Jack and Bert agree.)
4. Rajeev: I think what we have to do is prepare a way of growth (for the client).
5. (Nods, "yes" from Jack and Bert.)

Excerpt 1, representing less than one minute from the very start of a team's life, gives a clear view of the opening framework. The team's approach toward its organizational context (the professor and his requirements) is plain. The members are not going to read the material; they disagree with the professor's definition of the task and will define their project to suit themselves.

Their pattern of internal interaction is equally visible. When Rajeev made three consequential proposals—about the definition of the task, the team's lack of obligations to the professor, and the goal they should aim for—everyone concurred. There was no initial "storming" (Tuckman, 1965; Tuckman & Jensen, 1977) in this group. The clip also shows this team's starting approach toward its task: confidence about what the problem is, what the goal ought to be, and how to get to work on it. The team's stated performance strategy was to use strategic planning techniques to "prepare a way of growth."   **❞**

(Gersick, 1988, p. 18)

After making what I felt was tremendous progress, I sent my 45-page (long) manuscript, with high expectations, to the best journal I could think of. My first set of reviews, much like my first set of interviews, was strongly mixed. One reader seemed to love it, one was in between, and one seemed to hate it. Nevertheless, I was asked to revise and resubmit the article, an invitation that a UCLA colleague pegged (much later) as "hanging by a thread." Roughly stated, some key objections were that my findings were neither clear nor believable, and that I did not have a theory.

In the time between receiving this news and starting revisions, some fortunate events occurred. During a purely social conversation at a party, Warren Bennis suggested that if I wanted a good book, I should try anything by Stephen Jay Gould. I read *The Panda's Thumb* (1980). Later (I have forgotten why), I pulled my husband's copy of *The Structure of Scientific Revolution* (Kuhn, 1962) from our bookcase, and sat down to read it. I was astonished and delighted at the similarities among these theories, Levinson's, and my own. I now saw a larger theoretical context for my work: punctuated equilibrium. I also began to appreciate the opportunities for improvement identified by the journal editor.

> 66 The paradigm through which I came to interpret the findings resembles a relatively new concept from the field of natural history that has not heretofore been applied to groups: *punctuated equilibrium* (Eldredge & Gould, 1972). In this paradigm, systems progress through an alteration of stasis and sudden appearance—long periods of inertia, punctuated by concentrated, revolutionary periods of quantum change. Systems' histories are expected to vary because situational contingencies are expected to influence significantly the path a system takes at its inception and during periods of revolutionary change, when systems' directions are formed and reformed. 99

(Gersick, 1988, p. 16)

I think the questions raised by that first set of reviews forced me to make significant substantive improvements in the second draft of my manuscript. Two colleagues at UCLA, Barbara Lawrence and Bill McKelvey, helped me understand what the journal editor was saying, and how to respond. My husband, Kelin Gersick, helped me clarify my ideas, and showed me ways to shorten the paper when I was convinced it was down to bare bones. He offered steady encouragement—even sneaked his own optimistic prediction about publication into a fortune cookie for me, served after a birthday dinner. Unfortunately, the editor concluded that "the readers leave knowing full well what you the writer believe but not if they should believe it themselves." The new version was not accepted.

After complaining for at least a week, I decided to send the manuscript someplace else, just as it was. Bob Sutton advised me to choose the *Academy of Management Journal*. Janice Beyer, then editor, and the *AMJ* staff were wonderful. The manuscript they got was much better than the first version, but even though it seemed to intrigue them, it still left them skeptical. Among their key suggestions were that I spell out my method in better detail, that I clarify the differences between my model and traditional theory, and that I present the whole piece as explicitly exploratory. I think Jan identified some of the main problems in communicating a piece of research that was theory generating, not hypothesis testing, and that was not strictly normal science.

> 66 The traditional paradigm portrays group development as a series of stages or activities through which groups gradually and explicitly get ready to perform, and then perform, their tasks. All groups are expected to follow the same historical path. Proponents of existing models specify neither the mechanisms of change nor the role of a group's environment. In contrast, the paradigm suggested by the current findings indicates that groups develop through the sudden formation, maintenance, and sudden revision of a framework for performance; the developmental process is a punctuated equilibrium. The proposed model highlights the process through which frameworks are formed and revised and predicts both the timing of progress and when and how in their development groups are likely, or unlikely, to be influenced by their environments. The specific issues and activities that dominate groups' work are left unspecified in the model, since groups' historical paths are expected to vary. 99

(Gersick, 1988, p. 32)

TABLE 1 The Groups Observed

Teams[a]	Task	Time-Span	Number of Meetings
A. Graduate management students: 3 men	Analyze a live management case.	11 days	8
B. Graduate management students: 2 men, 3 women	Analyze a live management case.	15 days	7
C. Graduate management students: 3 men, 2 woman	Analyze a live management case.	7 days	7
D. Community fundraising agency committee: 4 men, 2 women	Design a procedure to evaluate recipient agencies.	3 months	4
E. Bank task force: 4 men	Design a new bank account.	34 days	4
F. Hospital administrators: 3 men, 2 women	Plan a one-day management retreat.	12 weeks	10

(Continued)

TABLE 1 The Groups Observed (Continued)

Teams[a]	Task	Time-Span	Number of Meetings
G. Psychiatrists and social workers: 8 men, 4 women[b]	Reorganize two units of a treatment facility.	9 weeks[c]	7
H. University faculty members and administrators: 6 men	Design a new academic institute for computer sciences.	6 months[c]	25

a. The three student groups were from one large, private university. Team H was from a small university.
b. Two other members attended only once; one other member attended two meetings.
c. The actual time-span (shown) differed from the initially expected span (see Table 2).
Editors' Note: A total of 72 meetings were observed.

(Gersick, 1988, p. 13)

I learned, with some difficulty, that it was not sufficient to say, "Look at this neat thing I found!" An intriguing finding may be interesting to take out and examine now and then, but without a theoretical context, there isn't much way to use it; it cannot join the circulating currency of ideas in a field. Beyond that, no one would be able to understand that I was proposing a different paradigm of group development unless I made the basic assumptions of the traditional paradigm explicit, and showed exactly how and why my ideas differed. I did more reading, and more thinking. I reexamined my old files and came up with a fuller description of my methods. I did some reframing. The article was finally accepted.

Reflecting on the Process

In retrospect, several factors were important for this research. One was time. Every step of the way—from finding the sample, to observing the groups, to transcribing the tapes, to writing the technical report and dissertation, to going through the publication process—took lots of time. For example, I spent one evening per group observation for a recent laboratory study (Gersick, 1989); observations for the field study took seven days to six months for each group!

Although I did do much of the work after coming to UCLA, I doubt I could have taken the time to do the whole project as a junior faculty member. Internal and external forces pressure one to get results much faster at this career stage. Graduate school provided the time to take on a big, open question, and to pursue it with the exploratory, qualitative field methods that enabled me to make a new discovery. I now agree even more strongly with Richard, that a dissertation is an opportunity to do special research, not something to get out of the way quickly so one can begin "real" work as a faculty member.

A second factor was a supportive context. The people in Yale's Organizational Behavior Program when I was there (1977 to 1984) were open-minded, happy to help students pursue their own interests, and committed to doing excellent work. They impressed us students with the importance of finding good answers to our questions—not with scientistic dogma about how study "must" be conducted. Furthermore, no one insisted (as I have heard a few times since) that research be undertaken *only* after a thorough search of the literature, and with a clear set of hypotheses to test. Normal science (i.e., hypothesis testing) has an important place in academic research, but not the only place.

Related factors were my lack of investment in the group development literature and my knowledge of alternative developmental models from entirely different areas (adult psychology, biological evolution). Indeed, my research was not theory centered at all, but problem centered. Had I set out to disprove stage theory, I might have come up with a negative conclusion (e.g., "No innate phases in group development"; Seeger, 1983), but not with a positive new model.

A final factor was the assistance I received from other people. People with whom I had only passing connections, and who were not necessarily "on my side," helped by listening to me talk or by reading my papers and taking the trouble to voice their questions and objections. People with whom I had ongoing relationships listened, argued with me about ideas, and offered advice and encouragement about how to handle various steps along the way—including the criticism.

The article has been out for a while now, and the response has been gratifying. Over the years, the work has put me in contact with people who became valued colleagues and friends. It has given me a lot to think about.

Commentary

Researchers Are Not Cats— They Can Survive and Succeed by Being Curious

Janice M. Beyer

There is considerable risk in pointing to exemplars of anything because, by so doing, we may invite microscopic criticisms from those who enjoy finding imperfections or uncritical imitation from those who want the assurance of legitimated paths. Since no piece of research is perfect, the first group may find flaws that lead others to ignore the virtues in the exemplar. Members of the second group may fail to correct the weaknesses in the exemplar and may even treat weaknesses as if they were virtues. For these reasons, it is important to recognize what makes the contributions in this volume exemplary.

Connie Gersick's article in the March 1988 issue of the *Academy of Management Journal* has several outstanding virtues:

(1) The study appears to spring from a genuine curiosity about groups and how they function.

(2) It both acknowledges and questions existing theory.

(3) It seeks new theoretical insights from immersion in the phenomena in question.

(4) It uses research methods flexibly and imaginatively, as a tool serving the questions pursued, rather than allowing them to constrict the range of inquiry.

(5) It is an unstinting effort; the author's curiosity drove her to do whatever it took to arrive at a credible answer to her questions.

Each of these is a virtue worth emulating.

Although conventional scientific training does little to foster it, curiosity is a genuine virtue and a great advantage for doing research. When scientists wonder about something, they not only tend to look for answers to questions other scientists never asked before, they become inventive about ways of finding out. Because they care deeply about what the answer is, their motivation is high and persistent. Unfortunately, most of us have had our curiosity dampened by warnings about dead cats and fellow academics who failed to make tenure. Those who follow where their curiosity leads them thus need considerable courage to face whatever professional and personal risks and disappointments lie ahead, and confidence in their abilities to impart scientific value to whatever they find out.

Evidence of Connie's curiosity emerges as she explains how the study originated:

> I was . . . interested not just in interpersonal issues or problem-solving activities, the foci of past research, but in groups' attention to outside resources and requirements, their temporal pacing, and in short, *in whatever groups did to make their products come out specifically they way they did, when they did.* (Gersick, 1988, pp. 11-12; emphasis added)

Her curiosity is very general and basic. She wants to know how groups work.

To lead to insights of value, curiosity must be informed. There is no point in reinventing the wheel. Connie's paper reflects knowledge and appreciation of the traditional, established research and theory on groups and group development. This knowledge prepared her to recognize and be curious about some large gaps in that literature. She did not focus on the ideas and evidence others had advanced. She digested that and went on to investigate what had been missed. As it turned out, the gaps were not as large as she initially thought; during the review process, one of the reviewers pointed out that someone else had been working on highly related questions. Fortunately, the other work was complementary and did not dilute the originality of her contribution.

Connie's methods helped to assure that what she found out would be original. She personally observed naturally occurring groups in great detail. With such rich, uncontrived stimuli, the probabilities were low that another observer would have focused on exactly the same aspects of the phenomenon that she did. Her curiosity was initially stimulated by some anomalies between what the literature predicted and what she had actually observed while participating in a larger study. To her great credit, she not only reexamined those data carefully to try to resolve the anomalies through new theory, but went out to collect more data to refine and support the insights. Without systematic, carefully recorded, fine-grained observations in the initial study, she would not have had data from which to generate new theory.

But having arrived at some new insights was not enough. She was still curious, wanting to know if her insights would hold in a wider range of situations. So she went back into the field to collect more data. This must have taken courage—she could have found out her insights were wrong. It also took some degree of confidence that the insights she had gained were worth pursuing. I don't know whether she received practical and emotional support from colleagues in these efforts; I suspect she did. Nevertheless, I admire her tenacity and the unstinting way she devoted her time to finding out what she wanted to know; far too few researchers can claim as much.

Analyzing qualitative data is also a very time-consuming and painstaking business. Connie was again both thorough and inventive. She had to adapt existing methods or invent new ones for her data and purposes. The constant comparative method is usually used when it is possible to collect new data to confirm or disconfirm emergent hypotheses. Connie imaginatively used it to analyze data she had already finished collecting, and then used another round of data collection to confirm and refine her ideas. Also, she rejected the idea of using existing category systems to code what happened in the groups as unsuitable to her inductive aims. Instead, she initially recorded as much detail as she could. Later she developed her own ways of systematically condensing and summarizing the various meetings so she could both detect common patterns and trace them back to the supporting detail.

At the end of this long process, Connie was able to find something interesting and credible to say about what she had observed. She had immersed herself in the phenomenon she was curious about by personally observing every meeting herself and personally coding and analyzing all of the transcripts. She went through her data again and again until she was intimately familiar with all of the details. Her thoroughness did not choke off her perceptiveness and imagination. On the contrary, it gave them value. She was able not only to detect a consistent pattern in the groups she observed, but to provide enough supporting detail to make that pattern credible to herself and others. Then, standing back a bit from her data, she was able to see conceptual similarities between that pattern and theory from another discipline. Her ability to link her insights to the more general notion of a punctuated equilibrium enriched her theory and grounded it in a more general set of ideas.

I don't know if Connie will continue to do this type of research; I hope she does. But whatever her research paths of the future, she will have gained immeasurably from the unstinting effort she gave to this one study. Like the students of Louis Agassiz who studied one fish painstakingly for a long time (Cooper, 1987), she not only learned a lot about her phenomenon from careful and painstaking personal observation, she learned about the process of learning. Her future observations, her imagination, and her critical thinking will always be informed by that effort.

When I was asked to become editor of the *Academy of Management Journal*, one of the questions I had to ask myself was whether the investment of time and effort I would make in the editorship would yield more or less payoff to the field and to me personally than any research or writing that I would not have time for during the period of my editorship. As I thought about the state of our field and the role editors can play, I realized I had been concerned for some time about the mindlessness of much of our research, which pursued increasingly trivial questions in increasingly sophisticated ways. It seemed like a narrow range of methods were driving the kinds of questions investigated and the kinds of data being collected. As an editor I might be able to redress the balance somewhat by publishing and thus encouraging research that dared to use methods as a tool to discover new ideas rather than to test the limits of old ideas one more time. I decided that if I could achieve this and other related aims as editor, the field would gain more than it lost.

Because *AMJ* already received a large number of submissions annually, I decided against special issues as a vehicle for encouraging unconventional research. I did not feel justified in doing anything that would be likely to increase the rejection rate on regular submissions. So I decided on a strategy of sending signals that *AMJ* was open to all kinds of methods and ideas, waiting for promising submissions, and then working with their authors to present their ideas and data more effectively. I had other aims (Beyer, 1985), including maintaining *AMJ*'s reputation for prompt decisions and methodological rigor, but did not see these as antithetical to my publishing studies using innovative methods. I knew everyone would not agree, but personally felt that all kinds of methods could be employed more or less rigorously.

66 DATA ANALYSIS

This study follows the tradition of group dynamics research in its qualitative analytical approach. I developed a case history for each of the first four groups after its product was completed, the unit of analysis being the group meeting. I did not reduce teams' activities to a priori categories for three reasons. (1) Existing category systems have measured the frequency of groups' activities without necessarily indicating their meaning; a large percentage of problem-orientation statements, for example, could mean either that a group did a careful job or that it had great difficulty defining its task. (2) A priori categories would have been unable to capture qualitative, substantive revisions in groups' product designs. (3) Category systems may be used for specific hypothesis testing but are inappropriate for inductive discourse analysis in theory development (Labov & Fanshel, 1977: 57).

Instead of using a priori categories, I read transcripts repeatedly and used marginal notes to produce literal descriptions of what was said and done at each meeting that were much like detailed minutes. These descriptions encompassed modes of talk, like production work, arguing, and joking; topics covered; teams' performance strategies, that is, implicit or explicit methods of attacking the work; any immediate or long-term planning they did; patterns of relations among members, such as roles, coalitions, and conflicts; and teams' discussions about or with outside stakeholders and authorities.

The entire course of meetings was searched to pinpoint milestones in the design of the products. This process was similar to that usually followed implicitly when a scholar develops a history of the body of work of an artist, writer, or scientist. I identified ideas and decisions that gave the product its basic shape or that would be the fundamental choices in a decision tree if the finished product were to be diagrammed. I also identified points at which milestone ideas were first proposed, whether or not they were accepted at that time. The expression of agreement to adopt a proposal and evidence that the proposal had been adopted were the characteristics of milestone decisions. When a proposal was adopted, either subsequent discussion was premised on it or concrete action followed from it. The milestones added precision to the qualitative historical portrait of each team's product. I searched the complete string of each team's meetings to identify substantive themes of discussion and patterns of group behavior that persisted across meetings and to see when those themes and patterns ceased or changed.

After the first four histories were complete, I searched them for general patterns by isolating the main points from each team's case, forming hypotheses based on the similarities and differences across groups, and then returning to the data to assess and revise the hypotheses. Analysis of data from the first four groups suggested a new model of group development, which I explored and refined in the second stage of the study. 99

(Gersick, 1988, pp. 14-15)

To help send signals that *AMJ* policy was changing, I chose a largely new Editorial Board. Some of the scholars invited I already knew; others I located by searching the recent literature for articles I thought demonstrated both rigor and originality. My search yielded a number of relatively junior scholars. Some I tried out first as ad hoc reviewers; a few I invited to join the Board from its inception. At the first meeting of the new Board I tried to communicate my aims and philosophy openly and in some detail. I urged members to cultivate a sense of appreciation and to focus on the potential of the data presented. If the data could tell the field something new and important, we could work with the author to help improve the rest of the paper. Subsequently, this strategy occasionally led us to encourage researchers to revise and resubmit only if they first collected additional data to strengthen an imaginative start on investigating a new area. Frequently it led us to suggest additional theoretical questions and methods of analysis.

I also carefully reworded the regularly printed "Information for Contributors" so it would not discourage submissions using any type of empirical methods. And I accepted all of the invitations I received to speak in various forums and editors' panels, using these opportunities to project a welcoming stance toward nonconventional ideas and methods.

66 RESULTS

An Overview of the Model

The data revealed that teams used widely diverse behaviors to do their work; however, the *timing* of when groups formed, maintained, and changed the way they worked was highly congruent. If the groups had fit the traditional models, not only would they have gone through the same sequence of activities, they would also have begun with an open-ended exploration period. Instead, every group exhibited a distinctive approach to its task as soon as it commenced and stayed with that approach through a period of inertia that lasted for half its allotted time. Every group then underwent a major transition. In a concentrated burst of changes, groups dropped old patterns, reengaged with outside supervisors, adopted new perspectives on their work, and made dramatic progress. The events that occurred during those transitions, especially groups' interactions with their environments, shaped a new approach to its task for each group. Those approaches carried groups through a second major phase of inertial activity, in which they executed plans created at their transitions. An especially interesting discovery was that each group experienced its transition at the same point in its calendar—precisely halfway between its first meeting and its official deadline—despite wide variation in the amounts of time the eight teams were allotted for their projects.

This pattern of findings did not simply suggest a different stage theory, with new names for the stages. The term "stage" connotes hierarchical progress from one step to another (Levinson, 1986), and the search for stages is an effort to "validly distinguish . . . types of behavior" (Poole, 1981: 6-7), each of which is indicative of a different stage. "Stage X" includes the same behavior in every group. This study's findings identified temporal periods, which I termed phases, that emerged as bounded eras within each group, without being composed of identical activities across groups and without necessarily progressing hierarchically. It was like seeing the game of football as progressing through a structure of quarters (phases) with a major half-time break versus seeing the game as progressing in a characteristic sequence of distinguishable styles of play (stages). A different paradigm of development appeared to be needed. **99**

(Gersick, 1988, p. 16)

I don't know what effects these efforts had, but I did begin to receive occasional submissions of work that used qualitative and other atypical methods. The first promising example was Harris and Sutton's (1986) paper on parting ceremonies. We worked with them so that their paper would be an exemplar for how to present qualitative data in a way that is convincing and shows its rigor. I published it as the lead article in the first issue composed of papers I accepted—again with a conscious intent to send signals that *AMJ* was open to all methods.

Connie's paper was submitted later that year. The initial reviews were mixed: The overall recommendations on a 5-point scale were 2 (doubtful), $2\frac{1}{2}$, and $4\frac{1}{2}$ (where 5 = accept as is). Each review provided about a page of comments for the author. Comments to me ranged from "This is the strongest manuscript I have seen in a year" to "the beginnings of a good review/conceptual piece . . . the data seems slight." The two negative reviewers had serious reservations about both theory and methods, rated respectively by both of them as "weak" and having "major problems." But they were sufficiently intrigued that they did not recommend outright rejection. The consulting editor was more positive ("It's refreshing to see something a little out of the mainstream"), and provided more than two pages of comments. After digesting all of the comments and reading the paper carefully myself, I decided to encourage a submission and provided another three pages of very detailed suggestions and questions; among other things, these encouraged Connie to shed some vestiges of positivist language and claims and to provide much more detail on her methods and data.

Connie's subsequent revision and letter of resubmission dealt with the various reservations and questions sufficiently well that only one reviewer still had serious reservations; the new overall ratings were 2, 4, and 5. I decided Connie was unlikely to be able ever to satisfy the remaining critical reviewer with the current study. (I wonder if his comments helped to spark her subsequent research.) The consulting editor recommended additional fine-tuning; I agreed and provisionally accepted the paper with very specific suggestions for further minor revisions. Her next revision was accepted and sent to the copy editor. The whole process, from Connie's initial letter of submission to the final acceptance, took from November 22, 1986, to August 3, 1987. The rest of the time until the paper's publication was consumed in copyediting, typesetting, proofing, printing, binding, and distribution.

This paper was one of those that helped my hopes for publishing genuinely innovative research come to fruition—at least enough to gratify me. The fact that the Organizational Behavior Division of the Academy of Management subsequently chose it as the best paper published in 1988 suggests that others share my feelings that intensive observation can yield important new insights. The fact that Connie Gersick's later research on the same topic won the Best Paper Award for research published in AMJ during 1989 suggests this initial research was a valuable learning experience. I hope other scholars follow her promising example.

Commentary

Time and Transitions

J. Richard Hackman

After Connie Gersick finished her dissertation research on time and transitions in work teams—the research that generated the *Academy of Management Journal* article on which I am commenting—she returned to me the tape recorder she had borrowed to use in the research. I thanked her for remembering to give it back, but then did a double take: Something was not right about that machine, it did not look quite the same as the others we had in the supply closet at the Yale doctoral program in organizational behavior.

Closer inspection revealed that the function keys on the recorder were different colors. The record, stop, and fast-forward keys were black, as they always had been. But the play and rewind keys were bright silver. The mystery was quickly solved: Connie had hit play-rewind, play-rewind, play-rewind so many times in analyzing the team meetings she had recorded that the paint on those keys had been worn away, exposing and putting a sheen on the original aluminum.

We joked about how much she would have to pay to have the borrowed machine repainted, but that tape recorder illustrates what was so right about this piece of research—and it offers a lesson to others who aspire to break new paths in their scholarly work. Connie had identified a few groups where, she was sure, the group development phenomena in which she was interested would be operating and visible to an observer. She then "captured" those groups with her tape recorder, and supplemented the recordings with personal observations and interviews. And then she disappeared into her tiny doctoral student office and stayed there for weeks—nay, months—playing and replaying those recordings, enduring the oppressive frustration of not understanding what was going on, until, finally, she did understand.

66 THE APPROACH OF THIS STUDY

> The ideas presented here originated during a field study of how task forces—naturally-occurring teams brought together specifically to do projects in a limited time period—actually get work done. The question that drove the research was, what does a group in an organization do, from the moment it convenes to the end of its life-span, to create the specific product that exists at the conclusion of its last meeting? I was therefore interested not just in interpersonal issues or problem-solving activities, the foci of past research, but in groups' attention to outside resources and requirements, their temporal pacing, and in short, in whatever groups did to make their products come out specifically the way they did, when they did. Since the traditional models do not attend to these issues, I chose an inductive, qualitative approach to increase the chances of discovering the unanticipated and to permit analysis of change and development in the specific content of each team's work. **99**

(Gersick, 1988, pp. 11-12)

Connie had completely immersed herself in her *phenomena,* emerging only occasionally for the onerous but necessary task of finding a job. Eventually the phenomena quit resisting and revealed to her their underlying structure. With the transcripts of her tape recordings in hand, all that remained was to demonstrate convincingly to others the new understanding she had achieved—a task that also presented quite a challenge, as will be seen below.

I do not recall exactly what prompted Connie to embark on this research project, one that from the start brimmed over with both promise and uncertainty. But I knew from her first days in our doctoral program that she was not going to be satisfied with conventional conceptual and methodological paradigms. It was that business about the *phenomena* that tipped me off. While many of her fellow students were able to be perfectly content once they had achieved a solid understanding of the theories that scholars had generated to explain some organizational phenomena, that was not enough for her. She had to first understand the phenomena herself, and *then* see if the theories did justice to them.

There was something about conventional "stage" models of group development that just didn't sit right with her. Maybe it was that they tended to be based on data from very special kinds of groups (T-groups or self-analytic groups) that operated in very special environments (no real boss, no client, no deadline, and an unusual organizational context). Or maybe it was that they did not fit with her own group experiences in the years when she was working as a college administrator. Whatever, it gradually became clear that Connie was not going to be satisfied until she had looked into the matter herself.

66 THE RESEARCH DOMAIN

Several features distinguish the groups included in the domain of this research. They were real groups—members had interdependent relations with one another and developed differentiated roles over time, and the groups were perceived as such both by members and nonmembers (Alderfer, 1977). Each group was convened specifically to develop a concrete piece of work; the groups' lives began and ended with the initiation and completion of special projects. Members had collective responsibility for the work. They were not merely working side by side or carrying out preset orders; they had to make interdependent decisions about what to create and how to proceed. The groups all worked within ongoing organizations, had external managers or supervisors, and produced their products for outsiders' use or evaluation. Finally, every group had to complete its work by a deadline. 99

(Gersick, 1988, pp. 12-13)

So one lesson we learn from this research is about the value of staying very close to the phenomena one is studying, rather than trying to do scholarly work at arm's length. Bob Grice, an experimental psychologist at the University of Illinois, used to put it this way: "Always handle your own rat." I tell my own students to "get your hands dirty." However expressed, the message is the same: If you aspire to breakthrough research, stay insistently close to your phenomena.

A second lesson to be learned from Connie's study of time and transitions in groups is that the research question should drive the methodology—not vice versa. Her study does not fit into any existing methodological paradigm of which I am aware: It is not a laboratory experiment, an interview study, a survey, or a field case study. Instead, Connie invented a unique research methodology specifically tailored to her particular research question. How often we do the opposite: We take as a given whatever methodology we are comfortable with or skilled in using and then adjust our research questions to fit. And how many opportunities for learning we let pass by when we do that.

66 This study must be interpreted with caution. It was hypothesis-generating, not hypothesis-testing; the model is oxpressly provisional. One person conducted the analysis. As Donnellon, Gray, and Bougon (1986: 54) pointed out, the use of a single judge is important in discourse analysis, where the goal is to create an in-depth understanding of a whole event, but it increases the need for further research. 99

(Gersick, 1988, p. 36)

A third lesson has to do with trusting oneself. Sometimes we tend to view science as a set of procedures that, if competently applied, will generate truth. That view may apply in some natural science disciplines (although I doubt it), but it certainly is not how learning occurs in the social sciences. Connie worked very hard, prior to beginning this research, to develop herself into a good research instrument. She knew herself—her strengths and her weaknesses—as an observer and as an analyst. By the time she started hitting the play and rewind buttons on her borrowed tape recorder, she was ready and able to trust herself to make sense of what was going on in those groups. Her work shows how intimately the person of the scholar is bound up in the knowledge-generation process in the social sciences. And it provides a small but important correction to those organizational scholars who may lean just a bit too far toward the popular image of the procedure-oriented natural scientist.

The final lesson I will draw from this research has to do with marketing. Colleagues sometimes have told me that when they contemplate a new study, they think specifically about the scholarly journal in which they hope to publish the results. From the moment that happens, I suspect, the editor of that journal is perched on the researcher's shoulder, whispering hints about what should and should not be done to achieve, at least, a solid "revise and resubmit." Connie had no such thoughts; there was no little editor on her shoulder. She simply did what she felt needed to be done to learn what she aspired to learn.

Not planning how she would market her work caused Connie great pain later. Right in the middle of her analyses, for example, she went off on a job interview at which she was severely admonished for having violated all the rules about how organizational research is done. And no job offer was forthcoming from that institution. That was discouraging to her, as was the rejection letter she received from the journal where she most wanted to publish her findings.

But Connie did get a job. And the article was published. And it won an award from the Academy of Management. And now lots of scholars and students of organizations are talking about the "Gersick model" of group development. Had Connie done all the right things, had she designed and executed this study the way research really is supposed to be done, the way we teach it in our methodology classes, it would not have turned out this way. And that, I suspect, is the most important lesson of all that this research and this researcher have to teach us.

Adapting to Environmental Jolts

Alan D. Meyer

This paper examines organizational adaptations to an environmental jolt — a sudden and unprecedented event (in this case, a doctors' strike) — that created a natural experiment within a group of hospitals. Although adaptations were diverse and appeared anomalous, they are elucidated by considering the hospitals' antecedent strategies, structures, ideologies, and stockpiles of slack resources. Assessments of the primacy of the antecedents suggest that ideological and strategic variables are better predictors of adaptations to jolts than are structural variables or measures of organizational slack. Although abrupt changes in environments are commonly thought to jeopardize organizations, environmental jolts are found to be ambiguous events that offer propitious opportunities for organizational learning, administrative drama, and introducing unrelated changes.•

Environments often surprise organizations. Trusted clients desert, dissatisfied customers sue, federal regulators file injunctions, and ecological activists boycott. These events exemplify environmental jolts, defined here as transient perturbations whose occurrences are difficult to foresee and whose impacts on organizations are disruptive and potentially inimical. The term "jolts" is used to distinguish external events from their disparate interpretations within organizations as opportunities, threats, crises, or catastrophes (Billings, Milburn, and Schaalman, 1980).

Minor earthquakes rarely topple well-designed buildings resting on solid foundations. Similarly, environmental jolts rarely threaten the survival of soundly designed organizations with well-maintained environmental alignments. However, seismic tremors often disclose hidden flaws in the architecture and construction of buildings, and environmental jolts trigger responses that reveal how organizations adapt to their environments.

A Severe Environmental Jolt

Early on the morning of May 1, 1975, voluntary hospitals in the vicinity of San Francisco were jolted simultaneously. The shock was due not to a shift in the San Andreas fault, but to an unprecedented strike by physicians. A major malpractice insurer had abruptly terminated the group coverage of 4,000 northern California doctors, and then offered to reinsure them as individuals at a 384 percent rate increase (Bodenheimer, 1975). Many doctors paid the higher premiums grudgingly; some elected to continue practicing without insurance; a few opted for early retirement. But, with a tenacity inspired by the highest premiums levied on any medical specialty, hospital-based anesthesiologists turned off their nitrous oxide tanks and went on strike. Most surgeons and referral physicians supported the strike, so elective surgery was curtailed immediately. These events caused alarming declines in hospital admissions, occupancy levels, and cash flows. The strike continued for exactly one month, and its impact was magnified by chronic excess capacity — only 40 percent of the hospital beds in the Bay Area had been occupied on an average day in 1974. Yet hospitals had acquired these beds by incurring debts that left many in tenuous financial positions. No hospital was jolted into

© 1982 by Cornell University.
0001-8392/82/2704-0515/$00.75

•

I am grateful for the valuable suggestions and benign criticisms of William Starbuck and Paul Nystrom. Raymond Miles, Charles Snow, and the anonymous ASQ reviewers also provided helpful comments on an earlier version of this manuscript.

Introductory Remarks:
Journey 3

It's the middle of June, and I'm in the homestretch of data collection for my dissertation at U.C. Berkeley. I'm doing a field study of hospitals in the San Francisco area, and some CEOs I interviewed last week mentioned the possibility of a strike by physicians to protest a hike in malpractice insurance rates.

With this 1975 research log entry, Alan Meyer embarked on a seven-year journey that ended with the publication of "Adapting to Environmental Jolts" in *ASQ*. Alan's dissertation research provided a rich baseline of quantitative and qualitative data on the population of 19 voluntary general hospitals of intermediate size in the San Francisco area for this naturally occurring experiment. But tired Meyer was not exactly thrilled with what he recognized as a unique research opportunity. When the rumored strike occurred, Meyer reluctantly decided to study three hospitals in depth and on site. His research commitment escalated as the symbolic protest evolved into a serious month-long dispute. Eventually, more data were collected on the population of hospitals, as well.

In the article, Meyer (1982) reports both the case analyses of adaptation at the three hospitals and regression results for the population as his response to the formidable "tasks of sifting, organizing, and reporting [the] hodgepodges of eclectic data" (p. 517) that the study had generated. In Journey 3, Meyer shares with us his experience of the "series of accidents, choices, and surprises overlaid with a combination of phenomenological, theoretical, and verificatory logic" (p. 517) that constitute the article. Meyer's commentary displays the same thoroughness and empirical groundedness as that found in the article. Meyer analyzed a total of 440 pages of research notes, manuscript drafts, review reports, and colleague comments to provide us with both real-time and reflective perspectives on his research process.

In his commentary, Karl Weick identifies the "jolts" article as a recapitulation of both the research process and much of the research content of organizational studies. In addition, he draws our attention to three "important tactics in the craft of research" that are displayed to advantage in Meyer's work. First is the use of comparisons of the three cases and of alternative theoretical positions around which Meyer organizes his presentation. Second is the immersion of Meyer in his phenomenon, to which Weick attributes Meyer's ability to convey to the reader the complex reality of the hospitals' adaptations. Third is the necessary, but all too infrequent, use of longitudinal research in the study of adaptive processes.

In her commentary, Linda Putnam sensitizes us to the rhetorical strategies that Meyer employs so successfully. She notes his creative use of the natural hazard metaphor, a use that "preserves the temporary, sudden nature of jolts while minimizing their deterministic outcomes." Thus Meyer provides structure to his writing without robbing it of the rich and differentiated social constructions of the strike within the various hospitals. Putnam develops a second rhetorical strategy, the notion of organizational irony, to analyze Meyer's presentation of the three case studies. This provides an analytic tool for understanding the counterintuitive, adaptive responses of the three hospitals to the strike.

Three features of the Meyer article drew our attention in considering it exemplary: the quality of the writing, the opportunistic nature of the study, and the mix of qualitative and quantitative data and methods. Meyer manages to present a very complex set of findings within the economical confines of 22 pages. Three case studies, theoretical discussion, three case analyses, and a set of regression equations are effectively communicated.

Meyer did not, of course, create the "opportunity" for this study, but he was able and willing to continue his research involvement and to follow the resulting leads. This required the mix of methods that Meyer employed so skillfully to develop and support his interpretation of the strike as an environmental jolt.

Ultimately, it is the dedication to the research craft represented by this article that we find exemplary. The use of multiple theoretical and methodological resources as required first to represent and then to examine the organizational experience of the doctors' strike stands as a model for empirical research.

JOURNEY THREE

From Loose Coupling to Environmental Jolts

Alan D. Meyer

This essay describes how I produced one 22-page journal article. When Peter and Ralph asked me to write it, I accepted straightaway—how could I pass up the chance to "open a window onto the process of doing good research"? Writing about the process, however, was much harder than I expected. It seemed that rather than opening a window, I was looking into a mirror. I found myself worrying about biases inherent in self-reported recollections of past events, ruminating about human beings' tendencies to take credit themselves for good outcomes while blaming bad outcomes on their environments, and generally struggling to set a course between the shoals of false modesty and tasteless puffery. After several false starts, I concluded that relying on introspection alone would probably evoke an essay on the research as I idealized it, not as I did it.

So instead I have taken a data-based approach. I first reconstructed the study's paper trail by arranging chronologically the documents summarized in Table 1. These data consist of 173 pages of entries in a loose-leaf research notebook made between 1975 and 1982; seven drafts of the paper, totaling 219 manuscript pages; and 48 pages of referee reports, correspondence with journal editors, and critiques provided by friends and colleagues. Next, I read all 440 pages and drew the time line shown in Figure 1 to highlight (a) key events in the researching/writing process, and (b) important inputs to the process from colleagues and reviewers. In the commentary that follows, the *italicized text* gives real-time descriptions of these events and inputs, and the nonitalicized text interprets them in retrospect. The last section of the essay offers some conclusions about conducting and reporting field research.

TABLE 1 Data Used in Evaluating the Research Process

Type of Data	Pages
Research notebook entries	
theoretical issues and topics	72
methodological issues and topics	22
empirical issues and data analysis	35
drafts of figures	23
drafts of tables	21
Manuscripts	
original and six revisions	219
Reviews	
ASQ commentary (editors and reviewers)	19
informal commentary (colleagues)	29
Total	440

66 A SEVERE ENVIRONMENTAL JOLT

Early on the morning of May 1, 1975, voluntary hospitals in the vicinity of San Francisco were jolted simultaneously. The shock was due not to a shift in the San Andreas fault, but to an unprecedented strike by physicians. A major malpractice insurer had abruptly terminated the group coverage of 4,000 northern California doctors, and then offered to reinsure them as individuals at a 384 percent rate increase (Boden-heimer, 1975). Many doctors paid the higher premiums grudgingly; some elected to continue practicing without insurance; a few opted for early retirement. But, with a tenacity inspired by the highest premiums levied on any medical specialty, hospital-based anesthesiologists turned off their nitrous oxide tanks and went on strike. Most surgeons and referral physicians supported the strike, so elective surgery was curtailed immediately. These events caused alarming declines in hospital admissions, occupancy levels, and cash flows. The strike continued for exactly one month, and its impact was magnified by chronic excess capacity—only 40 percent of the hospital beds in the Bay Area had been occupied on an average day in 1974. Yet hospitals had acquired these beds by incurring debts that left many in tenuous financial positions. No hospital was jolted into bankruptcy, but some lost sums in excess of half a million dollars.

The doctors' strike afforded a fortuitous natural experiment. By jolting hospitals away from their equilibria, it revealed properties that were not so visible during more tranquil periods. Links between the hospitals and their environments were highlighted, the integrity and resiliency of orga nizational structures were tested, and members' implicit values were manifested. Based on research conducted in 19 hospitals, this article describes how organizations adapt to jolts, and it shows how members imbue jolts with idiosyncratic meanings through processes of ideological interpretation. **99**

(Meyer, 1982, p. 515)

Events   Inputs

1975

Physicians' strike creates a   Ray Miles and Jeff Pfeffer recommend
fortuitous natural experiment   collecting additional data. Bob Biller
                                      advocates case study methods.

Ms. #1. Journalistic account
of four hospitals' reactions

1976

1979

Ms.#2. Draft entitled "Patterns of   Bill Starbuck critiques and
organizational adaptation" is   intensively edits the paper.
circulated to colleagues.

1980

Ms.#3. ASQ submission: "Tight couplings,
loose couplings, and environmental jolts"

Associate Editor (Salancik) returns   Paul Nystrom reinterprets reviewers' seemingly devastating
blind reviews, invites revision   comments as constructive criticism mixed with praise,
                                           interprets Salancik's letter as strong encouragement

Ms.#4. Revised version presented at   Janice Beyer provides praise, recommends
Academy of Management meetings   approaches to analyzing data.

1981

Letter to Associate Editor followed by   Jerry Salancik supports revision strategy, poses
phone call to discuss revision strategy   alternatives to loose coupling as conceptual frame.

Ms.#5. Alta Conference: Interpretive   Steve Barley, Peter Frost, Linda Smircich, and Karl Weick
Approaches to Studying Organizations   suggest ways to report data on linguistic and
                                           socially constructed phenomena.

Ms.#6. "Adapting to environmental jolts" 1982
First revision is submitted to ASQ

Associate Editor accepts ms.#6   Reviewers praise revision,
pending additional changes   suggest refinements

Ms.#7, revised and copyedited,
is published in ASQ

1983

Figure 1. Critical Events and Inputs in Researching and Writing "Adapting to Environmental Jolts"

1975: A Natural Experiment

It's the middle of June, and I'm in the homestretch of data collection for my dissertation at U.C. Berkeley. I'm doing a field study of hospitals in the San Francisco area, and some CEOs I interviewed last week mentioned the possibility of a strike by physicians to protest a hike in malpractice insurance rates. It occurs to me that such a strike might create a sort of natural experiment. My data in hand could serve as a pretest and the strike itself would be the experimental treatment, leaving a posttest and control group as the only missing pieces in a quasi-experimental design. By the last week of June, strike rumors are rampant, and I've discussed the natural experiment notion with Ray Miles and Jeff Pfeffer. Both strongly encourage me to collect additional data if the doctors go out. I'm thinking of mailing questionnaires to hospitals' chief executives, because the 25 field interviews I've just conducted have worn me out.

But when I tell Bob Biller I intend to use this method, he offers an analogy: "Sending questionnaires to CEOs would be about as likely to produce valid data as writing to the Romanoffs in 1918 and asking them, 'What happened last year?' " Instead, Biller urges me to study one or two hospitals intensively. When the strike begins I opt for three, expecting to spend an additional week in the field, two tops. But the strike lasts for a month.

I develop some straightforward predictions about hospitals' responses by extrapolating from their adaptive behavior before the strike. But as the strike progresses, the hospitals that actually fare best are ones whose responses directly contradict my predictions. Feeling puzzled and a little chagrined, I abandon the notion of a "natural experiment" as a vehicle for writing up the study. I summarize the three hospitals' responses in case-study form instead, and then turn to more promising writing projects. But the matter of the strike continues to tantalize me.

REFLECTION

Miles, Pfeffer, and Biller gave good advice. The additional time and effort needed to capitalize on this naturally occurring event have been amply repaid, and the decision to begin by using observational methods in a few hospitals instead of survey research methods in many hospitals was pivotal. Starting with a survey research approach would have led to an error of the third kind: asking the wrong question.

What baffled me at this stage in the project were flagrant inconsistencies between the quantitative and qualitative data I had collected. The cross-sectional correlations I had calculated didn't jibe with the dynamic processes I had observed. Viewed from a nomothetic perspective, relationships among organizational antecedents, responses, and outcomes continued to appear paradoxical and counterintuitive. But, when viewed up close from an idiographic perspective, many of these same adaptive responses displayed an impeccable logic. This tension between nomothetic and idiographic perspectives was the hook that kept me interested in the study over the next six years.

> **66** **Weathering the storm.** Memorial Hospital did not foresee the doctors' strike and remained stalwartly unresponsive for its duration. The administrator contended that "preparing for potential crises usually doesn't make much difference—although it is a convenient excuse for not doing your job."
>
> On the first afternoon of the strike, the administrator met with the controller. They reached two conclusions: first, that a prolonged strike would inflict greater financial hardships on physicians than on the hospital; and second, that layoffs and other aggressive cost-cutting measures could lead to unforeseeable work-flow bottlenecks, increase workforce turnover, and jeopardize cordial relations among members. Consequently, they decided to "weather the storm" and avoid laying off any employees. In an off-the-record meeting later in the week, medical staff members conceded that they did not wish to disable the hospital permanently and agreed to a broad definition of surgical emergency. During the month of May, occupancy fell to 50 percent of the normal level and net losses exceeded $120,000. However, Memorial's financial reserves were adequate, and the strike engendered no permanent changes or adverse consequences.
>
> Memorial's quiescent response to the jolt was perplexing because it was uncharacteristic. During more tranquil periods, the hospital placed great emphasis on cost-efficiency and consistently achieved healthy operating surpluses. Why would a profitable habitually efficient hospital forego aggressive cost-cutting and passively absorb a sizable capital loss?
>
> **A good experiment.** Community Hospital adapted to the doctors' strike rapidly and comprehensively. Members anticipated the malpractice insurance crisis, accurately projected its impact on the organization, and adjusted internal operations with such dexterity that the hospital actually made money during the strike.   **99**

(Meyer, 1982, p. 518)

1979: Writing and Revising

I've now taken a job, revised my journalistic first draft, titled it "Patterns of Organizational Adaptation," and asked my new colleagues at the University of Wisconsin—Milwaukee for comments. The paper's conceptual model is taken from Weick's (1976) paper on loose coupling. It presents case studies of the three hospitals' adaptations to the strike, and goes on to interpret these adaptations as logical consequences of preexisting "patterns of tight and loose couplings connecting components of organizations and their environments."

Bill Starbuck, whose office is next door to mine, has sent me a three-page letter. It warns that he will soon be giving me detailed editorial comments on my manuscript. Bill describes the philosophies, priorities, and procedures he is using in editing my paper, says that he is spending an average of two hours per manuscript page, and explains that he hopes the letter will keep me from becoming "irate or demoralized" when I see what he has to say about my creative product. It does.

Instead, I'm astonished. Bill has completely reworked the paper's first 10 pages—cutting and pasting sections of my original text to organize the argument logically, writing out by hand proposed new sections, inserting transitional paragraphs and sentences to link it all together. Appended to the refurbished manuscript are an additional 14 pages containing literally hundreds of explanations, comments, questions, and suggestions. A couple of weeks later, after the shock has worn off, I begin a major revision.

REFLECTION

Bill Starbuck's meticulous, interventionist approach to editing is unparalleled in my experience. I did not agree with all of his assertions about the paper or follow all of his suggestions in revising it. However, working through his comments taught me invaluable lessons about writing logically, clearly, concisely, and grammatically (these are Bill's editorial priorities). I discovered the value of active verbs, parallel phrasings, and seductive introductions. Bill showed me that microscopic copyediting can provoke macroscopic changes by highlighting flawed concepts. But the best insight was that clear writing is not just an adornment laid on at the end to show off research results in their best light. Because clear writing demands clear thinking, the greatest gains are achieved while a study's conceptual underpinnings are being established.

1980: Submission and Evaluation

I submitted my paper to Administrative Science Quarterly *in May, after pushing it through another revision and retitling it "Tight Couplings, Loose Couplings, and Environmental Jolts." Much of the energy invested in revising was lavished on the paper's introduction, where I delineate the benefits of viewing organizations as patterns of tight and loose couplings. The data remain primarily observational, and the analyses are entirely qualitative.*

Now, two and a half months later, the reviews have arrived in the mail. I notice that the cover letter was written by Jerry Salancik, an *ASQ* associate editor, rather than by the editor, Karl Weick, as I was expecting. My surprise turns into disappointment as I peruse the three reviewers' comments:

I found the literature review on pages 2-11 to be much too long, to add little to what has already been said by others, and to not address the specific problems of the paper.

The first nine pages are irrelevant to the main part of the paper. They simply repeat arguments made elsewhere for the utility of a particular sensitizing concept. The section contains too many problems to salvage it.

The reviewers' reactions to what I consider the paper's most seminal and well-articulated arguments sting, but their repudiation of the concept of coupling hurts even more:

The author's promise that the concept of loose coupling would be moved from the status of metaphor to explanation has not been fulfilled.

Assertions of tight or loose couplings are not always self-evident [or] believable. Some of the claims made about the power of the concept are dubious.

A basic problem with the ms. troubles me deeply. [This involves] substituting a new, general term into the mainstream of organizational theory where older, more specific ones exist. "Coupling," whether "loose" or "tight," seems to infringe, but in no way to compensate for the domain already occupied by the concepts of differentiation, integration and interdependence, and their specific formal and informal referents within complex organizations.

If ASQ rebuffs loose coupling—the notion championed by its own editor, Karl Weick—then my paper's chances don't look very good. Thoroughly discouraged, I leave for the airport to fly to Detroit, where I am scheduled to present the paper at the annual meeting of the Academy of Management. After my presentation in Detroit, Janice Beyer walks up and introduces herself. Jan tells me that she likes the paper and suggests an approach to presenting the qualitative data that I hadn't considered. Encouraged somewhat, I return home, photocopy the ASQ reviews, and ask Paul Nystrom, a senior colleague, to read them. My plan is to ask him to recommend another journal that might publish the paper.

"Congratulations!" Paul says after reading the reviews. "You've cleared the highest hurdle." He points out to me that Jerry Salancik wrote "the manuscript suggests a potential contribution," that Jerry invited me to "revise it for further consideration," and that Jerry has gone to the considerable trouble of writing a long letter spelling out specific goals for a revision. Paul goes on to convince me that each of the reviewers has given constructive suggestions for improving the manuscript, that their comments include praise as well as criticism, and that the changes requested by the different reviewers are not contradictory. All in all, he says, this adds up to about the most favorable outcome I have a right to expect.

REFLECTION

In the clearer vision afforded by hindsight, I agree. With the passage of time, the reviewers' comments seem insightful and charitable. In fact, after the *ASQ* review process had run its course, I discovered that each reviewer's first-round comments had pointed the way to one or more substantive changes that significantly improved the paper. For instance, Reviewer 1's insistence on precise operational definitions ultimately led me to develop a better scheme for comparing the hospitals, Reviewer 2's appeals to use archival data suggested methods for measuring hospitals' performance, and Reviewer 3's call for explicit comparisons before, during, and after the strike pointed the way to the summary model the paper eventually proposed.

66 Variables pertaining to strategy, structure, ideology, and slack had been measured for the original study. The available measures and each hospital's position relative to the entire sample are shown in Table 2. 99

TABLE 2 Antecedents to the Jolt: Strategy, Structure, Ideology, and Slack

| Organizational Antecedents | Organizational Characteristics and Rank Orders within the Sample* | | | |
	Memorial	Community	General	Definitions of lowest rankings
Market strategy				
Strategic type[1]	Defender	Prospector	Analyzer	
Innovativeness of market behavior[1]	L(3)	H(18)	H(14)	least innovative
Administrator's attention devoted to the environment[2]	L(1)	H(16)	H(19)	least attention
Boundary spanning[1]	L(3)	H(17.5)	M(11.5)	least extensive
Scope of services provided[3,4]	L(3)	L(4)	M(12)	narrowest scope
Scope of outpatient and longterm services[3,4]	L(4)	M(7)	M(13)	narrowest scope
Proportion of revenue from medicare[4]	M(8)	H(15)	M(6.5)	smallest proportion
Hospital structure				
Structural type[5]	Functional	Product	Division-alized	
Size[4]	L(5)	L(3)	H(18)	lowest patient census
Complexity[3,4]	M(8)	L(4)	H(15)	least complex

(Continued)

TABLE 2 Antecedents to the Jolt: Strategy, Structure, Ideology, and Slack (Continued)

Organizational Antecedents	Organizational Characteristics and Rank Orders within the Sample*			Definitions of lowest rankings
	Memorial	*Community*	*General*	
Formal job descriptions[7]	M(8.5)	L(3)	M(8.5)	smallest proportion of jobs
Decision centralization[7]	H(18.5)	L(4)	M(8)	least centralized
Medical specialization[4]	M(11)	L(6)	H(14)	smallest proportion board certified
Organizational ideology				
Dominant metaphor[6]	Lean and hungry	Entrepreneurial mob	Corporate system	
Perceived importance of environment[7]	L(1)	H(19)	M(8)	least important
Stories about strategic reorientations[9]	L(4)	H(13.5)	H(16)	fewest reorientations
Benefits expected from changes[7]	L(3)	H(16)	M(9)	smallest benefits
Subordinates' perceived capabilities[7]	H(17.5)	M(11)	M(8.5)	fewest capabilities
Benefits expected from participation[7]	L(2)	H(17)	H(16)	smallest benefits
Slack resource deployment				
Predominant kind of investment[6]	Capital reserves	People and innovation	Diversification and control	
Financial reserves[4]	H(16)	L(3)	M(7)	fewest days in working capital

(Continued)

TABLE 2 Antecedents to the Jolt: Strategy, Structure, Ideology, and Slack
(Continued)

Organizational Antecedents	Organizational Characteristics and Rank Orders within the Sample*			Definitions of lowest rankings
	Memorial	Community	General	
Human resources[4]	L(3)	H(15)	M(7)	fewest employees per patient
Medical technology[4]	L(4)	H(14)	M(10)	smallest investment per patient
Control systems[7]	L(6.5)	L(2.5)	H(17)	least sophisticated

Sources of Data:

[1]Ratings by panel of independent health care professionals.

[2]Structured interviews with chief administrators.

[3]Guttman scales measuring scope of general, outpatient, and long-term health care services (Edwards, Miller, and Schumacher, 1972).

[4]California State Health Facilities Commission data.

[5]Analysis of documents, interview notes, and nonparticipant observation.

[6]Index indicating proportion of available services that are separately organized, staffed, and budgeted.

[7]Administrators' responses to questionnaire items (Meyer, 1977).

[8]Verbatim language used independently by two or more informants.

[9]Content analysis of organizational histories.

*Rank orders are parenthesized and were used to trichotomize the sample into Low (1-6), Medium (7-13), and High (14-19) subgroups.

(Meyer, 1982, p. 523)

TABLE 4 Variance in Adaptation Explained by Strategy, Structure, Ideology, and
Slack*

Variables in the equation†	Antici-patory	Responsive			Readjust-ment Phase		Values of R^2 averaged across all three phases
	Fore-warn-ing	Occu-pancy lost	Lay-offs	Reve-nue lost	Resil-iency	Learn-ing	
Strategy variables	.38	.23	.00	.67	.42	.47	.36

(Continued)

TABLE 4 Variance in Adaptation Explained by Strategy, Structure, Ideology, and Slack* (Continued)

Variables in the equation†	Antici-patory Fore-warn-ing	Responsive			Readjust-ment Phase		Values ofR² averaged across all three phases
		Occu-pancy lost	Lay-offs	Reve-nue lost	Resil-iency	Learn-ing	
Structural variables	.19	.17	.00	.31	.29	.44	.23
Ideological variables	.22	.43	.43	.44	.39	.41	.39
Slack variables	.04	.00	.30	.36	.06	.12	.15

*Entries in the table are adjusted coefficients of determination, calculated through stepwise multiple regressions.
†The dependent variables were regressed separately on each group of predictor variables.

(Meyer, 1982, p. 529)

1981: Reorientations and Revisions

Along with the invitation to revise and resubmit my paper, Jerry Salancik asked for a number of improvements in my concepts, theory, methods, and data. A week ago, I finished mapping out a strategy for revising, put it down on paper, and sent it off to Jerry along with a couple of proposed figures and dummy tables. I want Jerry's reaction before committing to this particular course of action, so I telephone him. Jerry says the strategy looks responsive to the reviewers' concerns, but reiterates a point he raised earlier: "Coupling may not be the most crucial explanatory variable at work here."

I think this over for a week or so. What I'm trying to convey are configurations of crisscrossing relationships arising from multiple causes that have formed at several levels within organizations. Finally, I admit to myself that two years after I started trying to define tight and loose coupling operationally, the concepts still are eluding me. So I resolve to deemphasize coupling patterns, presenting instead organizational configurations constructed out of more operational concepts—strategy, structure, ideology, and slack resources.

Accepting this conceptual reorientation was hard, but the benefits are immediate and unmistakable: ideas jell, the writing flows, solutions to logical dilemmas present themselves, and new data sources materialize. The work I'm doing now is rapidly shifting the paper's methodological fulcrum from mostly qualitative case analyses to a balanced triangulation between qualitative and quantitative data. I'm collecting new survey and archival data, using them to anchor the three focal hospitals in the context of a larger sample and to conduct regression analyses that verify and extend the qualitative analyses. In short, I'm finally executing my five-year-old idea of presenting the study as a natural experiment.

In August, I go to Alta, where Linda Putnam and Mike Pacanowsky have organized a small conference bringing together people interested in interpretive approaches to studying organizations. This is my first direct exposure to scholars trained in ethnographic methods, rhetorical criticism, and language analysis. The conference inaugurates another burst of frenetic work on my paper. This time, however, instead of extending the analyses quantitatively, I am pushing in the opposite direction, building out from the three case studies to portray social construction processes that create shared values through language, ceremonies, dramaturgy, and other symbolic behaviors.

REFLECTION

During 1981, my concepts, methods, and data changed extensively, and the paper came together in almost its final form. In rereading my research notes for that year, it seems that a primary intellectual activity was synthesizing the stock of inputs I'd gleaned over several years from the literature, discussions with colleagues, and the reviewers. The notes also indicate that progress came in three discrete bursts. As described above, the first followed a shift in the paper's conceptual framework. The second followed my exposure to some new epistemological perspectives at Alta. A third productive burst was triggered by deciding to organize the article to reflect the chronological sequence of the research itself. Doing this let me present the undertaking as an unfolding process, changing the methods used in collecting, analyzing, and presenting data to match my evolving understanding of the topic.

> **❝ A lean and hungry organization.** Memorial's ideology cherished self-reliance, predictability, and efficiency. The controller's metaphor for the hospital was "a lean and hungry organization." Dense boundaries encircled a distinctive culture and insulated members from external change. The data in Table 1 suggest that Memorial's administrator ignored the environment because he believed that external events had minimal impacts on organizational outcomes. "Our approach," he said, "is to wait

until it's cast in concrete, and then do as little as possible. We don't try to be first—it's a waste of time and money."

Extensive delegation of authority to a stable work force nurtured shared values and consensual anticipations that supplanted explicit coordination. The administrator and controller had 12-year and seven-year tenures, and their values and personalities seemed eminently congenial. The personnel director observed that "people either quit after a week or they stay 10 years." He went on: "This is a Theory Y hospital, but it's also a pull-your-own-weight hospital. You're given tremendous freedom, but you have to enjoy working hard."

Table 1 indicates that Memorial's administrator valued his subordinates' capabilities but believed that the hospital was unlikely to benefit from participatory decisions or future organizational changes. His account of Memorial's history included a parable about the hazards that accompany strategic reorientations (Normann, 1971): internecine warfare had erupted while Memorial was devising a scheme to tap the market for geriatric care. Although the plan was abandoned, it took "five years to dispel the animosity." The moral of the story was that pursuing environmental opportunities can imperil a lean and hungry organization. **99**

(Meyer, 1982, p. 524)

1982: Publication

Jerry Salancik has accepted "Adapting to Environmental Jolts" for publication pending some additional revisions. The reviewers ask for a few clarifications and changes, and Jerry wants me to insert a theoretical overview up front to help readers follow the data presentation. When these changes have been made, the paper receives minor copyediting, and it is published as the lead article in ASQ's December 1982 issue.

Conclusion

I have extracted a few general principles from the experiences summarized in this essay, and arranged them according to stages in the research process.

THE DESIGN AND DATA COLLECTION STAGE

My study of environmental jolts sparked a continuing enthusiasm for field research. I still find it exhilarating to interact with top managers on their own turf in their own language. A collateral lesson is the importance of preserving these linguistic data verbatim, either on tape or in careful field notes. The potential value of such data extends far beyond providing anecdotal evidence or juicy quotes. For example, content analyzing transcribed interviews about the doctors' strike allowed me to adduce quantitative measures of several variables whose importance was not yet evident while the data were being collected. The "jolts" study also sold me on the value of using multiple methods—not merely to guard against common method variance, but as a means of motivating informants, tapping their higher mental processes, and enlisting their active participation in the research enterprise.

The highest cost of doing field research is the time required to collect and analyze data. It occurs to me, however, that the deliberate and sometimes leisurely pace that necessarily results can convey unexpected benefits. The long gestation period of the "jolts" study allowed me to accumulate a large assortment of theoretical notions, epistemological viewpoints, and kinds of evidence—and to infuse much of this material into the article I eventually published. Conversations with colleagues have turned up other examples of research projects believed to have succeeded in part because they progressed slowly enough to profit from their authors' intellectual and professional development.

THE WRITING STAGE

Thinking and writing are solitary processes, but clarifying one's thinking and improving one's writing are social processes. I often used my colleagues as sounding boards during the writing and rewriting of the "jolts" article. (Over the course of the project, 12 colleagues provided 29 pages of written comments.) My current practice is to start a new project by writing a rough draft, and to give an informal colloquium as soon as I feel ready to present the ideas coherently. I listen carefully to people's reactions and try to use them to sharpen my thinking. When I've revised the draft, I circulate it for the first time. I invite criticism, asking colleagues not to pull their punches. (Obviously, those who cast their colleagues in the role I'm describing here incur an obligation to reciprocate in kind.) As the feedback comes in, I try to approach every misinterpretation of my writing as evidence that I have failed to communicate clearly. Then I revise again. The revising is getting difficult now, because by this time I have usually developed an immodest affection for particular phrasings and passages. But it's worth the effort, because during the revision process I invariably hit upon new ideas, new data sources, different analyses, or different interpretations of results. A rule of thumb that I try to follow is to push every manuscript through three major revisions before submitting it to a journal.

THE PUBLICATION STAGE

Journal reviewers almost never appreciate my work as much as I think they should. Although this still occasionally hurts my feelings, it no longer surprises me. As Ben Schneider (1985) succinctly puts it, "Trying to publish in refereed journals is not a path to positive feedback" (p. 239). On several occasions, I have reviewed a manuscript that was later rejected by one journal only to have the identical manuscript arrive in the mail a month or so later with a different editor's request for a review for another journal. My first reaction is of great annoyance that the author has totally ignored the hard-won insights and comments I provided so generously in my initial review. The annoyance is soon tempered by empathy, however, because this is what I nearly did myself in the raw pique of my first-round reviews from *ASQ*.

Comments invariably appear more insightful and less mean-spirited a week or two after I first receive and read them. In fact, with the passage of even more time, many comments become constructive and actually improve my work dramatically. These experiences have convinced me that authors should (a) let reviewers' comments ripen before acting on them, and (b) *never* ignore a single comment made by a reviewer, no matter how incongruous, unseemly, or unfair it appears initially. I have also concluded that, like Jerry Salancik, most editors would actually rather help authors improve and publish their work than reject it.

> 66 I am grateful for the valuable suggestions and benign criticisms of William Starbuck and Paul Nystrom, Raymond Miles, Charles Snow, and the anonymous *ASQ* reviewers [who] also provided helpful comments on an earlier version of this manuscript. 99

(Meyer, 1982, p. 515)

AN ALTRUISTIC INVISIBLE COLLEGE

Some results of this analysis surprise me. In particular, I am struck by how many people contributed voluntarily to the "jolts" article, and by how crucial certain contributions were in shaping the final product. Research and scholarship are, of course, intrinsically collective pursuits. All academic workers belong to "invisible colleges" —intellectual networks that crystallize around shared interests. Nevertheless, I have become convinced that the sort of altruistic behavior I encountered while producing "Adapting to Environmental Jolts" is more common in the organizational sciences than in most other academic arenas. This unselfish concern for collegiality and for quality reflects favorably on our field, and bodes well for its future.

Commentary

Jolts as a Synopsis of Organizational Studies

Karl E. Weick

My graduate course in organizational theory is built around a notoriously long reading list. I've always entertained the fantasy that someday I will trim that list to just one article and we will spend the entire semester trying to understand it. So far, I know of only three articles that could support such intensive scrutiny. Meyer's (1982) "Adapting to Environmental Jolts" is one of them, and the other two are Hall's (1976) study of the demise of the *Saturday Evening Post* and Heimer's (1985) study of marine insurance decisions. All three articles, in just a few pages, present substantial samplers of both the most significant concepts and the most robust methodologies available in organizational studies, and ground these samples in descriptions of actual organizations that are rich enough to illustrate still other concepts. The way in which Alan Meyer has accomplished this provides a model of exemplary work.

In this brief comment I will focus on two things: the way in which this study exemplifies subtleties in the research process, and the relevance of its themes to current conceptual issues 10 years after it was published.

Subtleties in the Resource Process

The dimension of chronology in the research process, around which this entire volume is structured, is especially visible in Meyer's presentation of the jolts study. I want to highlight that chronology as well as point to subtle features of the research craft itself that are visible in the study.

Presentations of research findings are usually notoriously misleading accounts of how the research itself was conducted. The actual sequence of work is typically reordered, and propped up with massive omissions, to comply with the conventions of publication. Meyer's piece is a refreshing departure from that practice. Here, the sequence with which the argument is developed recapitulates the research process itself.

Sequentially, the article first presents adaptation to the doctors' strike in the voices of the hospital administrators themselves. Then there is a search for possible antecedents of what the administrators said, followed by tentative model building. The paper concludes with a final refinement and extension using quantitative indicators that approximate, with different notation, many of the things the administrators first presented in spoken language. At each step the writing becomes more specific, more concepts are added, and the author grows more confident in speaking on behalf of his informants. The reader is handicapped the same way the researcher is, moving from a puzzling set of observations concerning adaptation, through a set of possibly relevant antecedents that might bear on these puzzles, toward a section (starting on p. 528) where the adaptations and antecedents are merged.

The search for explanations is made more interesting by the addition of a subplot in which four "war-horse" organizational variables (strategy, structure, ideology, slack), each representing a somewhat different constituency within the field, begin to vie with each other as competing sources of variance in the gradually clarifying portrait of adaptation. This subplot serves to mobilize the interest of partisans of perspectives that emphasize cognitive versus structural determinants, macro versus micro levels of analysis, and deterministic versus volitional assumptions about human action. Thus the development of the "jolts" article recapitulates not only the research process, but also the process of problem framing that precedes the research process.

> 66 Most researchers believe in studying organizations while they are stable and in seeking attributes that many organizations have in common (Starbuck and Nystrom, 1981). But this study demonstrates the value of observing organizations undergoing jolts that highlight the attributes that distinguish organizations from each other. Ideologies, values, traditions, and myths can accord dignity to mundane tasks and instill the élan that transforms work organizations into beloved institutions (Clark, 1972). Such attributes help organizations obtain comparative advantages by

allowing them to develop more exquisite fits with ecological niches. But during tranquil periods these attributes can sink so deeply into the social fabric that they are invisible to the tools of survey research. They continue, however, to influence behavior unobtrusively and to perplex researchers expecting consonance between structure and behavior.

Most researchers presume that sudden environmental changes place organizations in jeopardy, and they show this by labeling the changes as crises, threats, or disasters (Starbuck, Greve, and Hedberg, 1978; Staw, Sandelands, and Dutton, 1981). But this study shows that sudden changes are ambiguous events that also benefit organizations. Scholars have exhorted organizations to experiment, be playful, and act randomly (Weick, 1969; March, 1976; Campbell, 1979). But hard-won success breeds resistance to change, and norms honoring consistency make administrative experiments risky. By plunging organizations into unfamiliar circumstances, jolts can legitimate unorthodox experiments that revitalize them, teach lessons that reacquaint them with their environments, and inspire dramas celebrating their ideologies.   **99**

(Meyer, 1982, p. 535)

Aside from the visibility of process, the jolt study is informative because it introduces a conceptual category, environmental jolts, that also has methodological virtues. Surprises, jolts, and discontinuities are all disruptions that, though stripped of inherent meaning, are staging areas that invite interpretations that are symptomatic of functioning elsewhere in the organization. Furthermore, as Meyer (1982) notes, they throw cause-effect relations into relief (p. 522) and expose tacit, taken-for-granted assumptions (p. 535). Jolts expose the organization for the researcher, in part, because they do the same for the incumbent with an agenda. Jolts invite intensified sense making by *both* parties.

Important tactics in the craft of research are illustrated by three additional facets of the study: comparisons, immersion, and longitudinal emphases. Perhaps the most important lesson involves comparison. It always takes two things to understand one: the object that is the focus of attention and something else with which it can be compared to highlight differences and similarities. The persistent comparison among three hospitals, picked for their disparateness in strategy, structure, and process, informs and enriches our understanding of each particular hospital. Not only is there a dramatic spread among the three in the degree to which they were forewarned of the strike (Meyer, 1982, Table 1), but there is a dramatic convergence of the three in the speed with which they rebound from the strike. The fact that the comparisons among these hospitals can be expanded into comparisons with an additional 16 hospitals (e.g., p. 520) exposed to the same strike and on which equivalent data have been collected increases our confidence in the conclusions drawn.

Meyer's immersion in the phenomenon seems to undergird the validity of the presentation, and is evident in such activities as his sitting in the cafeteria soaking up local color and gossip during the strike. The fact that he is apparently able to do this without calling much attention to his presence appears to be yet another instance of the generalization that younger ethnographers seem to get better data than older ones, because they are less threatening to informants (Weick, 1985, pp. 584-585). Whyte uncovers the street corner society at age 22, John Van Maanen gets inside police organizations at age 26, and both are joined by Meyer quietly drinking a cup of coffee in a hospital cafeteria while he learns about reactions to a strike at age 27.

But the immersion in the jolts study is also evident in a somewhat different way. There is an immediacy to the data, an accessibility to potential meanings, which seems to arise because the report avoids imposing greater and greater distance between the observer and the object of interest through a series of transformations imposed on indices that were cryptic to begin with. Instead, this study shows what the texture of an organization is like up close. This is a report of means, variances, and simple associations that need no further flourishes to suggest what might be going on. One is reminded of William Schutz's observation that the better something is understood, the simpler the words one needs to convey that understanding (profound simplicity).

The final point, about looking at processes over time, is self-evident. Structuring the argument around stages, events extended on both sides of a one-month strike, resilience, buffers, and learning allows Meyer to capture an organization in a dynamic rather than static form. If one is to understand adaptation and change, those phenomena must be allowed to unfold.

> 66 Strategy is conceptualized in terms of the breadth, volatility, and organizational surveillance of enacted market niches (Weick, 1977; Hannan and Freeman, 1978). The basic line of reasoning is that surveillance expedites perception of external stimuli, volatile markets inculcate adaptive capabilities, and broad niches diffuse external dependencies.
>
> Structural analyses focus on task allocations among subunits and mechanisms invoked to control and coordinate work (Ashby, 1960; Simon, 1969). The contention is that responses to exigencies will be facilitated or encumbered by task structures erected during periods of tranquility. Following contingency theory, structural formalization, specialization, complexity, and size are presumed to create rigidities inhibiting swift responses.

> Organizational ideologies are viewed as constellations of shared beliefs that bind values to actions (Beyer, 1981) and are manifested in languages, stories, and ceremonial acts (Pettigrew, 1979). When environments buffet organizations, ideologies espoused by elites should become especially salient (Hage and Dewar, 1973; Pfeffer, 1981), so the forthcoming inquiry seeks links between power holders' beliefs and organizations' responses.
>
> Cushions of slack resources are said to insulate organizations from external shocks (Thompson, 1967), fuel adaptive responses to them (Cyert and March, 1963), and foster organizational learning (Hedberg, 1981). Consequently, analyses will compare processes that create and deploy surpluses during tranquil periods with those that consume and exploit them during jolts.
>
> (Meyer, 1982, p. 522)

Current Relevance of the Findings

Returning to my opening claim that there is a one-semester course in organizational theory embedded in this single study on jolts, one can see this in at least two ways. First, the themes in the paper provide a synopsis of issues people perennially worry about when they study organizations. The four categories of antecedents—strategy, structure, ideology, slack—are recurrent in organizational analyses. For example, the well-known 7s framework used by Athos, Pascale, Peters, and Waterman includes three of Meyer's dimensions (strategy, structure, shared values-ideology), which leaves the question, What happened to staff, style, systems, and skills in the hospitals?

The theory adopted by each hospital to guide its action differed, not only in the ways identified by Miles and Snow (Defender, Prospector, Analyzer), but also in ways that are consistent with the Astley and Van de Ven (1983) matrix that divides the field into macro/micro and deterministic/voluntaristic emphases. Administrations at General and Memorial hospitals adopted a more deterministic view of their problem, whereas Community seemed to adopt a more voluntaristic view. If these assignments are plausible, then they suggest that General and Memorial may overestimate their constraints and underestimate their response alternatives, emphasize formal hierarchy over interaction and relationships, view the world more in terms of niches than networks, and be reactive rather than proactive. Community Hospital should show the opposite set of biases.

While several additional synoptic qualities of the jolts study could be cited, I want to conclude by mentioning several current issues in organizational studies that are exemplified in the work. We see several examples of what appear to be paradoxical positions (e.g., chaotic Community Hospital simultaneously shows distinct strands of decisiveness and coordination), interpretations systems (e.g., theories of action are encoded into ideologies that serve as perceptual filters), organizational learning (e.g., each hospital appears to learn the most when it acts in the manner most contrary to its normal functioning), institutional theory (e.g., a facade that increases societal legitimacy may also further internal agendas), professional organizations (e.g., complex tasks are delegated intact to individuals rather than broken down into smaller, more specialized activities), and loosely coupled systems (e.g., an organization becomes a shell within which there is a loose federation of heterogeneous components). The jolts study maintains its relevance to these current topics, in part because Meyer's descriptions incorporate diverse properties of organizations (e.g., both structure and process), but also because his descriptions themselves are rich in conceptual connotations that anticipate more recent distinctions.

Cumulation is difficult in a low-consensus discipline such as organizational studies, but the fullness of these data as well as the lacing of the descriptions with concepts exemplify one powerful means to foster whatever cumulation is possible. Thus we see a final sense in which this piece of work is exemplary, namely, it makes a contribution to the community at large.

Commentary

Embedded Metaphors and Organizational Ironies as Research Tools

Linda L. Putnam

Doing naturalistic research resembles, in many ways, the joys and frustrations of parenting. The excitement of helping a child learn parallels the exhilaration of making breakthroughs in a study. Similarly, the disappointments of false starts and redirected projects resemble the trial-and-error frustrations of disciplining young children. Naturalistic researchers, like parents, invest years of their lives in caring for and attending to the needs of their developing studies. These nurturing activities are evident in the detailed attention given to data collection and analysis, the time devoted to shaping ideas, the practice of soliciting insights and advice from peers, and the methodical preparation of manuscripts and research reports. It is not surprising that scholars often refer to their ongoing investigations as "labors of love." Moreover, just as parents eventually learn to rely less on prescriptions and more on their children's behaviors and reactions, naturalistic researchers also put down their texts, manuals, and formulas to let their data speak to them.

Doing naturalistic research, like parenting, runs the gamut of emotions, a factor that is often omitted in our sterile discussions of ethnography, intensive interviewing, and triangulating of multiple methods. These emotions often surface as a fervor that makes the research come to life for a reader, even when it is veiled in academic parlance. It is this passion intertwined with the use of metaphor and irony as theoretical tools that makes "Adapting to Environmental Jolts" a classic research contribution.

❝ **Triangulating on adaptations.** The objective of this article is to generate theory about organizational adaptations to jolts by triangulating between data from observations, anecdotes, surveys, documents, and archives (Denzin, 1970; Jick, 1979). By juxtaposing qualitative and quantitative modes of analysis, it seeks to compound their discrete advantages, offset their inherent liabilities, and achieve a deeper understanding of adaptation than either method could have produced alone. This strategy is especially appropriate for exploratory research because it yields "thick descriptions" of behavior in context that complement numerical data and facilitate their interpretation (Denzin, 1970).

The tasks of sifting, organizing, and reporting hodgepodges of eclectic data are formidable ones (Van Maanen, 1975). Methods of analyzing such data are not well formulated (Miles, 1979), and, in the absence of accepted analytical conventions, the credibility of findings hinges on "the capacity to organize materials within a plausible framework" (Weiss, 1968: 349). The organization of this article parallels the chronology of the research process. It reports a series of accidents, choices, and surprises overlaid with a combination of phenomenological, theoretical, and verificatory logic. Initially, it seeks to understand adaptation in three individual organizations on their own terms. It then examines antecedents and adduces an exploratory model of organizational adaptation to jolts. Finally, it employs quantitative techniques for refining and extending the model. ❞

(Meyer, 1982, p. 517)

The use of the term *passion* to refer to the rational, methodical process of conducting research may seem like an oxymoron. One key factor in any significant contribution to research, it seems, is the drive that invigorates the study. What compels Meyer to continue with this project? What gives this study a sense of zeal, mission, and enthusiasm? As Meyer readily acknowledges, his counterintuitive findings propel him to raise new queries and to pursue their responses. In addition to the fervor evident in this puzzle-solving endeavor, Meyer's article displays his devotion to the three hospitals under investigation. His case descriptions of the hospitals reflect an open acceptance of their modus operandi, idiosyncratic stances, and contradictory actions. Guided by notions of equifinality, he treats the hospitals as reacting in diverse yet effective ways. This unconditional acceptance of each hospital's normative practices illustrates how Meyer let his data influence the directions of his study.

Another feature that gives this study a sense of zeal is metaphorical language. A metaphor is a linguistic expression that depicts an experience or an abstraction as a concrete thing (Lakoff & Johnson, 1980). This symbolic expression constitutes a master trope for encoding and analyzing field data (Manning, 1979). But metaphors also function as conceptual schemes that organize human thought and action. That is, the selection of a particular metaphor to depict observable phenomena translates raw data into conceptual frames.

Typically, selecting conceptual frames is a major concern in naturalistic research. Some researchers generate these concepts through typologies, themes, and categories that emanate from the data (Lofland & Lofland, 1984; Spradley, 1980). Other investigators move back and forth between the data and the literature to uncover concepts that fit the research findings and the purpose of the study (Kanter, 1977; Kidder, 1981). In either instance, researchers are often "trying on" different conceptual clothes to find the most logical fit in size, style, and color.

What is rarely discussed in research reports are the "thinking units" that provide a systematic and coherent framework for interpreting findings. Thinking units are analytical tools that aid the researcher in deciding which concepts and explanations fit the data and yield important insights about organizational life. The metaphors in Meyer's article serve as conceptual arrangements for integrating disparate findings and for interpreting developments that surface over time. In an earlier draft of this article, Meyer cast responses to the doctors' strike as indices of tight and loose couplings. This metaphorical construction, however, favors structural explanations for adjustments to environmental jolts over alternative views.

After the Alta paper on organizational stories and linguistic symbols, seismic tremor emerged as the dominant metaphor or the master trope for environmental jolts. Through juxtaposing heterogeneous metaphors or thinking units (e.g., systems-structural explanations with social construction-interpretive explanations), Meyer centers on some of the paradoxes between deterministic and strategic choice models of the environment (Astley & Van de Ven, 1983; Weick, 1989). Specifically, Meyer treats environmental changes as sudden and temporarily disruptive shock waves in the form of *upheavals* or *ruptures* that *shake the foundations* of organizations. In periods of tranquility, organizations *cushion impacts, insulate,* and *buffer* components. Lean and hungry organizations store up financial reserves to *absorb the shock* and to *weather the storm.*

Employing a natural hazard metaphor to typify organizational environments is not unique. Other researchers have characterized the environment as *turbulent, stormy,* and *volatile* (Huber & Daft, 1987; Starbuck, 1976). What signifies Meyer's use of it is his developmental process for tracking organizational adjustments and his view of ideologies and social constructions as factors that enact environments and

shape organizational responses. Through constructing hazards as opportunities or morality plays, the dominant metaphor shifts away
from deterministic events such as disasters and crises toward such
reactions as "banding together," "acting as seasoned troopers," and
"engaging in learning experiments." Moreover, the loci of this metaphor are the tremors (i.e., the shock waves) rather than the jolt itself
(e.g., the epicenter of an earthquake, the eye of the storm). Responses
to tremors, then, are enacted through sets of activities in which scanning, scrutinizing, detecting, and overlooking set the stage for alternative choices. This shift to social construction of an evolutionary process
preserves the temporary, sudden nature of jolts while minimizing their
deterministic outcomes, usually one of misfortune and devastation.

What is still absent from Meyer's use of this metaphor is the way in
which jolts are premeditated. The "accidental" quality of a natural
hazard metaphor may conceal the fact that strikes are enacted as
subjective decisions and that participants, bystanders, and publics
socially construct these events as well as react to shock waves from
them. Thus both the enactment and the interpretation of the jolt may
impinge on organizational strategies, ideologies, and responses to
them. Meyer's discussion of the intergroup conflicts and lingering
dissonance at Doctors Hospital hints at the problem of treating strikes
as sudden, accidental occurrences rather than as social enactments of
interorganizational events.

> 66 Comparative research has so strongly emphasized objective measures
> of structures and resource measures of effectiveness as to imply that
> structures and amassed resources comprise the essence of organiza-
> tions (Starbuck, 1982). But this study proposes that whereas ideologies
> and strategies exert strong forces guiding organizations' adaptations,
> structures and slack resources impose weak constraints. Qualitative
> analyses depicted adaptations as more consistent with social realities
> constructed through processes of ideological interpretation than with
> objective realities imposed by environmental events. Quantitative analy-
> ses implied that ideological and strategic variables were better predictors
> of organizational perceptions, responses, and consequences than struc-
> tural variables and measures of organizational slack.   99
>
> (Meyer, 1982, p. 534)

Irony, as a metaphor of opposites, is another mode of discovery that
Meyer employed in conducting his study. Irony is seeing something
from the viewpoint of its antithesis. As a thinking unit, it is similar to
Davis's (1971) use of opposition as a double dialectic for generating
interesting theories (Weick, 1979). As a principle of discovery in social

sciences, irony challenges our suppositions about typical behavior and hence contributes to the development and revision of theory. Two basic elements that typify irony are an unanticipated link between incongruent actions and a transcendence in which these opposites are united at a higher level (Brown, 1977).

The ironies that Meyer employs in his study are the unexpected and seemingly counterintuitive ways in which the three hospitals react to the strike. In particular, the cost-efficient, fiscally conservative organization opts for a major capital loss; the chaotic, overextended hospital implements well-organized and efficient contingency plans; and a large, complex bureaucracy absorbs the shock of this environmental jolt with minimal effort. Although Meyer begins his paper by treating these inconsistencies as "ironies of fate," his research suggests that these incongruent reactions emerge from the process of adapting rather than from predetermined antecedents. The contradictions, then, surface from the evolving situation or the ripening of events rather than from amassing slack resources, employing particular scanning strategies, or adopting particular organizational structures.

Meyer's interpretations transcend these ironies by showing how each organization's adjustment fits logically into its typical market strategies and corporate ideologies. Of particular salience is Meyer's finding that Memorial's ideology reveals a dilemma between cost-effectiveness and its devotion to self-reliant, highly committed employees. That is, the inconsistency between Memorial's typical modus operandi and its response to the doctors' strike evolves from an ideology that unites employee commitment and self-reliance with conservative fiscal management.

Transcendence for Community and General hospitals stems from enacting diverse, numerous, and volatile environmental sectors. Hence effective forewarning and learning offer plausible explanations for novel or even incongruent responses to environmental jolts. Treating the environment as a dilemma, opportunity, or aberration is a type of transcendence that explains why but not necessarily how Community and General hospitals adapted their internal operations efficiently or how employees and clients absorbed the layoffs and cutbacks without resentment and ill feelings. In effect, Meyer accounts for the counterintuitive responses of the hospitals, but these accounts provide only partial transcendence for reactions that run counter to organizational routines, values, and norms.

In summary, "Adapting to Environmental Jolts" makes a number of significant contributions to research. Through astute integration of qualitative and quantitative data, it crafts a rich tapestry that depicts the evolution of organizational reactions to environmental jolts. The case comparison methodology triggers new queries that uncover the importance of organizational ideologies and market strategies in effective adaptation. Use of metaphor and irony as thinking units yields insights that defy taken-for-granted assumptions about the roles that organic structures and slack resources play in adjusting to environmental changes. Finally, this study reflects the nurturing and compassion that make it a labor of love for the reader as well as the researcher.

© *Academy of Management Journal*
1988, Vol. 31, No. 3, 461–487.

UNTANGLING THE RELATIONSHIP BETWEEN DISPLAYED EMOTIONS AND ORGANIZATIONAL SALES: THE CASE OF CONVENIENCE STORES

ROBERT I. SUTTON
Stanford University

ANAT RAFAELI
Hebrew University of Jerusalem

It has been proposed that the emotions expressed by role occupants influence the behavior of others. We hypothesized a positive relationship between employees' display of pleasant emotions to customers and sales in retail stores and tested that relationship in a sample of 576 convenience stores. An unexpected negative relationship was observed. A subsequent qualitative study suggested that sales is an indicator of a store's pace, or the amount of time pressure on clerks and customers, and that pace leads to displayed emotions, with norms in busy settings supporting neutral displays and norms in slow settings supporting positive displays. Reanalysis of the quantitative data confirmed that clerks in rapidly paced stores with high sales and long lines were less likely to display positive feelings than clerks in slow-paced stores.

People want to be happy! Be happy and they will be glad they came to your store.

Loyal, regular customers are a source of steady sales for your store. Smile!! Service with a smile and a friendly attitude will keep them loyal and keep them coming back!

—From "Effective Customer Service Increases Sales," a training program used by a chain of convenience stores

Much theory and research has focused on the role of emotion in organizational life. Emotions are typically viewed as intrapsychic states caused by factors such as job characteristics (Hackman & Oldham, 1980), stress (Kahn, 1981), relationships with supervisors (Bass, 1982), or compensation (Lawler, 1981). Such studies most frequently have examined the determinants of job

We wish to thank Mary Kay Benson, David Bowen, Larry Ford, Connie Gersick, James Jucker, Benjamin Schneider, Caren Siehl, Barry Staw, Lorna Weisenger, Tim Whitten, and John Van Maanen for their help with this article. We thank the Department of Industrial Engineering and Engineering Management at Stanford and the Mutual Fund of the Hebrew University of Jerusalem for supporting this research. Portions of this paper were prepared while Robert Sutton was a fellow at the Center for Advanced Study in the Behavioral Sciences. He is grateful for financial support provided by the Carnegie Corporation of New York and the William and Flora Hewlett Foundation.

Introductory Remarks:
Journey 4

"Untangling the Relationship Between Displayed Emotions and Organizational Sales: The Case of Convenience Stores," by Robert I. Sutton and Anat Rafaeli. Published in *Academy of Management Journal*, 31 (1988), 461-487. Copyright 1988 by the *Academy of Management Journal*. Excerpts from this article are reprinted in this volume by permission.

Anat: Now we not only have ideas, we have data. Once we make the scales and run the regressions, the paper is almost done. The introduction is already pretty much written; all we need to do is modify a few pages from our theory papers.

Bob: You bet. This paper is going to make our careers, and it isn't even going to be very much work.

Anat Rafaeli and Bob Sutton were two junior scholars who made a small splash at the Academy of Management meeting with a paper on emotional work in organizations. They knew that to sustain interest in their novel and intriguing ideas they had to turn from theoretical argument to empirical demonstration. Thus they were primed to recognize immediately the value of in-house research done by Larry Ford, a colleague from Sutton's grad student days at the University of Michigan. Ford's employer, a retail chain of convenience stores, had decided to evaluate the effectiveness of the company's courtesy training program. The chain's research department had the resources to finance a national random sample of salesclerk-shopper interactions coded by nonparticipant observers.

Sutton and Rafaeli started this empirical project with a rather straightforward hypothesis: that friendly sales personnel would lead to increased sales. Because the conceptual and empirical examination of emotional issues in the workplace was rather novel in 1988, such a demonstration could be judged as an appropriate, if incremental, demonstration of the practical importance of their approach. The study promised to be not only simple, but easy, because they stumbled on an incredible data set. However, the simple, easy demonstration became a headache—nay, a nightmare—for the authors.

They were wrong. Friendly personnel did not sell more. In fact, they sold *less*. In their article and commentary, the authors describe how they reacted, once they grudgingly accepted this empirical reality. Ultimately, Rafaeli and Sutton switched their focus from the explanation of sales to the explanation of expressed emotions. A series of qualitative studies suggests that total sales is a proxy for the pace and time pressure on sales clerks. The clerks in high-sales stores are simply too busy to be friendly. In slow stores, the clerks have the time and the motivation (to reduce boredom) to be friendly. A reanalysis of the quantitative data set confirms this.

In his commentary, Richard Mowday draws our attention to several exemplary aspects of this study. He notes the importance of management-academic cooperation, persistence, and multiple methods in the research process. Barry Staw, in his remarks, has two main points to make about the Sutton and Rafaeli article. First, he discusses how they have violated the "sacred ritual" of reporting research as a linear process. Second, he shows how their work opens up the field for research into the role of emotion in the workplace.

One of the metaphors for the research process is that of exploring the uncharted frontiers of knowledge. Such journeys are bound to lead to a fair share of dead ends. Sometimes we can get over or around the obstacles by applying additional energy, thought, and other resources to the problem; sometimes we cannot. In this case all the extra creativity, sweat, and careful analysis paid off. Rafaeli and Sutton unraveled a bit of the mystery at the source of their original disappointment. In our opinion, they actually achieved more than an original confirmation would have done. The study, as conceived, would have provided modest support for the authors' research program on emotions, but the rather obvious hypothesis hardly would encourage many to see emotions research as an important new paradigm for increasing our understanding of organizations. Sutton and Rafaeli's decision to share explicitly the confusion and groping that underlay this study is unusual and admirable. By presenting the missteps and recovery along their research path in the published article, they convince the reader that emotional work in organizations is not something obvious. It is subtle, contextual, and relates meaningfully to key organizational variables.

How We Untangled the Relationship Between Displayed Emotion and Organizational Sales: A Tale of Bickering and Optimism

Robert I. Sutton

Anat Rafaeli

The story of how we developed this manuscript is, in many ways, the story of the research relationship between the two of us. We met at Stanford University in 1984. We had both just finished our dissertations. Anat was a visiting scholar and Bob was a brand-new assistant professor. Our initial conversations revealed common backgrounds in organizational psychology and, more important, that we were each cursed with a high need for achievement and with considerable impatience about making such achievement.

We began by working together on a study of workstation characteristics as sources of stress. This initial paper was successful in that we finished it, felt that we had done competent work, and eventually got it published. This scholarly adventure was also successful because we learned that we had fun working together. We soon developed a work style characterized by loud (and often rude) conflict. This style had several advantages. We were so critical of each other that we identified and repaired many problems before our papers were ever submitted. Further, once a paper was submitted, the reviewers' suggestions often concerned issues that we had already spent hours arguing about, which meant we had well-developed ideas about changing the paper and well-developed responses to suggestions that we believed would weaken rather than strengthen the paper. The greatest advantage, however, was that we were rarely interrupted by students, faculty, and staff members: They were hesitant to knock on the door because they didn't want to walk into the middle of our ugly little war.

We argued about many issues while writing the workstation characteristics paper, including which conceptual approach should be used in the introduction, exactly what words should be used in each sentence, and whose turn it was to sit in the comfortable chair. But our most frequent (and nastiest) arguments arose because we were having trouble developing intrinsic interest in the topic. A typical exchange went as follows:

> *Anat:* This is so boring. I can hardly wait to become the world's expert on workstation temperature and employee satisfaction.
>
> *Bob:* Shut up and quit complaining. I'm not very excited about this paper either, but we both want it on our résumés and it will never get done if you keep whining.

The Topic of Expressed Emotion Emerges as a Source of Entertainment

We soon began to reward ourselves for making progress on our workstation paper by talking about expressed emotion. Anat had lived in Israel, Ohio, New York, and California during the previous five years. She was intrigued by the striking differences in friendliness that she had encountered in the four places. Bob had just read Arlie Hochschild's *The Managed Heart* (1983), which argued that, as with other behaviors, employees were paid to express certain emotions and suppress others, and that displaying such false emotions harmed employees in a variety of ways. We began exploring these ideas by developing a conference paper for the Academy of Management meetings and developing ideas for a theory paper.

We continued to believe, however, that our research on workstation characteristics was more important than the "fun stuff" we were doing on expressed emotion, *until* the 1985 National Academy of Management meetings in San Diego. About 50 people attended the session on physical characteristics of work in which our paper was presented. The only strong reaction we can recall was our embarrassment when the discussant, Jeffrey Pfeffer, pointed out an important flaw in our arguments. In contrast, more than 300 people attended Stanley Harris's session on emotion in organizations. The big audience was there, no doubt, to see Andrew Pettigrew, John Van Maanen, and Karl Weick—not us! But it was clear that our paper was well received and that the audience was interested in the topic. We were ecstatic when Pettigrew said that our paper was "the top of the pops." At that moment, we knew that our stream of research on physical characteristics of work was never to be. We turned to developing ideas about how to study the expression of emotion in organizational life.

We've Got the Theory—
Will We Ever Be Able to Get Any Data?

Our first task when we returned to Stanford was to complete a theory paper, "The Expression of Emotion as Part of the Work Role," which we eventually published in the *Academy of Management Review* (Rafaeli & Sutton, 1987). We also had been approached by Barry Staw, who asked us to do an essay on emotion for the *Research in Organizational Behavior* series that he edits with Larry Cummings (see Rafaeli & Sutton, 1989, for the outcome of this adventure).[1] We were ecstatic during the fall of 1985 because it seemed that we were going to receive occupational rewards for studying a topic we found fascinating. We ran around the halls of the Department of Industrial Engineering and Engineering Management at Stanford, ranting at anyone who would listen about the great new ideas that we were developing.

Despite such optimism, we continued to argue. We fought mostly about how we were going to test the ideas that we were developing. We had dozens of tentative plans for collecting data about the expression of emotion, including a variety of experimental and quasi-experimental designs. We also started doing numerous little field stimulations. For example, following a suggestion by Gerald Ledford, we routinely asked waiters and waitresses who seemed to be displaying required good cheer, "What is the worst thing on the menu?" This proved to be an effective technique for provoking their genuine inner feelings. Anat also asked waiters and waitresses, as well as salesclerks and telephone operators, "Why are you being so nice to me?" and was surprised by how often she was told, "Because I'm paid to be nice," or "I'll get fired if I don't," or even "You might be one of those people who are paid by management to spy on me."

> 66 Recent theoretical work, however, has emphasized that employees' emotions are displayed as well as felt (Hochschild, 1979, 1983; Rafaeli & Sutton, 1987, 1989). A variety of forces may explain variation in organizational members' displayed emotions. Internal feelings certainly influence such behavior: satisfied employees may display genuine broad smiles and laughter during interactions with co-workers and customers; dissatisfied or tense employees may frown and groan during such transactions.

Yet there is an imperfect match between the emotions people feel and emotions they express on the job because employees are often expected to display emotions that are unrelated, or even in conflict, with their true feelings. Many organizations use practices, including recruitment and selection, socialization, and rewards and punishments, to assure that their members will conform to normative expectations, or "display rules" (Ekman, 1980: 87-88), that specify which emotions should be expressed and which should be hidden.

A primary reason that organizations develop and enforce display rules is that displayed emotions are thought to operate as "control moves." Goffman (1969: 12) defined control moves as an individual's strategic manipulation of expressions, including emotional expressions, to influence the behavior of others. Along those lines, the emotions displayed by employees in organizational settings can function as control moves that influence the behavior of clients and fellow organizational members (Rafaeli & Sutton, 1987).

Writings intended for managerial audiences also imply that the emotional front is a meaningful organizational attribute. Indeed, some recent managerial folklore suggests that employees who display good cheer to customers can enhance sales and customer loyalty (Ash, 1984; Hochschild, 1983; Peters & Austin, 1985; Peters & Waterman, 1982; Richman, 1984). The emerging literature on customer service (Czepiel, Solomon, & Surprenant, 1985; Parasuraman, Zeithamal, & Berry, 1985) also implies that belief. Those writings suggest that, when all other factors are held equal, the display of positive emotions by employees can, in the aggregate, act as control moves that bring about gains for an organization. The implication is that to the extent each potential customer associates a positive emotional front with a given organization, a larger proportion of the potential population will patronize that organization.

Theories of learning may explain why displaying warm feelings to customers can promote sales. Encountering employees who display warm, socially desirable feelings may be reinforcing for most people. Initial encounters with friendly employees may mark the start of an operant conditioning cycle (Skinner, 1953) in which the emotions displayed by employees are the reinforcers and patronizing the organization is the reinforced behavior. The probability that a given customer will visit an organization a second time is increased by employees' display of positive emotions. The organization's emotional front may also reinforce customer behavior indirectly through vicarious learning (Bandura, 1977). A customer may watch other customers encounter positive emotions or may visit a service organization after reading that its employees are nice, friendly, or polite.   **99**

(Sutton & Rafaeli, 1988, pp. 462-464)

Larry Ford Gives Us
the "Perfect" Data Set

This was all good fun, but we weren't making any progress toward the development of a solid, publishable empirical paper. Then a happy accident happened. Bob discovered that Larry Ford, who had been a coauthor and good friend in graduate school, was conducting a study of employee courtesy in his capacity as director of field research for a national chain of convenience stores. It turned out that Larry had designed and was implementing a study that would allow us to test our most treasured hypothesis. We were taken with the idea that expressed emotions could serve as "control moves," which Goffman (1969) defined rather elegantly as "the intentional effort of an informant to produce expressions that he thinks will improve his position if they are gleaned by an observer" (p. 12). We extended this notion to expressed emotions in organizations, and argued (along with dozens of other writers, including Tom Peters) that when employees tended to express good cheer to customers, their organizations would be more profitable.

We were ecstatic because the data Larry gathered seemed perfect for testing this hypothesis. It contained observations of more than 11,000 customer service transactions in a national random sample of 585 stores. Data collection focused on four components of displayed positive emotion: greeting, smiling, establishing eye contact, and saying "thank you." Data about numerous control variables such as store ownership, region, store stock level, and average number of customers standing in line were also collected. Detailed records about store sales were also gathered routinely by the company. It was easy to convince Larry to let us use these data because of his friendship with Bob. And it was easy for Larry to convince the executives in his firm to release the data—they were spending millions of dollars trying to enhance courtesy because they believed that, by doing so, they could increase store sales. Moreover, even though Larry had designed and implemented the study, he agreed not to join us as a coauthor of the scholarly publication because "it doesn't help my career in the real world at all." [2]

We thought we were set. Oh, sure, there were a few potential problems including data at different levels of analysis, the use of a cross-sectional rather than a longitudinal design, and complex technical problems of reading and analyzing data from a different system.

But we were so confident in our hypotheses and in Anat's ability to conduct these analyses that we even stopped arguing for a while. Instead, our private conversations were filled with optimism and enthusiasm, and perhaps a touch of arrogance. For example:

> *Bob:* This is the best data set of its kind. Larry is such a great researcher and he is just giving us these wonderful data.
>
> *Anat:* Now we not only have ideas, we have data. Once we make the scales and run the regressions, the paper is almost done. The introduction is already pretty much written; all we need to do is modify a few pages from our theory papers.
>
> *Bob:* You bet. This paper is going to make our careers, and it isn't even going to be very much work.

Our confidence persisted during the early stages of data analysis. We were undaunted by the various problems associated with aggregating the data and building the scales. We knew our hypothesis was correct and that all we had to do was run the numbers. In fact, our only doubts were raised by several colleagues and family members who suggested we were studying something trivial: After all, everyone knows that stores with friendlier employees sell more merchandise. They wondered why we were so excited about studying something that was so obvious.

Oh No. We Can't Be Wrong. There Must Be Something Wrong With These Data!

We were set to run the regressions. We expected to spend a day or so preparing our tables to be typed. We assumed that it would take only a few weeks more to write the paper. But the output generated by the regressions was like a blow to the head: No matter how we analyzed the data, expressed positive emotion seemed to have a consistently *negative* relationship with store sales, which was exactly the opposite of our hypothesis.

We had several reactions. First, we avoided each other for a few days. This is notable because (except for occasional spells of laughter, trips to get food, and the episode of overconfidence described above) we had developed a style of work that involved detailed and nasty arguments peppered with personal insults. We spent hours sitting in front of a Macintosh computer, fighting for physical control over the mouse while we struggled to craft sentences and paragraphs. Second, we checked the way in which we had constructed the scales and the raw data that Larry had sent us dozens of times, but could find no errors. Anat also tried again and again to run slightly different regressions in the desperate hope that "maybe this one variable will save our paper." Third, Bob called Larry and asked him (actually accused him) of sending us data that were reverse scored as a result of a coding error. Larry, who is accustomed to Bob's irrational emotional outbursts, laughed at Bob and assured him that the data were correct. But Larry is also a skilled and careful data analyst. He ran some analyses of his own to double-check, and he too found the unexpected negative relationships.

We were soon convinced that the data were right and that our hypothesis was wrong. We began to talk seriously about giving up the paper, and were so depressed that we talked a bit about abandoning future research on expressed emotion. Anat even had private thoughts about turning motherhood into a full-time career.

Jim Jucker Proposes the "Manhattan Effect"

We begged for help and complained to any colleague who would listen in our efforts to cope with these unexpected findings and the depression they had provoked. Luckily, Jim Jucker, our colleague at Stanford, returned from a trip to New York a couple of weeks after we had obtained our unexpected findings. When we complained to him about our findings, he mentioned how annoyed he had been by the obnoxious service people he had encountered in New York City. He then said something like, "You know, I bet the people in the busy stores in your sample are like New Yorkers. They are so busy and so irritated that they don't have the time or the inclination to smile." This simple idea came as revelation. A quick check of our findings indicated that not only were stores with greater sales less likely to have employees who displayed good cheer, stores with longer lines of customers were also less likely to have friendly employees. Taken together, these two results suggested that, like New York City, fast-paced settings do not support the expression of good cheer. Moreover, when corporate executives learned about our findings, they enthusiastically adopted Jim Jucker's notion of the "Manhattan effect." They were particularly attracted to this label because the corporation had been unsuccessful in its attempts to operate profitable stores in Manhattan.

Our initial inclination was to change the introduction so that it proposed new hypotheses that fit the data. We were disturbed by the prospect of writing a paper that did not reflect the process by which we had conducted our research, but we also had begun to learn an unstated, but powerful, occupational norm: When your hypotheses aren't confirmed, you don't admit it, you change the hypotheses in your introduction to fit the data. We had learned this lesson from conversations with more experienced colleagues and from suggestions made by anonymous reviewers of our papers. We also learned that this practice is not limited to the so-called soft sciences. When Bob described it to a friend who was a genetics researcher, he replied "Of course, we always write our hypotheses after we get our results. It is more efficient that way!"

We had two incentives, however, for avoiding this unsavory practice. The first was self-serving. We had written one paper and were considering writing another that included our argument that expressed emotions are control moves. If we published a paper that contained an opposite, or unrelated, argument about the relationship between expressed positive emotion and store sales, it would appear as if we had not read our own work. The second incentive was more noble. We wanted to write a paper that reflected the process by which we had actually learned about expressed emotions. There were risks to this strategy because we believed that some editors and reviewers would have negative reactions to a paper that had a nontraditional structure. But we also believed that, if the paper ever got published, it would be better than if we had simply changed our hypotheses to fit the data.

The Qualitative and Inductive Phase

When we began thinking about writing the paper in this manner, however, we realized that—although the notion of the Manhattan effect had caused us to reverse our independent and dependent variables—we lacked sufficient theoretical understanding of the meaning of the unexpected findings. Thus we decided that, rather than just sitting in our offices and imagining what these stores were like, we would gather some qualitative data and include it in the paper.

We had already started some haphazard data gathering, including store visits and conversations with Larry Ford. We decided to make this data gathering more systematic. We conducted four case studies, had more focused conversations with managers and executives in the corporation about our findings, attended a customer service workshop for store owners and managers, and made approximately 40 additional informal visits to these stores. Bob also worked as a clerk for a day in one of the stores. These qualitative data proved to be essential for helping us to refine our revised conceptual perspective. For example, while we had thought about how a crowded store suppresses the display of positive emotion, we had not thought about the ways in which a slow store supports the display of good cheer. During the day that Bob spent working as a clerk, he learned that customers were an important source of entertainment, and that clerks are more friendly during slow times because they are genuinely pleased to see customers and want to encourage customers to engage in conversation.

The Structure of the Manuscript

Once these qualitative data were gathered, we turned to writing the manuscript. By this time, Anat had returned to Israel, but we communicated and argued via electronic mail and occasional telephone calls. We decided to structure the paper so that it reflected the two complete cycles of induction and deduction that we had traveled through in order to reach our final conclusions. Although literally hundreds of nuances have been changed since we wrote the first draft, the structure of the paper has not been changed. The introduction presents the armchair theory building that we used to develop the initial hypothesis that store sales would be greater to the extent that clerks displayed positive emotions during transactions with customers. The quantitative and deductive study is then presented as a test of this hypothesis. Next, the paper states explicitly that the failure of this deductive phase provoked a new round of induction, specifically, the qualitative study and the development of a new conceptual perspective. Data from this second inductive phase are then used to provide grounding for our new hypothesis: that store pace (indicated by store sales and line length) would be negatively related to the display of positive emotion. This perspective is then tested and confirmed in a reanalysis of the quantitative data.

The Paper Is Rejected

We submitted the paper to the *Administrative Science Quarterly*, but not before having several arguments about its prospects. Bob was very optimistic, arguing that he thought it was the best paper he had ever written. Anat was fairly pessimistic, arguing that the structure of the paper was so strange that *ASQ* reviewers would stop reading it after the completion of the first cycle of induction and deduction, and conclude that the paper obviously didn't have firm enough conceptual grounding because our hypotheses were wrong. Bob's optimism persisted until about a month after the paper was submitted. He presented the paper to a group of faculty and students at the University of California, Berkeley. The presentation was very well received. But Barry Staw, who was one of the strongest supporters of the paper, also expressed concern that *ASQ* might not be willing to publish a paper in which the final conceptual perspective is not presented until about page 20 of the manuscript.

Anat and Barry were right. It has been more than three years since *ASQ* rejected the paper, but it is still painful to read the associate editor's opinion that "the point is that this seemingly simple situation is rich and complicated and that your theorizing does not even address it seriously." We briefly considered changing the paper so that it appeared as if we had thought of the correct hypothesis to start with. Nonetheless—despite our depression over this rejection—we both continued to believe that it was more intellectually honest and more interesting to retain the original structure of the paper. We did, however, make numerous changes. We decided to act as if we were revising the manuscript along the lines suggested by the three *ASQ* reviewers: Their 11 pages of careful comments were very helpful in revising the paper. But we decided not to pay attention to the comments made by the associate editor. We believed then, and still believe, that his numerous comments were of little value during the revision because they were inspired by his negative reaction to the structure rather than the content of the manuscript.

The Paper Finds a Home in
the *Academy of Management Journal*

We decided to send our paper—which we believed was improved considerably—to the *Academy of Management Journal*, which had already published our quantitative paper on workstation characteristics, along with two qualitative papers that Sutton and his colleagues had written on organizational decline. We thought the editors might be interested in publishing a paper that combined quantitative and qualitative methods. And, indeed, the *AMJ* reviewers and editors were supportive of the manuscript. We were especially impressed by both the quality and the number of comments made by the editor, Janice

Beyer, and the associate editor, Richard Mowday. Both of them indicated that they liked the paper and made explicit that—although one reviewer was a bit uncomfortable with the unconventional structure of the paper—the structure should be retained. Nonetheless, they hounded us about the nuances of the paper. By the time the paper was published, they had offered hundreds of suggestions and comments aimed at refining every paragraph, and nearly every sentence. For example, the paper originally contained little text about the context in which the data collection occurred. In retrospect, we believe that the manuscript is considerably stronger because we followed Richard Mowday's suggestion and added a "Research Context" section. It describes the great emphasis that the corporation had begun to place on customer service through means including training for both new and experienced employees, written rules requiring the display of good cheer, cash incentives for displaying good cheer, and the collection of customer service data.

66 RESEARCH CONTEXT

These data were collected as part of an evaluation of employee courtesy in a large national chain of convenience stores. The corporation's human resources staff conducted this research as part of a chain-wide effort to enhance employee courtesy; top executives had decided that they could gain an advantage over their competitors by improving customer service in their stores. A primary reason that executives made this decision was that they had read *In Search of Excellence* and were swayed by Peters and Waterman's arguments that staying "close to the customer" (1982: 156) and having a "service obsession" (1982: 157) are characteristics of excellent firms.

During the year before these data were collected, the human resources staff had changed employee handbooks and the classroom training provided to new employees so that—rather than vaguely encouraging clerks to be friendly to customers—the training clerks received instructed them to greet, smile at, establish eye contact with, and say "thank you" to every customer.

A variety of local and corporate-wide practices were used, both before and after the collection of the data, to reward clerks who acted friendly during transactions with customers. Clerks in most regions were informed that "mystery shoppers" would be used to observe levels of employee courtesy. In some regions, clerks who were caught displaying the required good cheer to customers received a $25 bonus. In other regions, clerks who were observed greeting, smiling, establishing eye contact, and saying "thank you" could win a new automobile instantly.

The corporation held a contest, costing over $10 million, in which the owners of franchised stores and the managers of corporation-owned stores could qualify to enter a drawing for a million dollars if their clerks

consistently offered good cheer to customers. The corporation also
awarded large bonuses (over 25 percent of base salary) to regional
managers when a high percentage of sales clerks in the stores they
managed were observed greeting, smiling at, establishing eye contact
with, and saying "thank you" to customers.   **99**

(Sutton & Rafaeli, 1988, pp. 464-465)

Aftermath

"Untangling the Relationship Between Displayed Emotions and
Organizational Sales: The Case of Convenience Stores" appeared in
September 1988 in the *Academy of Management Journal.* Our experience
with this paper led both of us to make constructive changes in our
views of the role of qualitative data in organizational research. This
study was Anat's first experience with qualitative research, and it
taught her the virtues of a set of methods that she once viewed as
without scientific rigor. She was so impressed with the role played by
the qualitative data in this paper that, after the manuscript was complete, she spent three months working part-time in an Israeli grocery
store doing an ethnographic study (see Rafaeli, 1989). Thus it caused
her to stray far from her doctoral training in quantitative methods at
Ohio State's program in industrial and organizational psychology.

In contrast, the study helped Bob renew his faith in quantitative
methods. Bob's qualitative dissertation on organizational death was
done, in part, because he became disillusioned with the methods that
he learned, used, and once nearly worshipped as a resident of the
University of Michigan's deeply quantitative Survey Research Center.
Bob was often asked why, after doing a qualitative thesis, he was still
writing quantitative papers. He often provided obnoxious answers
such as "It's a bad habit I can't break" or "It is easier than qualitative
research; I need to give my mind a break." The experience with this
paper caused him to appreciate the virtues of both sets of methods, to
believe sincerely that qualitative data are best for induction and that
quantitative data are best for deduction. Now, when he is asked
whether quantitative or qualitative methods are more valuable to the
field, he replies: "That is a silly question. It is like asking whether the
transmission or the engine is more important for running a car. It
doesn't work unless you have both."

The aftermath has also included some sweet extrinsic rewards. The
paper was published as lead article in the September issue, a sign that
the *AMJ* editors thought that it was important. Both of us have since

been promoted to associate professors with tenure, and several of the people who wrote letters evaluating our work have reported to us that their letters focused special attention on the quality of this paper. We were absolutely ecstatic about receiving the award for the best paper published in *AMJ* in 1988. And we are very pleased to have our paper be included in this book on exemplary research.

Yet, despite all of these lovely rewards, we still are plagued by lingering doubts about this paper and its subsequent effects on our research. We both still worry that the relationship between store sales and expressed emotions is a trivial topic. We worry that by focusing on four simple behaviors—smiling, greeting, establishing eye contact, and offering thanks—we offered an oversimplified view of expressed positive emotions. We also worry that we have focused too much on the expression of good cheer in our empirical work and not enough on the expression of unpleasant emotions.

These concerns about the drawbacks of our past empirical work led us to conduct a pair of qualitative studies on the expression of emotion. Anat studied interrogators who are paid to gain confessions from suspected criminals, and Bob studied bill collectors who are paid for getting payments from debtors. As we turn to the task of writing up these qualitative data, however, we have occasional worries that our best work together has already been done. During these moments of uneasiness, we wonder if all of those lovely extrinsic rewards will cause us to become arrogant, overconfident, or lazy, or—worst of all—to stop arguing. We believe that the quality of our work will suffer if we stop bickering and are left with only our optimism.

Notes

1. As of this writing, we have collaborated on six articles, two chapters, and one book review, are planning two new articles, and have had vague discussions about writing a book. The order of authorship of our papers is one of the points that we have had constant negotiations about throughout our research relationship. In hindsight, it seems that we have placed little weight on estimates of who has contributed more when we try to make a decision about who will be listed as first author of a given paper. Instead, we consider the full set of papers that we have written in the past, are currently writing, and expect to write in the future, and then argue about "whose turn it is to be first author." For example, Anat was initially listed as first author of this commentary until Bob noticed that doing so would mean that Anat would have been listed first on three papers in a row. In addition to "whose turn it is," we also consider who would most benefit from being listed as first author. For example, at the time we started working together, Anat felt that she was known primarily for her quantitative research papers, while Bob felt that he was known primarily for his theory papers. As a result, Anat was

listed as first author of the theory papers we published in the *Academy of Management Review* and *Research in Organizational Behavior*, while Bob was listed as first author of the two empirical papers we published in the *Academy of Management Journal*. It would have been impossible for us to estimate who "deserved" to be first author of any of these papers on the basis of the amount of time we spent. We both simply worked as hard as we could on each paper until it was done.

2. When Bob learned that this paper was going to receive the "Best Paper" award, he called Larry and said, "Congratulations, your research has just won an award from the Academy of Management, even though you won't get any credit for it." Larry only laughed, and cracked a few jokes about the misguided standards used by the awards committee. He was too gracious to express misgivings about not being listed as an author. But Bob now feels lingering guilt about not including Larry as an author of this paper.

Commentary

Out of the Tangled Thicket:
Persistence in the Face of
Failed Conventional Wisdom

Richard T. Mowday

This paper feels like an old friend. When it was first submitted for publication to the *Academy of Management Journal* back in April 1987, I participated in the review process as the consulting editor. Although Janice Beyer, then editor of the journal, had the wisdom to accept the paper for publication, the task of managing copyediting, reviewing page proofs, and handling production details fell to me when I followed her in that role. Later, I served on the committee that selected this paper as the best article published in the 1988 volume of *AMJ*. Over several years and for a variety of reasons, I have read this paper many times. Like an old friend, Sutton and Rafaeli's work has reinforced my initial positive feelings about it on each occasion I have had to revisit it.

Empirical research that gains recognition beyond the fact of publication invariably has an interesting story to tell and provides insights on topics of theoretical and practical significance. In addition, it has something to teach us about the research process and how our own work might be improved. Without wishing to minimize the importance of the research findings reported in this paper, I have chosen to confine my comments to several valuable lessons about research that the authors remind us of.

Cooperative Research

The majority of research in our field has its origin in theory or had a goal of building on and extending previously reported empirical

129

findings. Most research remains true to the literature, even when previous findings are abstract and far removed from the phenomena they attempt to describe.

In contrast, this study has its origin in the practical concerns of managers faced with the task of evaluating the effectiveness of a corporate program designed to increase retail sales. Following conventional management wisdom at the time (see Peters & Waterman, 1982), a multimillion-dollar program had been initiated to encourage cashiers to greet customers, establish eye contact, and otherwise act in a friendly manner. Data collected by corporate staff to determine whether the program was successful provided the foundation on which Sutton and Rafaeli built.

Academic researchers are often accused of ignoring practical problems (Porter & McKibben, 1988). One has to admire the authors for entering into a cooperative relationship with management that served both their interests well. Management received an expert evaluation of its belief that friendly cashiers increase store sales, even if not the answer that was expected. The researchers gained access to a data base that allowed an examination of ideas that emerge from the literatures on displayed emotions and effectiveness in service industries. Sutton and Rafaeli remind us there is much to gained from a cooperative research relationship between academics and managers.

Persistence

The typical research study tests a set of research questions or hypotheses derived from theory or previously reported findings. The goal is to provide a rigorous test of the predictions that will produce an answer in which we can have confidence. If things turn out as expected, as they usually do, the findings are written up for publication. If things don't turn out as predicted, the results are still written up. A question is asked, an answer obtained. Then, it's off to the next project.

When I first reviewed this paper, its most attractive feature was the authors' persistence when the initial findings contradicted their basic prediction. Courtesy and good cheer on the part of cashiers were not positively associated with store sales. In fact, the simple relationship was negative. An important contribution of the authors to this research effort was to undertake an additional investigation to understand this unanticipated finding.

Sutton and Rafaeli have an interesting story to tell, and I think it is because their research has several characteristics in common with a good detective novel. The detective, confronted by a crime requiring investigation, sifts through a series of clues until an explanation is found. When an obvious clue turns out to be a false lead, the detective cannot be content with knowing what does not explain the crime. That won't solve the case. Instead, the detective must continue to evaluate additional facts until the culprit is apprehended. In much the same way, the authors persisted when their initial expectations proved incorrect. This quest was probably made more interesting by the fact that it was conventional management wisdom that was brought into question. In fact, one reviewer was attracted to this paper because it allowed "an initial theoretical jab at the simplemindedness of the 'smiles are money' school of thought."

TABLE 3 Qualitative Evidence About the Influence of Store Pace on Displayed Emotions

Sources of Data	Evidence About Displayed Emotions in Stores During Busy Times	Evidence About Displayed Emotions in Stores During Slow Times
Four case studies	One store manager reported that clerks were less likely to be friendly during busy times. Customers are "more stressed and tense," as another store manager put it. Observers also noted that clerks tended to become less friendly during busy times. In both stores that were low on expressed positive emotion, there was a tendency to wait longer to open a second register than in the two stores that were high on the expression of positive emotion. Thus, during busy times, lines tended to be longer in the two "unfriendly" stores than in the two "friendly" stores.	The store managers reported that clerks were likely to be friendly during slow times; the observers noted that clerks tended to become more friendly during slow times. The observers also noted that extended conversations took place between clerks and regular customers during slow times, especially in the two "friendly" stores.
Day spent working as a clerk	The field notes reveal the following: [when the line of customers got long] "I never looked up at the customers. I never established eye contact. I never said thank you. I was breaking the rules, and I knew it. But I couldn't help it."	The field notes reveal the following. [during slow times] "There were regular customers. And my co-workers and I would often engage in brief, friendly banter, and sometimes even extended conversations, with these folks."

(Continued)

TABLE 3 Qualitative Evidence About the Influence of Store Pace on Displayed
Emotions (Continued)

Sources of Data	Evidence About Displayed Emotions in Stores During Busy Times	Evidence About Displayed Emotions in Stores During Slow Times
Conversations with managers	The negative relationship between positive emotion and performance was attributed to the "Manhattan effect," the notion that New Yorkers are less polite than people in other parts of the country because they are under greater time pressure.	There was widespread agreement that lack of courtesy should not be tolerated when it was slow because there are no excuses for such behavior.
Customer service workshop	A store manager remarked, "Customers who are in a long line don't care if we smile or not. They just want us to run like hell."	There was a general discussion about slow and busy stores. All agreed that it was easy to smile, greet, establish eye contact, and thank customers when it was slow, but being courteous was thought to be a challenge when it was busy.
Store visits	We noticed that clerks and customers tried to move as fast as possible when the store was busy. Everyone was less friendly. We also found that our own irritation from waiting in long lines was sometimes expressed to clerks.	We noticed that clerks tended to be more friendly when there were fewer customers in the store; customers and we ourselves also tended to be more friendly during slow times.

(Sutton & Rafaeli, 1988, p. 475)

 In short, we proposed that stores with a high proportion of busy times would be less likely to have clerks who greeted, smiled at, established eye contact with, and said "thank you" to customers. Specifically, we expected that (1) store sales would be negatively related to the expression of positive emotion and (2) a store's average line length would be negatively related to the expression of positive emotion.

These expectations were tested in the same data set used for the first quantitative analyses; multiple regression analyses were again used in the sample of 576 stores. A hierarchical procedure similar to that used in the first quantitative analysis was employed. The first equation included seven control variables—ownership, supervision costs, stock level, customers' gender composition, clerks' gender composition, clerks' image, and region—as predictors of the display of positive emotion. This analysis yielded a multiple R of .40 and an adjusted R-square of .15 ($p < .001$).

In the second equation, we added the predictor variables of line length and total store sales to the seven control variables used in the first equation. Table 4 presents the results of this equation: a multiple *R* of .44 and an adjusted *R*-square of .18 were obtained. Table 4 indicates that both store sales and average line length were significantly and negatively related to the display of positive emotion. The significant beta weights for both total store sales and average line length indicate that these variables make a significant contribution to the variance explained by the model. That is, the increment in *R*-square is statistically significant. These results support our revised perspective. **99**

(Sutton & Rafaeli, 1988, p. 479)

Multiple Research Methods

Another attractive feature of this study is the blending of quantitative (deductive) and qualitative (inductive) research methods. The initial study quantitatively evaluated data collected by management from observation and company records. The subsequent qualitative investigation undertaken by the authors used a variety of data collection techniques, including limited participant observation. It is a sad comment on our field that most researchers come no closer to the phenomena they wish to study than handing out questionnaires to a group of anonymous subjects. Sutton and Rafaeli, in contrast, were willing to become more actively involved in the cashier's role, attempting to understand the demands of the job in the context in which they occur. The result was a far richer and deeper understanding of the relationship between displayed emotion and store sales.

Although I find the blending of quantitative and qualitative research attractive, it is interesting to speculate on what might have happened had the order of the studies been reversed. Had the qualitative investigation preceded the quantitative one, it is likely a quite different prediction would have been deductively tested. Managers and researchers have an important lesson to learn about the benefits of getting closer to the phenomena they wish to understand.

Ethical Considerations

Even though at least one reviewer thought it unnecessary, I found Sutton and Rafaeli's explicit consideration of the ethical dimensions of their research refreshing. The fact that the study involved observation of people without their prior consent raises an interesting ethical concern. The authors' willingness to address the ethical implications of their methodology explicitly is worthy of emulation by others. Ethical considerations in research should not only be apparent in writing about methodology, they should be explicitly considered in design and should inform research practice.

> 66 In closing, we would like to return to the methods used in this study. The observational methods used here are not widely employed in organizational research. Thus, questions may arise about whether it is ethical to secretly observe employees. Procedures used in the present research were, however, consistent with ethical guidelines on the conduct of nonreactive research and contrived observations (Salancik, 1979; Sechrest & Phillips, 1979; Webb et al., 1981). The American Psychological Association discourages "covert investigations in private places" (American Psychological Association, 1973: 13). The convenience stores used in the present research are, however, public places. Moreover, the corporation's use of incognito observers and our own use of that method during the qualitative phase were only partly covert. Although specific, informed consent was not obtained from each clerk observed, all clerks had been informed that encounters with mystery shoppers were part of the job: the corporate training program explained the use of mystery shoppers and the expected expressive behaviors. Furthermore, the names of individual clerks were not recorded in either the quantitative research conducted by the corporation or in our own qualitative research. Thus, in terms of a harms-benefit analysis, such data were not, and could not, be used to harm any individual clerk. 99

(Sutton & Rafaeli, 1988, p. 484)

Conclusions

My own future research will benefit from this article because it helps me understand there are theoretically interesting issues to be explored in the practical concerns of managers, that the research process does not end when initial predictions are disconfirmed, and that multiple methods facilitate a deeper understanding of the problems we study. Of course, these insights are not entirely new (see Campbell, Daft, & Hulin, 1982), but they are made more salient and persuasive by example.

Finally, although it was Sutton and Rafaeli who were published and won an award for their research, it is important to recognize that their effort would not have been possible had not management committed to putting its ideas to the test of empirical research. When millions of dollars are spent in support of a promotional campaign, one can understand a certain reluctance about evaluating the consequences. The implications of incorrect predictions by managers are probably far more severe than for those made by researchers. Without the willingness of managers to study the question, a very useful research contribution would have been lost.

Commentary

Do Smiles Lead to Sales?
Comments on the Sutton/Rafaeli Study

Barry M. Staw

So what is so special about the Sutton and Rafaeli article? Didn't they just try to correlate smiling to sales in a chain of convenience stores? Well, yes. But, in trying to test the common assumption that expressing positive emotion increases customer sales, Sutton and Rafaeli have contributed an exemplary study in terms of both method and theory.

One of the main strengths of the Sutton and Rafaeli study is its use of both quantitative and qualitative methods. Although all of us in organizational research nod approvingly when multiple methods are extolled, we each tend to specialize in a single methodology. Survey researchers seldom do experiments, experimenters seldom analyze archival data, and almost none of us utilizes both quantitative and qualitative methods. It is difficult to find a topic that has been addressed with a variety of methodological approaches, since research topics, subfields, and styles of research are all so highly intercorrelated. For example, issues such as job satisfaction and performance usually attract quantitative organizational psychologists, while organizational socialization and careers have tended to interest more qualitative sociologists.

When the field of organizational behavior was beginning in the 1950s, there was less of an orthodoxy in method. People observed, participated, counted, and cross-tabulated. There was ready admission that each methodology was flawed. The consensus was that social research was a groping for knowledge with crude tools, almost like trying to measure a sponge with a rubber ruler, as Donald T. Campbell was so fond of saying. Now there is not only a clearer reliance on single methodologies (with scholars proclaiming, "The appropriate analysis is . . . "), but there has developed a strong norm for the presentation of results. Articles typically review existing work, propose a hypothesis to fill a knowledge gap, present data validating the hypothesis, mention a few limitations of the findings, and call for further research. This sequence has become almost a sacred ritual, with violators told to keep revising and resubmitting their manuscripts until they look like all the rest. Rarely is social research presented as it is conducted, capturing the conflicted search for concepts, the false starts, and the disconfirmation of one's hypotheses.

66 DISCUSSION

Our initial conceptual perspective focused on expressed positive emotions as control moves that influence the shopping behavior of customers. We hypothesized that stores in which employees were more likely to offer positive emotions to customers would have greater sales. But a quantitative study of 576 convenience stores revealed a negative relationship between displayed positive emotions and store sales.

Our revised perspective emphasized that store sales reflect store pace and that store pace is a cause, rather than an effect, of expressed emotions. We found some empirical support for the revised perspective. But our sample included only one variety of convenience stores; the service ideal associated with these stores has not traditionally included friendly service. Emotions expressed in organizations in which a different service ideal is present may act as control moves that influence sales. That is, a warm emotional front may promote sales when customers expect that it should and will be a central part of a firm's service. Examples of organizations where customers expect to receive good cheer from employees include Nordstrom's (Peters & Austin, 1985), Disneyworld (Tyler & Nathan, 1985), and Delta Airlines (Hochschild, 1983). Furthermore, expectations of fast service need not exclude warmth and friendliness; McDonald's is an example of a national chain in which the service ideal includes both rapid and friendly service.

The convenience stores studied are settings in which transactions between employees and customers are very brief. Expressed emotions may also be more powerful control moves during long transactions between employees and customers. When waiters serve customers in restaurants, for example, the interaction may last anywhere from 30 minutes to one and a half hours (Mars & Nicod, 1984), far longer than the 2 or 3 minutes that a typical customer spends in the stores we studied. There is more time during a long transaction for the customer to notice and react to the emotional behavior of an employee; thus, the operant conditioning cycle we discussed earlier is more likely to become established.

Our initial conceptual perspective had a far different focus than our revised perspective. The initial perspective emphasized control moves and corporate display rules. The revised perspective emphasized store pace, widely held norms for convenience settings, and employees' inner feelings. Nonetheless, some integration of those two perspectives on the expression of emotion in organizational life may have benefits for both organizational theory and managerial practice.

First, the qualitative evidence suggested that the concept of control moves might still be useful for understanding the convenience stores we studied but that future research might benefit from considering how expressed emotions influence variables other than sales volume. Evidence about busy times suggested that an emotionally neutral demeanor discouraged customers from initiating extended conversations. Presenting a neutral demeanor can act as a control move because it helps clerks influence the behavior of their customers and thus helps clerks provide fast service. Further, evidence about slow times suggested that pleasant displays can encourage customers to engage in conversations that are an important source of variety in a boring job. Thus, the display of good cheer during slow times may be a control move that promotes individual rather than organizational goals.

Second, organizational theorists have not extensively studied the emotions displayed by organizational members (Hochschild, 1983; Rafaeli & Sutton, 1987). One central question for this emerging area is the extent to which leaders can prescribe employees' expressive behavior. Our initial perspective emphasized emotions expressed on the job as the outcome of corporate practices. But our revised perspective emphasizes that, although corporate display rules do constrain displayed emotions, store norms and inner feelings can sometimes be a more powerful influence over such behavior. 　　　　　　　　　　　　　　　　　　　　　　　　　　　**99**

(Sutton & Rafaeli, 1988, pp. 482-483)

66 Finally, we learned much about the role of expressed emotion in organizational life from this research because it entailed two complete cycles of induction and deduction. Unfortunately, however, it is not normative in the organizational studies literature, nor in other scholarly areas, to report unsuccessful efforts at induction or deduction. Studies that find no significant relationships are usually not published. Moreover, we occasionally hear of studies in which the findings contradict initial hypotheses but that are written as if the unexpected results were predicted at the outset of the investigation. The tendency to report only successful predictions persists even though failed predictions offer important lessons about the research process and about organizational life (Mirvis & Berg, 1977). We hope that, in some small way, this research is a step toward changing those norms. 　　　　　　　　　　　　　　　　　　　　　　　　　**99**

(Sutton & Rafaeli, 1988, p. 484)

The Sutton and Rafaeli article has successfully violated most of our norms. Their piece starts as a conventionally ambitious study testing the relationship between displayed positive emotion and store sales. It capitalizes on a large field study conducted by a nationwide convenience store chain using "mystery shoppers" to note the emotional demeanor of its sales personnel. The main hypothesis was that display of good cheer would be positively associated with store sales. When this result did not hold up and, in fact, a negative relationship was shown, the real fun began. At this point Sutton and Rafaeli threw down their printouts and started collecting more qualitative data. They served as observers of clerks' behavior in stores with various combinations of high and low sales and high and low display of positive affect. They interviewed the clerks and higher-level management, attended a customer service workshop, and even worked themselves as store checkout personnel. The insights from these qualitative data were then used to reformulate the study's hypothesis, reanalyze the data, and show why sales and affect are negatively related.

Basically what Sutton and Rafaeli found was a "Manhattan effect." Norms for service seemed to vary with the pace of the store. In busy environments customers expected fast, efficient service and not friendly socializing. A conspiracy almost seemed to exist, in which smiling service was not expected by customers and not delivered by store personnel. Probably the busy pace served as an exogenous reason or justification for lack of good cheer. But there may also have been a perceptual discounting process in which customers saw a trade-off between friendliness and service. High degrees of friendliness may have even created the impression of bad service, while a more curt demeanor might have implied efficiency in operations.

Have the Sutton and Rafaeli data thus put to rest the assumption that positive affect contributes to sales? Certainly most store managers would not readily throw out the hypothesis, even if they were to wade through this journal article. I also doubt that Hochschild would drop her central premise that women are used by industry to generate sales through emotional work. Even Sutton and Rafaeli would probably not generalize their data to all forms of retailing, let alone to other service relationships. What these authors have contributed, then, is more of an opening of the broad question of the consequences of affect than a set of definitive answers.

In the face of the Sutton and Rafaeli data we are now forced to ask more pointedly about the role of emotion in organizational behavior. It can be argued that most service transactions are much more than the transferral of goods from seller to buyer; they are a conveyance of assurance (e.g., legal service), social support (e.g., psychological consultation), positive self-image (e.g., hairstyling), and even direct mood elevation (e.g., entertainment). Within organizations, interaction among participants also involves more than the transmittal of information. It is an exchange of persuasion, trustworthiness, power, and even passion. As we know from the work of Ekman and others, the meaning of information can come as much or more from the emotions expressed as from any of the objective facts involved.

In the delivery of services that are based on speed, such as those in convenience stores, fast-food outlets, or toll booths, one might argue that positive emotion is less of a factor for customer satisfaction than in more leisurely pursuits such as travel and restaurant dining. Yet one is hard-pressed to argue theoretically that positive emotion is *necessarily* associated with customer satisfaction in a broad range of settings such as banks, supermarkets, and hardware stores. Some banks, for example, have successfully marketed positive affect with slogans like "Big-city efficiency with small-town friendliness." In contrast, many prestige stores seem to be successful with an aloof stance toward the customer, conveying status and an air of "quality beyond reproach." Thus it seems difficult to draw definitive rules for settings in which positive affect should or should not be conveyed. Norms governing affect may be specific to each type of service and may be alterable by a concerted campaign or effort by the organization. There are also, as Sutton and Rafaeli note, substantial regional differences in expressed emotion. Behavior that is normal for one geographical area may be considered insulting in another part of the country, with even larger differences expected to exist across cultures.

In summary, if norms for emotional expression are localized by industry, region, and subculture, have we learned anything substantively from the Sutton and Rafaeli piece? We now know, of course, how sales and emotional expression covary for one part of retailing, but only the boldest or most rash would generalize this relationship beyond convenience stores. In fact, one might suppose that the Sutton and Rafaeli data could even be used to discourage potential investigators of emotion because its supposed relation to tangible outcomes (i.e., sales) has been called into question. However, I would hope that Sutton and Rafaeli's challenge to our everyday assumptions about good cheer may stimulate future cross-industry research. And, as further studies come forth, other means of emotional expression (such as aggressiveness, hostility, warmth) may also attract attention. In the end what could be achieved is not only an inventory of when and how emotions are expressed in organizations, but how these expressions relate to other organizational processes such as communication, decision making, the maintenance of power, and leadership. The Sutton and Rafaeli piece has given us a taste for these spoils, but also has demonstrated that flexibility in method may be necessary to get them.

Resolving Scientific Disputes by the Joint Design of Crucial Experiments by the Antagonists: Application to the Erez–Latham Dispute Regarding Participation in Goal Setting

Gary P. Latham
Graduate School of Business Administration
University of Washington

Miriam Erez
Faculty of Industrial Engineering and Management
Technion, Israel Institute of Technology
Haifa, Israel

Edwin A. Locke
College of Business and Management
University of Maryland

In this monograph we describe a unique method for resolving scientific disputes: the joint design of crucial experiments by the antagonists themselves with the help of a mediator. This method was applied to the issue of the effect of participation on goal commitment and performance. In research on this topic, Latham and his colleagues had obtained markedly different results from those obtained by Erez and her colleagues. With Locke serving as a third party mediator, Latham and Erez designed four experiments to resolve the discrepancies. The experiments were conducted at the University of Washington and the University of Maryland. The results revealed that the major reason for the difference was that Erez gave very brief *tell* instructions to her assigned goal subjects, whereas Latham used a *tell and sell* approach. Four additional factors also contributed to the earlier difference in findings: goal difficulty, setting personal goals before goal treatments were introduced, self-efficacy-inducing instructions, and instructions to reject disliked goals. It was concluded that (a) the differences between Latham and Erez can be explained on the basis of differences in specific procedures, and (b) the method used to resolve this dispute should be used by other investigators.

In this monograph we present a method of resolving scientific disputes that may be unique in the history of psychology, and we demonstrate its application to a current scientific dispute. The method involved the joint design of "crucial experiments" by the antagonists, using a third party as a mediator.

Typically, when there are disagreements regarding a certain finding or relationship in science, the disputants attack one another in the literature. Each may claim that the other used a flawed procedure, an invalid design, inappropriate analyses, or that the findings were valid but misinterpreted. The rest of the scientific community then lines up on either side (or in the middle).

At this point, several things can happen. The disputants may each conduct further experiments until one side wears the other down or persuades the scientific community that his or her view is correct. This occurred in the controversy surrounding motivator–hygiene theory with its critics winning the day. Sometimes a controversy continues because of strong convictions that may, in part, be ideologically based. A case in point is the heritability of intelligence dispute, which continues to this day. In other instances, the scientific community may simply lose interest in the issue on the grounds that it is not worth pursuing. An example is the controversy over intrinsic motivation; industrial and organizational psychologists have, in recent years, basically ignored it.

What has rarely been done in scientific disputes is for the disputants themselves to work together to try to design one or more crucial experiments to resolve the differences in their findings. It is not difficult to understand why one rarely if ever sees this method used. It can be ego threatening to work with an antagonist after he or she has made opposing scientific claims in print; the antagonists face the risk that their work may be shown to be wrong. Furthermore, the disputants may not like each other personally, thus making any attempt at joint research impractical. Finally, the dispute may be based on ideological issues, thus limiting what can be accomplished through the systematic collection of data.

Preparation of this article was funded in part by a Ford Motor Company Affiliate Fund grant to the first author. All three authors contributed equally to this article.

We thank John Dimitejevich, Barbara Finnegan, Shirley Ring, and Kimberly Tilghman for their help in conducting and analyzing these experiments, and Ayala Cohen for her statistical advice.

Correspondence concerning this article should be addressed to Gary P. Latham, Graduate School of Business Administration, DJ-10, University of Washington, Seattle, Washington 98195.

Introductory Remarks:
Journey 5

Latham: I felt both excitement and irritation.

Erez: I was excited to have this unique opportunity . . .

Locke: I welcomed the opportunity . . .

Thus the coauthors of this article remember their reactions to a dinner in which the three discussed the anomalous and contradictory results of the independent work done by Latham and Erez. Latham and his colleagues had established over a series of 10 laboratory and field investigations that participation in goal setting has no independent motivational effect on goal commitment or performance. The work of Erez and her colleagues, however, did find an effect. Locke brought the disputants together over a dinner table at a Society for Organizational Behavior meeting.

What many would consider a threat these authors chose to define as an opportunity to search collaboratively for a resolution of the anomaly. With the help of Locke in the role of mediator and referee, the disputants investigated their differences over the effectiveness of assigned versus participative goal setting. With the persistence of detectives, the three participants examined old experimental protocols, their memories, and the recollections of an ex-student to uncover possible causes of the Latham-Erez dispute. They identified a series of differences in their research that may account for their opposing results. Having done so, they carefully designed studies that capitalized on the advantages of factorial design in a laboratory setting. Little was taken for granted. Extraordinary attention was paid to the operationalization of constructs and experimental manipulations. Reliable manipulation checks were provided. Multiple control variables were assessed.

Ultimately, they discovered that the source of the dispute centered not on the effectiveness of participation, but rather on the different meaning of assigned goals for the two disputants. In the Latham studies, goals had been assigned with a "tell-and-sell" procedure that featured an assurance that the goals were achievable. In contrast, Erez had assigned goals with a "tell" procedure that lacked any additional comments. Subjects exposed to Latham's procedure were characterized by goal commitment and performance levels similar to those of participative subjects. In contrast, subjects with "tell" instructions reported lower levels of commitment and usually performed at a lower level as well.

Latham, Erez, and Locke are not coauthors in the usual sense. Though they have worked together closely, they have distinctly different roles. Both the article and their commentaries reflect this difference in allowing their individual voices to be heard. All three describe their human and their intellectual experiences of this project.

While the authors tend to focus on the substantive issues of the dispute, the commentators focus on the process of the dispute resolution. Larry Cummings and Christopher Earley explore the characteristics of the resolution process. They highlight aspects of that process that will need to be considered by other disputants who may use this technique. John Campbell points to the external generalizability of the conflict resolution strategy. Along the way, he raises important issues of construct validation. Finally, he shifts our attention from the technique itself to our consciousness of ourselves as a research community. He reminds us that we are not omniscient observers of organizational life. We, too, exhibit organized behavior in need of study and understanding.

We chose to include this exemplar for several reasons. First, it provides a template for those conducting research in the laboratory context. Second, it demonstrates the advantages of paradigmatic research programs. Finally, it serves as a possible model for the resolution of disputes in organizational studies.

We often characterize the choice between laboratory and field investigation of phenomena as the trade-off of control in the laboratory experiment for the realism and meaning of the field setting. This series of studies demonstrates the truth and limitations of this simple dichotomy. The authors achieve control in the lab, but that control does not come easily. The studies illustrate the difficulties. For example, how did the experimenter interact with the subjects? It matters if he or she is friendly or not. Thus the goal-setting result is that specific, difficult goals yield better results when assigned by friendly supervisors. Much of the difference between Latham's and Erez's findings can be attributed to differences in the meaning of assigned goals. They demonstrate that interpreting meaning is not only an issue in qualitative field research.

The Latham, Erez, and Locke contribution illustrates the utility of a strong paradigm. The goal-setting paradigm was first articulated as a program of research by Locke (1968). It has proved to be a durable and successful program that continues to generate new research more than 20 years later. The relatively specific participation question has been explored and honed over a period of years by a number of investigators in a variety of settings, using several methodological approaches. This series of four studies builds on that base and provides evidence that cumulation is possible in organizational studies. This work clearly exemplifies the puzzle-solving nature of normal science (Kuhn, 1970) or the positive heuristic of a research program (Lakatos, 1970).

Both the authors and the commentators see potential applicability of this dispute resolution technique to other questions. We share that belief. The irony of using a participative method to handle a dispute over the value of participation does not escape the authors. Locke notes: "The design of the present series of experiments themselves [was], interestingly, an example of the cognitive benefits of joint decision making or pdm [participative decision making]" (Latham, Erez, & Locke, 1988, p. 770).

One of the benefits we have received in preparing this book has been our experience of the depth and breadth of goodwill among the members of the organizational studies research community. We suspect that techniques such as the one illustrated here would work well in this community. Perhaps journal editors and other gatekeepers might consider providing the catalytic situations and structures necessary for more collaborative problem solving.

Resolving a Scientific Dispute with Dr. Miriam Erez: Genesis, Process, Outcome, and Reflection

Gary P. Latham

Genesis

In 1969 I was hired by the American Pulpwood Association's Harvesting Research Project as their first staff psychologist. My job was to find ways of increasing the productivity of pulpwood producers in the southeastern United States. Serendipitously, we discovered through a survey of wood practices that goal setting correlated positively with cords per man hour (Ronan, Latham, & Kinne, 1973). Further, when we randomly assigned producers who had not used production goals in the past to a group that was trained to set specific difficult but attainable goals, the productivity and job attendance of their logging crews were significantly higher than those of the control group (Latham & Kinne, 1974).

In doing my doctoral work with Gary Yukl, I became convinced from the work of Rensis Likert that participatively set goals would result in even greater crew productivity than assigned goals. The results of my doctoral dissertation showed that this was indeed the case with uneducated woods workers (Latham & Yukl, 1975). My dissertation also showed that the goal was higher in the participative than in the assigned condition for these employees.

66 CONCLUDING REMARKS: LATHAM

Conducting the present series of studies was as exciting as it was illuminating. It was science at its best. It involved systematically reviewing one another's studies, formulating hypotheses, arguing over proper procedures for testing hypotheses, implementing the procedures, re-implementing the procedures, analyzing the data, and reanalyzing the data because someone thought of an alternative statistical test.   99

(Latham, Erez, & Locke, 1988, p. 767)

Upon completing my doctorate, I became Weyerhauser Company's manager of human resource research. Subsequently, field experiments that I conducted with word-processing operators (Dossett, Latham, & Mitchell, 1979; Latham & Yukl, 1976; Yukl & Latham, 1978) and research engineers and scientists (Latham, Mitchell, & Dossett, 1978) led me to question my belief in the importance of participation in goal setting. Only in those instances where participation led to higher goals than those that were assigned was performance significantly better in the former condition. Thus it appeared that it was the difficulty level of the goal rather than the process by which it was set that affected performance.

On a Sunday morning in 1978 I was awakened by a phone call from a man whom I revered but had never before met. Rensis Likert informed me that he had read my work and had wondered if his principle of supportive relationships (Likert, 1967) might explain my findings. That is, it occurred to him that the goals in my studies had been assigned within a supportive atmosphere. He asked me to measure the degree of supportiveness in my future work.

I decided to conduct research in a laboratory setting, where I would be free to manipulate the variables that had been suggested as causal explanations in my field experiments. In brief, my former graduate students and I found that when goal difficulty was held constant, goal commitment and performance were indeed the same regardless of whether the goal was assigned or set participatively (Latham & Saari, 1979a); when the assigned goal was higher than the participatively set goal, performance was also higher even though goal commitment was the same in the two conditions (Latham, Steele, & Saari, 1982). Further, there was no main effect for participation in decision making on a motivational task (one that required no learning) regarding ways of completing it; rather, there was a main effect only for goal setting (Latham & Steele, 1983).

Supportiveness in these studies was held constant and high across conditions. In one study I actually manipulated supportiveness

(Latham & Saari, 1979b). In that study, supportiveness led to higher goals being set than did nonsupportiveness. Goal commitment was the same in the two conditions, but performance was higher in the participative than in the assigned condition. The subjects asked performance-related questions in the participative condition, which increased their understanding of what was required of them.

On the basis of 11 laboratory and field experiments that my colleagues and I had conducted, I believed the issue had been solved. As Herb Meyer had concluded in 1965 in the *Harvard Business Review*, it is not so important how a goal is set as it is that a goal in fact be set. Thus in the early 1980s, when Miriam Erez started publishing results different from mine (e.g., Erez, Earley, & Hulin, 1985), I felt angry and frustrated. I felt angry because years of work were now being called into question. I felt frustration because I did not know why her results were different from mine.

Coincidentally, Erez was on a sabbatical at the University of Maryland during 1985-1986, where she became friends on both professional and personal levels with Ed Locke. I too was and am a friend at both levels with Ed.

In the fall of 1985, Miriam attended a meeting of the Society of Organizational Behavior as a guest of Ed. At Ed's suggestion, the three of us went to dinner and brainstormed explanations for the differences in our findings. He then proposed to serve as a mediator between us if we would do a series of experiments to test our explanations.

I felt both excitement and irritation. I was excited on two accounts. First, Ed is a stickler for detail. I knew with his assistance that we would discover the reasons for the discrepancy in findings. He would force us to make explicit every detail of our research. Since both Miriam and I trusted Ed, and since both of us respected his research skills, I knew that what I would be asked to do would be fair. Second, I was excited because, to my knowledge, the idea of using a mediator to design studies to resolve a scientific dispute had never been proposed previously. This unique aspect in itself all but guaranteed an interesting project regardless of the outcome of the research. By this time I had left Weyerhauser for the University of Washington; publications now had extrinsic, in addition to intrinsic, value for me.

> 66 Typically, when there are disagreements regarding a certain finding or relationship in science, the disputants attack one another in the literature. Each may claim that the other used a flawed procedure, an invalid design, inappropriate analyses, or that the findings were valid but misinterpreted. The rest of the scientific community then lines up on either side (or in the middle).

At this point, several things can happen. The disputants may each conduct further experiments until one side wears the other down or persuades the scientific community that his or her view is correct. This occurred in the controversy surrounding motivator-hygiene theory with its critics winning the day. Sometimes a controversy continues because of strong convictions that may, in part, be ideologically based. A case in point is the heritability of intelligence dispute, which continues to this day. In other instances, the scientific community may simply lose interest in the issue on the grounds that it is not worth pursuing. An example is the controversy over intrinsic motivation; industrial and organizational psychologists have, in recent years, basically ignored it. **99**

(Latham, Erez, & Locke, 1988, p. 753)

I was also irritated at two levels. First, I felt that I would be "nit-picked" by Ed and Miriam to do "this and that" when there was other unrelated research I had planned for that year. Further, at the risk of sounding arrogant to the reader, I was confident that my findings would be replicated because they were based on both laboratory and field experiments. The laboratory experiments had been conducted by people other than me, thus eliminating the possibility of experimenter bias; further, some of these laboratory experiments had been conducted by "blind" experimenters. Finally, the field experiments had been conducted by disinterested parties who were interested only in the outcome—productivity. Thus the feeling conflicting with excitement was despair. There was no face-saving way of avoiding a situation that I believed should never have come to pass. On the whole, however, my feeling of excitement in attempting to solve a mystery outweighed any feelings of irritation.

Process

The process was painstakingly slow in that every word that would be uttered by the experimenter had to be written down in script form. I found an MBA student in finance who was unaware of goal-setting theory to serve as a "blind" experimenter. Miriam, who was at the University of Maryland, did likewise. The process of agreeing on the experimental tasks, procedures, manipulation checks, and data analyses went surprisingly fast, because the three of us share similar, if not identical, approaches to research philosophy and design.

66 The face-to-face discussions were followed by extensive telephone calls and written correspondence. Thus, every experimental condition, includ-

ing the choice of tasks, the experimental manipulations (including verbatim instructions), and all questionnaire measures (most of which were
common to all the experiments) were agreed on by the three researchers
prior to the experiments. In addition, the experiments were conducted,
not by the protagonists themselves, but by research assistants who were
unaware of the hypotheses of the studies. The experimenters were told
truthfully that the researchers did not know how the studies would
come out.   **99**

(Latham, Erez, & Locke, 1988, p. 754)

In conducting my two of the four experiments, I experienced two
frustrations. First, the research assistant, due to poor supervision on
my part, set the goals differently in the "task important" condition and
the "task unimportant" condition. We included the results in the
write-up, namely, that performance and goal commitment were the
same in the two goal-setting conditions regardless of the subject's
perceived importance of the task. Ed, quite rightly, insisted that I
repeat the experiment. Miriam insisted that the goals be extremely
difficult, because she believed that this was a factor that could account
for the differences between us in our previous research. I was reluctant
to do so because I believe goals should be difficult but attainable. Ed
sided with Miriam; my confidence that my results would be replicated
was now shaken.

Happily for me, my research assistant found that although a self-
report measure of goal commitment was higher in the participative
than in the assigned goal conditions, performance was the same.
Unhappily for all of us, the two experiments did not solve the mystery
of why Miriam's earlier work was in conflict with mine.

66 Experiment 2 also differed from Experiment 1 in that very hard or
impossible goals were encouraged in the participative condition. This
was done because in Experiment 1, 77% of the people attained their goal.
In Experiment 2, the goal was 30% higher than the premeasure ability
score prorated over 30 min. Consequently, only 21% of the people
attained their goal. This procedure was followed because the authors
noted that in the Latham experiments, the subjects/employees in the
participative condition were requested to set a goal that they perceived
as difficult but attainable, whereas in many of the Erez studies, especially
in the second phase of her two-phase design, the goal was far out of
reach. Thus, it was hypothesized that participation in setting the goal
might be critical to goal commitment and performance only when very
hard goals are set.   **99**

(Latham, Erez, & Locke, 1988, p. 758)

Three major surprises came from our work. First, consistent with our brainstorming meeting, a reading of our scripts suggested that my dispute with Miriam was not in regard to the effectiveness of participatively set goals. Both of us had shown repeatedly that they resulted in significantly higher performance than that of a control group. Rather, our dispute was over the effectiveness of assigned goals. The scripts made clear that Miriam assigned goals in a curt manner; mine were assigned with a rationale for the goal. We borrowed N. R. F. Maier's terminology describing the effective way to assign goals in a performance appraisal, namely, "tell and sell" for describing my approach to goal assignment and "tell" for describing Miriam's.

> **66** Typical instructions used in laboratory experiments by Latham (e.g., Latham, Steele, & Saari, 1982) were as follows:
>
>> Thank you for agreeing to participate in this study. Weyerhauser Company has employed us to ____. You are now familiar with the task. I would like you to do the following ____. This goal is difficult but attainable.
>
> These instructions were given in a polite, friendly manner so that the experimenter was seen as supportive. Contrast this with the instructions typically given by Erez:
>
>> Now that you have already had a practice session to get familiar with the task, you are asked to next attain a score of ____. You will have ____minutes.
>
> Three differences between these two sets of instructions may be significant: (a) Latham provided a rationale for why the task was an important one; (b) Latham provided a statement to the effect that the goal was reachable, using a *tell and sell* rather than only a *tell* approach; and (c) Latham stressed a warm and friendly rather than an abrupt tone (i.e., high supportiveness). **99**
>
> (Latham, Erez, & Locke, 1988, p. 755)

In the third experiment, conducted by Miriam, I insisted that she measure experimenter supportiveness. As I suspected, supportiveness was not constant across conditions. Her results replicated my work in that supportiveness, goal commitment, and performance were the same in her tell-and-sell and participative conditions; this was not true for the tell condition. The late Rensis Likert had been right. When goals are assigned with an explanation in a supportive atmosphere they are effective; when goals are assigned curtly, the atmosphere is not viewed as supportive and the goals are not effective for increasing performance.

The second surprise occurred as a result of Miriam's inability to get the range in self-reports of goal commitment that she had obtained in her earlier research. Ed, upon learning the name of the research assistant who had worked with her several years ago, interviewed him along with Miriam by telephone on every detail of the previous experiments. It was discovered that in Miriam's previous work the research assistant had instructed subjects that they could reject goals they did not agree with.

The third discovery also came from reading Miriam's scripts. Whereas I had always held self-efficacy-type instructions constant across my tell-and-sell and participatively set goal conditions, Miriam in her own experiments had given only those people in the participative goal conditions instructions designed to increase their self-efficacy in order to encourage them to set difficult goals. She had not done this for the people in the tell condition. The fourth and final experiment reported in our monograph confirmed that self-efficacy-inducing instructions significantly affected or mediated performance and/or goal commitment.

> 66 Following procedures previously used by Erez and her colleagues, subjects in the present tell-and-sell and pdm conditions were told that they could be expected to improve on the task as a result of practice (learning) and gaining momentum, whereas subjects in the tell condition were given no such persuasive encouragement. With self-efficacy strength held constant across the tell-and-sell and pdm conditions, goal commitment and subsequent performance in the two conditions were not significantly different.   99

(Latham, Erez, & Locke, 1988, p. 763)

Production

One conclusion of our monograph is that failure to put all of one's procedures in writing can mislead both authors and readers. Consequently, we included all the procedural details of my two experiments. Miriam wrote the details of her two experiments, and all three of us had a separate discussion section. We then exchanged drafts for critique. The process was relatively straightforward, with little or no argument among us. We included a footnote stating that all three of us deserved equal credit as first author.

The first public appearance of our work was at the International Congress of Applied Psychology held in Jerusalem in 1986. There we discussed what we were doing and how, but we had only preliminary results. Audience feedback requested that we include in our write-up where we agreed and where we still disagreed despite the results of our four experiments. We did so.

The second appearance of our work was in a debate format at the annual meeting of the Society of Industrial-Organizational Psychology in Atlanta in 1987. There audience feedback requested that our write-up emphasize the role of a mediator to resolve scientific disputes. Hence this aspect, as we anticipated at the genesis of our research, was heavily weighted in our article.

Because of the length of our manuscript, we narrowed our choices of journals to which we might submit it to two in the United States. We chose American journals because both Israeli and North American universities are biased favorably by publications in them, and because they have a wide readership. The *Journal of Applied Psychology* was our first choice because to have a monograph published in it is considered highly prestigious. Both Ed and I had served on the Editorial Board of this journal. Our knowledge of the journal's policy led us to believe that our paper had a good chance of being accepted. We were not disappointed. The paper was accepted with minor revisions. The length of time from genesis to product was two years; the length of time from genesis to publication was three years.

Aftermath and Reflection

In the time since the paper's publication, the feedback has been very positive in terms of requests for reprints. More significantly, in August 1989 we were informed that our article had won the award for best paper in the Organizational Behavior Division of the Academy of Management.

The importance of the manuscript, in my opinion, is twofold. First, it suggests a relatively sane way of resolving a scientific dispute. Picking a mediator that the antagonists trust is far more productive for them and the field than carping back and forth in the literature about who is right. The answer is unlikely to emerge unless the combatants are willing to discuss their "honest differences." Second, the mono-graph lays to rest, or should lay to rest, the debate on the motivational effects of assigned versus participatively set goals. When supportive-ness, goal difficulty, and self-efficacy instructions are held constant, and when the goal is assigned with a rationale so that it is not viewed as capricious, assigned goals are as effective in increasing performance as are participatively set goals. At best, when the goal is extremely difficult, participatively set goals may influence a self-report of goal commitment favorably relative to an assigned goal.

My respect for Dr. Erez remained high throughout this process. She was straightforward in what she did and why she did it. My major disagreement with her is on the importance one should attach to a self-rating of goal commitment that has no relationship to actual performance.

Because of my observation of employees, and because of my respect for giants in our field such as the late Ren Likert, I am continuing to pursue the issue of participation in the goal-setting process. I believe that proponents of participatively set goals have been correct for the wrong reasons. On tasks where motivation, as defined by effort or persistence, is relatively unimportant, I believe that participation increases understanding of how to perform effectively. The cognitive effects of goal setting were first suggested by Campbell, Dunnette, Lawler, and Weick (1970). Our monograph suggests that the cognitive benefits of goal setting constitute an area long overdue for systematic research.

Reflections on the Latham/Erez/Locke Study

Miriam Erez

Genesis

My research interest has mainly been focused on the motivational effects of goals on performance. In particular, I have been interested in the self-regulatory processes that link goals to performance. Some of my early empirical findings demonstrated that feedback and goal acceptance, which are part of the evaluation process, are necessary conditions for goals to affect performance (Erez, 1977; Erez & Zidon, 1984). Following these findings, I became interested in ways to improve goal acceptance.

The seminal work of Kurt Lewin (1943, 1951) provided the necessary theoretical framework for my research. Lewin developed the technique of group participation as a means to overcome resistance to change. His first study on participation aimed at changing consumers' attitudes and eating habits (Lewin, 1943). Lewin found that group participation was effective where other methods failed, and that it helped to overcome resistance to change.

While I was reviewing the line of research developed by Lewin, I met Fred Kanfer, a professor of clinical psychology at the University of Illinois, who introduced me to a new research area of self-management methods in clinical psychology (Kanfer, 1980). I learned that acceptance of therapeutic goals is a necessary precondition for most treatments, and that attempts to change client behaviors solely through external control are commonly rejected. It is more likely for a goal to be accepted if it is perceived to be under a person's control than if it is perceived as externally imposed. In an attempt to integrate the research in clinical psychology with that in social and organizational psychology, we developed a conceptual model postulating that the amount of control a person has over the situation ranges on a continuum from assigned goals to self-set goals, with participation lying between the two poles. Therefore, participation is expected to elicit more goal acceptance than the no participation condition (Erez & Kanfer, 1983).

Two lines of research in social and clinical psychology proposed that participation is mainly effective if goal acceptance is at risk. Such an approach coincides with the work of Vroom and Yetton (1973), who developed a contingency model of managing participation in organizations. They proposed that the expected level of goal acceptance on the part of subordinates should serve as a criterion of whether to implement participation. They advised managers to use a participative approach when they had no confidence that their decisions would be accepted by their subordinates.

The three sources of research summarized above guided my conceptual and methodological approach to the study of participation. I reasoned that goal acceptance mediates the relationship between participation and performance, and I decided to test for a two-step model in which participation affects goal acceptance, which, in turn, affects performance (Erez, Earley, & Hulin, 1985).

In the process of developing the research method, it was important to get variance in goal acceptance in order to test for its mediating effect. From a statistical perspective, the causal relationships among participation, goal acceptance, and performance could be tested only if there were a variance in acceptance. To create such variance I had to think of experimental conditions that might cause resistance to goals. For example, I predicted that goal acceptance would tend to decrease with increased goal difficulty, if there is a conflict between an externally set goal and a self-set goal, or if the task itself is not intrinsically motivating. Thus I implemented all of the above factors in my research. The methodology I used was found to be effective. In all of my studies the level of goal acceptance was moderate rather than high, and there was high variance in goal acceptance.

When the empirical findings proved to support the two-step model, I was intrigued by the differences in the results between my own research and the series of studies conducted by Gary Latham and his colleagues. I noticed that Latham generally reported high levels of acceptance, whereas in my own research, as well as in the classical research by Lewin, the level of commitment was moderate to low. I wondered whether goal acceptance might explain the differences in the effect of participation on performance in the two lines of research.

Process

To my great satisfaction, I had the opportunity to meet with Ed Locke and Gary Latham to brainstorm explanations for the differences in our findings. Locke, after encouraging us to design crucial experiments to test for the potential explanatory variables, offered to serve as a mediator. His role was found to be crucial for the successful operation of the joint experiments.

I was excited to have this unique opportunity to take a constructive approach, and to work together with Locke and Latham in an attempt to discover the factors that would explain the differences in our results. I took the approach of a non-zero-sum game, since I had the feeling that the differences in goal acceptance between the two lines of research would explain the differences in the effects of participation on performance.

I must admit that when I told my colleagues that I was going to work on this joint project, some of them discouraged me and advised me to withdraw from it. They argued that the project was of a zero-sum game, and they worried that we could end up fighting each other rather than resolving the scientific dispute. I assessed my own feelings and thoughts, because there was no precedent from which I could learn. Three factors influenced my decision not to withdraw: My curiosity to discover the reasons for the differences in our results, trust that we were capable of doing it, and expectation that the collaboration of the three of us would lead to interesting results.

Brainstorming generated a number of factors that might have caused the differences in the results. Four of these factors were related to goal acceptance: task importance, goal difficulty, instructions— "tell" versus "tell and sell" versus participation—and setting personal goals prior to the externally set goals. An additional factor, advising subjects that there is no need to accept impossible goals, was added in Experiment 4. This factor was used before to overcome the demand characteristics of the experiment that imposed compliance with the instructions (Erez et al., 1985). In real-life situations, such demand characteristics do not exist, since employees recognize their rights and use external frames of reference to evaluate whether the goals assigned make sense or not.

TABLE 1 Summary of Independent Variables Explored in Each
Experiment

Experiment	Variable
1	Task importance, group decision,[a] and participation values[b]
2	Task importance,[c] group decision,[c] and participation values[b]
3	Tell vs. tell and sell vs. pdm instructions, set personal goals before manipulations vs. no-set, and participation values[b]
4	Tell vs. pdm instructions, self-efficacy instructions, instructions to reject goals, two-phase design with increasing goal difficulty, participation values[b]

[a]There was no individual decision comparison group. Previous studies were used as
a comparison base.
[b]Participation values was an individual difference factor.
[c]Goal difficulty was increased.

(Latham, Erez, & Locke, 1988, p. 756)

One additional factor that differentiated between our two lines of
research was group composition. I conceived of participation as a
group discussion among five members who have similar position
power. In Latham's research, participation usually took place in a
dyadic setting between one superior/experimenter and one subordi-
nate/subject who did not hold the same position power.

It is plausible that my schema of participation is different from
Latham's because mine is anchored in the cultural values of Israel,
which are more group oriented and egalitarian than North American
values (Hofstede, 1980). It should be noted that I did not make a
conscious choice between a group composition of five versus two.
Groups of five members were natural in my case.

We designed a total of four experiments to test hypotheses about
each of the variables that could explain the differences in our results.
The method and the results are summarized in detail in the manuscript, and will not be repeated here. However, some points in the
process deserve further attention. The process of designing the set of
studies involved jointly determining which variables to include and
how to operationalize them. Each of us had to make compromises in
order to proceed with the process. The first two experiments were
designed to test for the effect of task importance on the relationships
among group participation, goal commitment, and performance. I
compromised on the nature of the task in the first two experiments.
Latham preferred to use the brainstorming task, which requires sub-

jects to generate a certain number of uses for a given object. I thought that the brainstorming task had the connotation of a creativity test; it enhances intrinsic motivation and thereby goal acceptance. For this reason, I preferred to use the class scheduling task, which is not intrinsically motivating. We ended up using the brainstorming task in the first two experiments, and the class scheduling task in the other two experiments.

In the first experiment, we discovered two problems that were resolved in the second experiment. First, the experimenter set the goals differently for the groups of high and low task importance. As a result, we could not compare the two conditions. Second, the goals were too easy, because 77% of the subjects were able to attain them. The second experiment was designed with a higher level of goal difficulty, and with identical instructions for all groups on how to set the goals. Participation had a positive effect on goal commitment, and the lowest level of goal commitment was expressed by subjects in the assigned goals and low importance condition. However, there was no significant effect of participation on performance.

TABLE 5 Ideas Generated by Experimental Condition in Experiment 2, Adjusted Group Means

	Goal condition		
Task importance	*Participative*	*Assigned*	*Do best*
Important			
M	125.29	106.55	52.65
SD	41.96	37.36	25.50
n	9	10	13
Unimportant			
M	119.83	110.10	59.58
SD	43.89	49.90	17.90
n	9	10	13

66 In the perceived task important condition, which is analogous to all the laboratory and field experiments conducted by Latham, there was no significant difference, $t(17) = 1.09$, *ns*, in the performance of those with assigned versus participatively set goals. Similarly, in the task unimportant condition, which is analogous to the Erez laboratory experiments, performance was not significantly different in the two goal-setting conditions. **99**

(Latham, Erez, & Locke, 1988, p. 759)

Experiment 3 aimed at testing the effect of instructions for setting the goals (participation, tell and sell, tell), and of the conflict between personal goals and externally set goals. In addition, Latham wanted to include a measure of experimenter supportiveness. In this experiment, we compromised on the measure of goal difficulty. Locke and Latham argued that goal difficulty should be set relative to the person's ability, and therefore they proposed to set a goal as a multiplier of the performance level in the practice trial. I preferred to set a goal in absolute terms, and to control for ability. The use of a multiplier led to the setting of impossible goals for the high-ability subjects. The multiplication of their high performance scores in the practice trial by a certain multiplier resulted in much higher goals than they were able to obtain. Only 19% of the high-ability subjects were able to obtain their goals, compared with 55% of the low-ability group. Thus future research should pay more attention to the manipulation of goal difficulty.

Results of Experiment 3 demonstrated that participation led to higher perceptions of participation, supportiveness, and task interest, and to lower perceptions of experimenter's autocratic style compared with the two other conditions. There were no significant differences between the participation and the tell-and-sell styles in goal commitment and performance, and both had significant advantages over the tell condition regarding actual performance.

TABLE 6 Manipulation Checks: Means and Standard Deviations in Experiment 3

Condition	n	Perceived participation M	SD	Perceived brevity M	SD	Task importance M	SD	Task interest M	SD	Experimenter supportiveness M	SD	Experimenter nonautocratic style M	SD	Compliance M	SD
Tell	34	3.42	1.81	4.05	1.33	3.71	1.61	3.17	1.30	4.62	1.25	3.63	1.63	5.39	1.35
Tell & sell	54	3.86	1.35	3.19	1.38	3.68	1.52	3.40	1.46	4.03	1.37	3.49	1.84	5.58	1.19
Pdm	47	4.97	1.32	3.46	1.26	3.88	1.36	4.04	1.35	5.98	1.00	4.84	1.31	5.54	1.19

Note: Pdm = participation in decision making.

 RESULTS

Manipulation checks. The manipulation effect of participation was measured by the items pertaining to perceived influence on setting the goal. In addition, the goal-setting conditions were compared with respect to subjects' perceptions of brevity of instructions, task importance, task interest, the experimenter's supportiveness, and autocratic style. The means and standard deviations for the manipulation checks are presented in Table 6.

The following significant effects were found, using independent t tests to compare groups. Participation: Tell versus pdm, $t = 4.08$, $p < .001$; and tell and sell versus pdm, $t = 4.08$, $p < .001$. The tell and tell-and-sell conditions were not significantly different, $p > .05$. Brevity: Tell versus pdm, $t = 1.98$, $p = .05$; tell versus tell and sell, $t = 2.85$, $p < .01$; and tell and sell and pdm were not significantly different, $p > .05$. Task importance did not significantly differ across experimental conditions. Task interest: Tell versus pdm, $t = 2.89$, $p < .01$; tell and sell versus pdm, $t = 2.24$, $p < .01$; and tell versus tell and sell were not significantly different, $p > .05$. Experimenter supportiveness: Tell versus pdm, $t = 5.17$, $p < .01$; and tell and sell versus pdm, $t = 7.74$, $p < .01$. Tell versus tell and sell were not significantly different, $p > .05$. Experimenter's autocratic style: Tell versus pdm, $t = 3.54$, $p < .01$; tell and sell versus pdm, $t = 4.03$, $p < .01$; and tell versus tell and sell were not significantly different, $p > .05$.

In sum, the tell groups experienced less perceived participation, less task interest, less supportiveness, greater brevity of instructions, and more experimenter autocracy than did the pdm groups. The tell-and-sell groups were typically either intermediate between the tell and pdm conditions or closer to the tell conditions. **99**

(Latham, Erez, & Locke, 1988, p. 761)

Locke proposed that in the fourth experiment we should separate the effect of self-efficacy from the effect of participation because he thought that the instructions I used for participation were confounded with enhanced self-efficacy. Locke interpreted the statement in the instructions that "people improve on this task with practice and also get momentum when working continuously for a longer time period" as an enhancement of self-efficacy. I included the sentence in the instructions because I wanted to motivate subjects to set high goals in the participation condition. Thus Experiment 4 was designed to test for the separate effects of participation and self-efficacy, and to test for the effect of goal difficulty by designing a two-phase experiment with an increasing level of goal difficulty in the second phase. Without the self-efficacy instructions, subjects in the participation conditions set lower goals compared with Experiment 3. Results of Experiment 4 demonstrated that self-efficacy magnitude differed between the two participation conditions, but not self-efficacy strength. Commitment and performance were lower in the tell condition than in the two participation conditions. Commitment and self-efficacy mediated the effect of participation on performance in both Experiments 3 and 4.

Contributions of the Research

The unique contributions of the present research are threefold. First, we have developed a constructive process for resolving the scientific dispute.

Such a research process coincides with the constructivist approach of theory building proposed by McGuire (1980). Constructivism asserts that in the case of existing differences between theories, empirical research should be conducted to reveal the conditions under which each is true. Although such an approach to theory building exists, it is rarely implemented to resolve scientific disputes.

Second, the study illuminates the crucial effects of the research method, procedures, and manipulations on the empirical findings and conclusions. The method sections in scientific journals often appear in small type, and they do not always describe all the details of research methods and procedures. Very often, researchers are even unaware of contextual effects because they are part of the context and have no external reference point. By working together, the two researchers provided each other with the reference points needed to define the unique characteristics of each other's procedures.

Such a process demonstrates that the research design and method define the boundary conditions for the predictions made by the researchers. The most striking part of this process for Locke was the number of differences in procedure and design that can occur when two people are allegedly studying the same phenomenon. The number of little differences between studies can add up and have a significant effect on the differences in empirical findings and hence on conclusions.

The third significant contribution is the identification of the boundary conditions for effective participation. The common characteristic of most of the factors identified in the joint studies is that they affect goal commitment. Goal commitment served as a mediator of the relationship between participation and performance, as shown in Experiments 3 and 4, and in support of previous research (Erez & Earley, 1987; Erez et al., 1985). However, when goal commitment was high in all experimental conditions, as in Experiment 1, there was no effect of participation on performance. When goal commitment is endangered by the organizational conditions, participation and self-efficacy may counterbalance such effects.

Aftermath and Reflections

As a result of the joint studies, there is a convergence between Latham and myself on the following matters: I agree with Latham that the tell-and-sell style is as effective as the participation approach in enhancing goal commitment and its consequent performance. It was the tell style that was found to be less effective. It conveyed a higher level of perceived brevity and a lower level of supportiveness than the other two conditions. Latham's belief that "the way a goal is set is not as important as the fact that a goal is set" was based on a comparison between tell and sell and participation. However, the way a goal is set does make a difference if the goal is set in a tell style.

Further, Latham has recognized the theoretical importance of the two-step model, and the role that goal commitment plays in the relationship between participation and performance. However, we disagree on the practical implications of the two-step model for the following reason: Latham argues that a high degree of goal commitment occurs in most field and laboratory settings regardless of the method by which the goal is set. My argument, in contrast, is that the practical contribution of participation should be tested not when employees are highly committed to reaching their goals, but rather when unmotivated employees, with a low level of commitment, endanger the productivity level of the organization. In a decade of massive layoffs (Hirsch, 1987), a trust gap, and lack of mutual commitment between employees and employers (Farnham, 1989), the enhancement of goal commitment might be crucial to organizations. Participation was found to be effective in enhancing employees' perceptions of supportiveness and goal commitment, compared with the tell style.

Although the present studies did not examine the cognitive effects of participation on performance, for practical considerations I would like to note that participation may be found to improve employees' knowledge, understanding, and strategy use (Campbell & Gingrich, 1986; Erez & Arad, 1986; Locke & Schweiger, 1979; Latham & Steele, 1983).

Future Research

Future research should continue to examine the effects of participation under conditions that were beyond the scope of the current research, such as the following.

The cognitive effect of information. Participation generates information sharing and clarifications. The process of knowledge and information sharing may not be replicated by the tell-and-sell style because the latter involves a one-way flow of communication, and it might not capture the points that need clarification on the part of the employee. Participation may enhance knowledge and understanding that cannot be replicated by other techniques. The cognitive effect of knowledge may enhance perceptions of self-efficacy and intrinsic motivation. Future research should examine the direct and indirect effects of the cognitive factors of participation.

Task. The tasks used in most research are independent by nature. Future research should examine the effect of participation when a collaborative effort among participants is required in interdependent tasks.

Extrarole behavior. Attention has recently been given to extrarole behavior, such as prosocial organizational behavior, organizational citizenship, and task revision (correction of a faulty task or misdirected work role). Staw and Boettger (1990) suggest that participation schemes might enhance task revision, since they may heighten responsibility and empowerment in employment settings. Future research may empirically examine the above argument.

Group composition. The groups in the present line of research were not natural ones, in the sense that the people did not know each other and did not work together on a long-term basis. The effect of participation might change between natural and artificial groups.

Stress. Stress is part of many real-life work situations. It would be interesting to examine the extent to which stress moderates the relationship between participation and performance. For example, two of Latham's studies took place under a threat of layoffs (Latham, Mitchell, & Dossett, 1978; Latham & Yukl, 1976). The studies by Meyer and his colleagues took place under a threat of performance appraisal. People under stress or threat may become motivated to reach their goals, regardless of participation, if they believe that goal attainment will eliminate the source of stress. On the other hand, one might argue that the enhancement of supportiveness in the participation condition may have a positive effect on stress reduction and performance. Future research is needed to learn about the moderating effect of stress on the relationship between participation and performance.

Reflections on the
Latham/Erez/Locke Study

Edwin A. Locke

Although I had never done a study of participation until the mono-graph with Latham and Erez, the subject had always interested me. When I was a student in graduate school I was taught that participation was a useful and effective technique for gaining commitment. In my first major goal-setting paper (Locke, 1968), I noted that a number of participation (pdm) studies had confounded pdm with goal setting, but I also noted that there was evidence to indicate that pdm facilitated goal commitment.

When Latham started doing research on pdm and goal setting and not getting positive results, I began to get a bit suspicious of the enthusiastic claims for pdm. Thus I welcomed the opportunity to review the literature on pdm thoroughly when I was asked to do a chapter for Staw's *Research in Organizational Behavior* series (Locke & Schweiger, 1979). Dave Schweiger and I decided to reexamine the literature from scratch. We were really shocked when we discovered the messianic flavor of much of the writing on the topic. There seemed to be a substantial number of people who believed that pdm simply *had* to work because it was an axiomatic good. (There are still many such people writing today.) The result was in many cases a rather shocking distortion of the evidence. A symptom of this was that people seemed to be less interested in trying to *understand* the phenomenon of pdm than in trying to prove it was great.

Since I did not see pdm as a moral issue, I welcomed the opportunity to help Erez and Latham discover the reasons for the disagreements in their findings. I think we did this pretty successfully. Latham, like myself, was interested in pdm as a paradigmatic issue—that is, does it work? Erez, I believe, based on her cultural background, perceived

165

participation in a favorable way, but I give her credit for being a good scientist. I give both of them credit for being willing to put their ideas on the line in a high-risk venture. Both they and science are the better for it.

Where do we go from here? I have thought for many years that pdm research was somewhat on the wrong track, in that I think its greatest payoff is probably cognitive rather than motivational. My bet is that the real benefit of pdm comes from the supervisors and managers getting good ideas from subordinates about how to do the work, solve problems, make decisions, and so on. The major contingency here, then, is the locus of knowledge between supervisor and subordinate. There is good reason to believe that in many, if not most, work situations subordinates know things that supervisors do not know. Tapping into such knowledge should, therefore, make for better outcomes. There may be motivational benefits *resulting* from the knowledge that your ideas are being listened to and actually used as well.

I believe that we also need to think outside the square more in pdm research. For example, has anyone ever considered the possibility that assigned goals or tasks could result in *higher* commitment than those set participatively (or delegated)? Take the case of a highly competent and highly respected and perhaps charismatic leader who assigns a subordinate a seemingly preposterous goal and tells him or her that it can and must be attained. This could lead to much higher commitment than setting the same goal, perhaps in an unrealistic fit of optimism, participatively or on one's own. In the latter case, the employee can say, "I set it, so I certainly can change it." But what can he or she say in the former case except, "The boss is counting on me. I have to do it." Isn't this the essence of leading people to perform beyond expectations (Bass, 1985)?

Let's *study* participation instead of closing all doors in advance because of ideological blinders.

Commentary

Comments on the Latham/Erez/Locke Study

Larry L. Cummings

P. Christopher Earley

Given the nature of scientific discovery and reporting, discrepant research findings often arise. A common method of dealing with these discrepancies is for investigators to continue their own research streams and use journals as an outlet to perpetuate their own perspectives. A more fruitful means of reducing these discrepancies is illustrated by the work of Latham, Erez, and Locke (1988). The purpose of our commentary is to express an appreciation for five characteristics of the process employed by these authors to resolve the dispute between Latham and Erez.

Collaborative Reasoning

One of the more innovative aspects of Latham, Erez, and Locke's research concerns the willingness of the scholars to challenge one another in a commonly agreed-upon series of critical studies. As the authors point out in their paper, one of the more fruitful ways of integrating opposing scientific viewpoints is through the mutual design and conduct of critical experiments intended to promote better understanding of the opposing views. For example, Carlsmith, Collins, and Helmreich (1966) collaborated in order to understand more fully the nature of cognitive dissonance (supported by Carlsmith) and incentive theory (supported by Collins) interpretations of the relation

167

of pay justification to motivation. The dissonance position argued that increases in pay level would have a debilitating effect on motivation, whereas the incentive position argued that pay would be positively related to motivation. Through careful reasoning concerning the key aspects of each scholar's research design, Carlsmith et al. determined that task characteristics moderated the applicability of the dissonance and incentive approaches to justification research. Although quite rare, the integrative approaches presented by Carlsmith et al. and Latham et al. are highly desirable, because they may be essential if we are to gain a full understanding of some organizational phenomena.

Another important characteristic of Latham, Erez, and Locke's collaborative reasoning is particularly evident in their concluding remarks. For example, the antagonists conclude that the process of scientific inquiry can be every bit as important as the outcomes of such a process. They conclude that the process is important because it provides a basis for replicability and establishes the boundary conditions for the predictions made in the research. A less immediately obvious consequence of their collaborative reasoning is an implicit acceptance of one another's paradigms and scientific methods. We find evidence of this based on mutual acceptance of key decision points in the design of the studies (e.g., selection of variables, choice of task, operational definitions of constructs).

Detailed Reasoning

The paper consistently presents the fine-grained details of the reasoning of each of the two antagonists. It provides sufficient detail to generate a feeling in the reader that one could actually replicate the experiments from what is presented in the text. While some events in the research sequence remain implicit, sufficient description is presented to allow relatively complete understanding of the procedures followed in collecting and analyzing the data.

In addition, the details of the reasoning by Latham and Erez when arguing their points of difference are very clear. The specific points about which disagreements exist are clearly articulated. For example, the authors determined a key difference in their respective operationalizations of assigned goal setting. Latham implemented a "tell-and-sell" approach in which participants were assigned a goal and provided a supporting reason for the goal, whereas Erez implemented a "tell" approach in which participants were assigned a goal but were not provided additional supporting information.

> 66 We believe that the tell versus pdm difference is the major causal variable that explains the results; we consider it to be the single most potent factor in this set of experiments. In Experiments 1 and 2, there was virtually no difference in the effect of pdm versus assigned goals when the goals were assigned in Latham's usual tell and sell style. In contrast, in Experiments 3 and 4, there were consistent differences between the tell and pdm groups in both commitment and performance (except for the performance of the high-ability subjects in Experiment 3). In contrast, the tell and sell condition (Experiment 3) did not differ significantly from the pdm condition in either goal commitment or performance. 99

(Latham, Erez, & Locke, 1988, p. 766)

Third-Party Mediator

Yet another noteworthy dimension of this research concerns the participation of a neutral third party. Locke enacted a variety of roles in the study, ranging from arbitrator to process facilitator to source of creative insight concerning the studies. For instance, Locke's presence provided a mechanism through which disagreements in operationalization might be resolved and/or clarified. At times, even the most open-minded parties will suffer from a paradigmatic myopia that can be overcome only through the observations of an outsider who is not ideologically committed to a particular framework. As a process facilitator, Locke aided Erez in conducting her component of the collaborative studies at his home institution while she was there on leave. Finally, as a source of creative insight, he identified subtle differences in operationalizations that might otherwise have been overlooked by the individual antagonists.

Too often, investigators blur the specifics of their own research methods or forget particular interventions that may be of critical importance. For instance, the second author of this commentary was contacted by Locke during the design of these studies for details concerning how Erez ran her studies, since the second author had collected data for Erez during his graduate training. During this discussion of the research methods employed in Erez's work, Locke deduced that a critical difference existed in instruction sets being used by Latham and Erez (p. 764). If it were not for Locke's insight into a rather subtle difference in Latham's and Erez's research methodologies, a major reframing of the key research question would not have been discovered. This reframing suggested that the key question was not how the participative goal-setting manipulation differed in the Latham and Erez studies; rather, the key was how the *assigned* goal-setting manipulation differed.

> 66 In addition, we wanted to replicate the wide range of commitment previously attained by Erez and her colleagues. By talking to Earley, the experimenter in the Erez et al. (1985) study, we learned that he had encouraged subjects to reject their assigned goals if they did not agree with them. Because we originally had only the published instructions to go by, we had not incorporated this oral instruction into Experiment 3. 99

(Latham, Erez, & Locke, 1988, p. 764)

> 66 CONCLUDING REMARKS: LOCKE

> To begin my remarks I would like to extend my sincerest compliments to my co-authors who put themselves on the line in the name of science. Remarkably, despite the ego-threatening nature of this cooperative enterprise, I rarely had to assert my authority as mediator and never in any major way. In designing the experiments and measures (e.g., manipulation checks), suggestions from one party were readily accepted by the other party. Similarly, in writing up the experiments, although there was a lively exchange of ideas and some initial differences of opinion as to what the results meant, we had little trouble agreeing on the data analyses and on the content of the manuscript. In the concluding sections, each party emphasized somewhat different aspects of the experiments, but still a broad core of agreement remained. All of us did extensive editing of the final version, but again, most editorial suggestions were readily agreed to by the other parties. 99

(Latham, Erez, & Locke, 1988, p. 769)

Openness

Until now we have discussed the rationale and facilitating conditions leading up to the research. Such work might still not have been fruitful had the three parties not been open to mutual influence. We can view the nature of collaborative research as an ego-threatening one in which investigators subject themselves to potential ego deflation in at least three ways. First, the ideologies and beliefs of the investigators can be threatened if a particular framework fails to be supported. Such a situation is demonstrated by the failure of Latham's and Erez's positions to converge fully in the discussion of their studies. It appears that the scholars are in more agreement than they were prior to conducting this work, but their agreement is still not total. Their individual commentaries still seem to reflect ideological preferences. Second, the prior research conducted by the scholars is called into question by the joint research.

There is a tendency for us to view the resolution of the opposing views as a zero-sum game, but Latham, Erez, and Locke provide an example of an integrative solution to such a process. After the dust settled, it was evident that both Latham and Erez had engaged in strong scholarship and that their new collaboration provided even more insights into goal setting. Finally, we can view this type of collaborative research as ego threatening within the domains of the current research. For instance, Latham and Erez initially pursued task importance as a critical variable even though this turned out to be an unproductive avenue. The detailed exposure of the reasoning, ineffective as well as effective, behind the design of the studies demonstrates their willingness to admit they might have been wrong or misled. Without the openness expressed by these authors, who put their egos and reputations on trial, we think that the contribution of this research would have been greatly inhibited.

Programmatic Research:
Linear Versus Iterative

Perhaps the most interesting aspect of this research concerns the overall dynamic of its structure. Unlike many programmatic research themes, these studies did not simply build linearly on one another; rather, they developed interactively. For example, each individual study has its own findings and revelations, but only in the summary of all four studies does the reader gain a full insight into the key aspects of participative and assigned goal setting. Based on the summary presented in Table 13 as well as the concluding comments of the authors, it is apparent that differences of opinion remain (e.g., practical significance of the various goal-setting methods), yet the authors have an enriched appreciation for one another's research.

TABLE 13 Summary of Results in Experiments 1-4

| | | Effect | | |
		Little or no effect	Some effect (e.g., commitment but not performance)	Large effect (e.g., commitment and performance)
Variable	Experiment			
Task importance	1,2	X		
Group decision	1,2	X		
High goal difficulty	2,4		X	
Tell vs. other instructions	3,4			X
Set/no-set	3		X	
Participation values	1,2,3,4	X		
Two-phase design	4	X		
Self-efficacy instructions	3,*4		X	
Instructions to reject goals	4			X

*Not manipulated separately from participation in decision making.

(Latham, Erez, & Locke, 1988, p. 767)

It is clear from our commentary that we believe this work is exemplary and critical for resolving disputes between research antagonists. The collaborative and detailed reasoning used, as well as the intervention by a neutral third party, provided a forum in which creative insights were gained. It is also important to recognize the role played by the openness of the parties and the interactive nature of the program that produced the research. It is our hope that this type of discourse will continue to be used for resolving scientific debates.

Commentary

Experiments as Reforms

John P. Campbell

Latham, Erez, and Locke's monograph, which certainly should become a classic, is set in a very important context. The well-known Cook and Campbell (1979) essay argues convincingly that for an experiment to provide useful evidence about the issue in question, the treatment itself must possess construct validity. That is, we must label the independent variable accurately and be able to explain correctly what it means. For example, the Hawthorne studies did not provide an accurate characterization of what was actually manipulated, and arguments have ensued ever since about what really "caused" the results (e.g., Landsberger, 1958).

The experiments reported in the monograph are directed at a very specific substantive issue. That is, within a Locke-type paradigm for studying the effects of goals on performance, do goals that are set via a participative process have different effects from goals that are simply assigned in some way? Other goal-setting contexts (e.g., the effects of goals on skill acquisition), other goal-setting issues (e.g., *why* specific goals usually beat general goals), or other uses for participation (e.g., overcoming resistance to change) were not under consideration. However, *because of* (not in spite of) its very specific focus, the monograph has very broad implications for graduate training and the conduct of research. The following comments attempt to outline two of these broader implications and suggest three additional contexts in which it would be profitable to use the protagonist confrontation strategy.

> 66 From the point of view of the experiments themselves, what struck me the most was the number of differences in procedure and design that can occur when two people are allegedly studying the same phenomenon. In this case there were at least nine differences in the procedures or designs of the Erez and Latham studies. Some of these were quite subtle (e.g.,

173

self-efficacy instructions). Many were not evident from reading the
printed version of the studies (e.g., differences between tell and tell-and-
sell instructions; telling subjects to reject disliked goals). If such differences occurred in these studies, one can assume that they also must
occur in studies of other phenomena.   99

(Latham, Erez, & Locke, 1988, p. 769)

First, these experiments speak directly to one of the most fundamental problems in all of behavioral science: the ambiguity of meaning in
the verbal descriptions of "theory," "models," or "hypotheses." A
classic example is the decomposition by King (1970) of the basic
Herzberg hypothesis into five alternative specifications, all of which
were consistent with the Herzberg language but by no means the same
in terms of what they asserted to be true about job satisfaction. Similarly, in the domain of personnel selection one can get nods of agreement or start heated arguments depending on how the notion of
validity generalization is described (see, e.g., Schmidt, Hunter, Pearlman, & Hirsh, 1985). For whatever reasons, it must be more reinforcing, both in graduate school and beyond, to underspecify the nature
of the variables we use and the form of their functional interrelationships than it is to attempt a full explication. This is *not* an argument for
a retreat to logical positivism and the comfort of operational definitions. It is instead an argument for construct validation (Cronbach &
Meehl, 1955) as a way to approach the explication of surplus meaning
in the variables we use, including the independent variables in an
experiment. Surely the concept of participation can be explicated in
such a way that its meaning goes far beyond any specific operationalization. Further, it surely must be reasonable to expect that if this
surplus meaning were well articulated there would be a widely shared
understanding of what participation entails. It should then be possible
to consider a description of a particular intervention and then say (a)
Yes, this is participation, (b) No, it's not, or (c) I can't tell for reasons x,
y, and z. Research in motivation, be it operant or cognitive or trait
based, and research in leadership, from whatever perspective, are
replete with underspecification of variables and functions. Just ask
anybody what the words *motivation* and *leadership* mean. Our world
should not be that way.

In an even larger sense, the Latham, Erez, and Locke procedure is
quite consistent with the view of McGuire (1983), who presents an
eloquent argument that our business is not to "test" theories but to
determine the conditions under which a particular assertion is true and
the conditions under which it is not true. That is, we should not design
research to test a theory but to determine when and where the most

critical substantive relationships suggested by a theory hold or do not hold. While it is difficult to know what "supporting a theory" means, to "understand" something is to be able to specify the conditions under which a substantive relationship will in fact occur.

The "joint design by antagonists" strategy would appear to have wide applicability beyond the design of how the independent variable should be operationalized. It is my firm belief that the articulation of the substantive research question itself would benefit immeasurably if there were more confrontations over what the question should be and what it means (see, e.g., Campbell, Daft, & Hulin, 1982). My colleagues and I argued a while ago that people doing research on behavior in organizations tend to talk about research needs and research priorities in very general and rather ambiguous ways (Campbell et al., 1982). Consequently, research results seem not to accumulate very well. Perhaps this is a product of the historical tendency for research to be produced by single investigators working in relatively autonomous settings; and perhaps the field would benefit if there were more organized confrontation right from the beginning.

If the independent variable is fair game, then why not the dependent variable? For example, what should the dependent variable be if the research question is whether specific goals improve performance compared with "do your best" goals? What is the meaning of performance in this context? We in fact have no theory of performance, or specification of performance as a construct (Campbell & Campbell, 1988). Consequently, to what degree can we specify when a particular operationalization of performance will be differentially influenced by specific versus do-your-best goals and when it will not? Similarly, what is (or should be) the meaning of the dependent variable in studies of motivation or leadership? Unfortunately, trying to shed light on this issue with Latham, Erez, and Locke's strategy may soon exhaust the supply of reasonably neutral third parties.

Finally, it may be of some interest to turn the authors' strategy back on themselves. That is, what is the substantive meaning of their treatment, which they refer to as "joint design by antagonists"? If another set of antagonists tried to use the same strategy, would it work the same way? How would we know when it works and when it doesn't? Under what conditions will it work and under what conditions won't it? Will we know the strategy when we see it in other contexts?

> 66 It remains to speculate as to the general applicability of this method and as to the conditions under which the method will work successfully. Generally, we believe that the method is applicable any time the following conditions are present.

First, we believe that the disagreement must be accompanied by a lack of full knowledge of the procedures followed by each party in conducting his or her experiments. This is something we did not anticipate at the outset, but it is probably the case that many experiments are reported without every relevant detail being included in the write up. The only way to discover such omissions is through joint collaboration.

Second, we believe that there should be a third party whom both antagonists trust and respect, so that if differences of opinion do occur in the process of designing studies or analyzing the data, they can be resolved. The mediator in this case did not ever have to become heavy-handed, but he did have to make some decisions and to ask each party to reconsider certain opinions and conclusions.

Third, the differences between the antagonists cannot be too deep or too much at the philosophical level. In such cases, the antagonists would probably not be able to agree on what variables to study, how to operationally define them, or how to interpret the results when they emerged, regardless of what they were. For example, it is unlikely that a die-hard behaviorist and a firm believer in the cognitive approach to psychology could successfully collaborate to resolve their differences, because the differences are not primarily scientific.

Fourth, the antagonists must have a strong scientific curiosity and an honest desire to discover the truth, rather than being concerned primarily with protecting their pet theory against attack. Their self-esteem must be based on using the correct process to discover knowledge, rather than on getting the desired outcome (e.g., being right). They must be willing to look at the facts objectively.   99

(Latham, Erez, & Locke, 1988, p. 770)

Depending on how joint design by antagonists is characterized, it could lead back into a different body of literature and pose a different set of research questions directed to the strategy itself. For example, is it an exercise in conflict resolution, which implies that a genuine difference in goals or values must be reconciled through compromise, mediation, or some other strategy? Is it a demonstration of individual versus group problem solving? Is it an example of team building or third-party intervention (i.e., an organization development technique that tries to correct faulty we-they perceptions)? Or is it simply a straightforward procedure for providing the necessary factual information in sufficient detail to eliminate design errors across investigators? If it is the last of these, then one doesn't need a confrontation mediated by a neutral third party. A Delphilike written exchange of detailed descriptions of methods should do the trick. In the end, the Latham, Erez, and Locke monograph should help remind us that our own research enterprise is an institution worthy of study using the same models, procedures, and accumulated literature that we use on "them."

War and Peace: The Evolution of Modern Personnel Administration in U.S. Industry[1]

James N. Baron, Frank R. Dobbin, and P. Devereaux Jennings
Stanford University

This paper charts the transformation of the employment relationship in different industries during the second quarter of this century and is based on a representative sampling of U.S. business organizations. The first section documents changes in the control systems that prevailed in U.S. industries between the Depression and the end of World War II. The descriptive analyses generally corroborate portraits that have recently been provided by neo-Marxists of how and where technical and bureaucratic controls evolved. The second section sketches an explanation for the rapid diffusion of bureaucratic controls that apparently occurred between 1939 and 1946. It examines the role of three key constituencies in shaping modern systems of work force control: labor unions, personnel professionals, and the state. In particular, the analyses underscore the large role of government intervention in manpower activities during World War II in bureaucratizing employment. This effect of the state blurs the distinction between "efficiency" and "control" explanations of bureaucratic controls and internal labor markets, calling attention to institutional sources of change in organizations' employment structures. The concluding section highlights the implications of the findings for efforts to understand the employment relationship.

Recent research has examined how organizational and institutional arrangements shape labor market outcomes, rekindling interest in how and why employment practices vary across sectors of the economy. Differences among firms and industries in work arrangements, control systems, and the presence of internal labor markets are claimed to account for

[1] We gratefully acknowledge generous research support provided by the Stanford Graduate School of Business. Teri Bush provided invaluable assistance in preparing the manuscript. Suggestions from H. Aldrich, R. Althauser, Y. Cohen, P. DiMaggio, T. DiPrete, N. Fligstein, M. Hannan, S. Jacoby, T. Kochan, J. Meyer, D. Palmer, J. Pfeffer, G. Strauss, and *AJS* reviewers were very helpful. Requests for reprints should be sent to James N. Baron, Graduate School of Business, Stanford University, Stanford, California 94305–5015.

Introductory Remarks:
Journey 6

"War and Peace: The Evolution of Modern Personnel Administration in U.S. Industry," by James N. Baron, Frank R. Dobbin, and P. Devereaux Jennings. Published in the *American Journal of Sociology, 92* (1986), 350-383. Copyright 1986 by The University of Chicago. Excerpts from this article are reprinted in this volume by permission.

"Jim Baron was rummaging through old personnel documents in the library . . . ." Thus Jennings, Dobbin, and Baron describe the serendipitous beginning of the project that led to publication of "War and Peace." Baron's rediscovery of long-forgotten Conference Board surveys of personnel practices in U.S. industries unleashed a research process that constantly threatened the authors' sense of intellectual equilibrium. They wanted to recover the understandings of the original respondents and organizational actors and researchers. Against this they balanced their desire to address a contemporary organizational debate regarding the emergence of bureaucratic personnel practices. The debate pits the functionalist explanation rooted in efficiency against the radical emphasis on managerial control of the workplace. The data ultimately included surveys in 1927, 1935, 1939, and 1946, as well as a diverse set of historical documents.

The authors utilized these data to make two key contributions. The first relates to the evidence for the radical account. The radical perspective has largely emerged out of case studies of particular firms and industries. The research paper establishes the external generalizability of the pattern of technical and bureaucratic control practices that feature in radical accounts. Baron, Dobbin, and Jennings document the emergence of this pattern in most U.S. industries. The second contribution is their questioning of the parameters of the debate. Both perspectives emphasize internal organizational imperatives as the source of change in personnel practice. The data simply do not allow Baron, Dobbin, and Jennings to limit their search for explanations to internal mechanisms. As Pamela Tolbert succinctly puts it in her commentary, a fuller explanation "locates the source of the institutionalization of personnel structures in the interwoven interests of the state, industrial managers, unions, and an emergent occupational group."

This contribution depended on the authors' attention to the complex interplay of theory, data, and historical context. Theoretical controversy motivated the search for data and initial attempts to analyze it. Insights from institutional theory helped to direct the search for historical documentation of important aspects of context and subsequent data analysis. The data themselves constrained the domain of theoretical issues that could be addressed. For example, the data could not be disaggregated to the organizational level. Initially confusing patterns in the data analysis drove the search for both additional understanding of the historical context and utilization of diverse theoretical resources.

In their commentary, the authors describe the difficult road to mastery of the meaning that these archival data have for us when interpreted within the historical context. They weave a fascinating and convincing story relying on careful reasoning, the relatively simple data analyses that the data quality will support, and relevant historical documentation. Pam Tolbert and Woody Powell contribute to our appreciation of this research by placing the authors' contribution within the larger theoretical context of organizational studies. Tolbert emphasizes the relevance of the research to current concerns and praises the authors' sensitivity to the theoretical complexity of the phenomenon they study. Powell focuses on the authors' break with traditional explanations for the growth of personnel systems. Both commentators point to another important characteristic of exemplary research: the fact that it is never finished. Exemplary research opens up inquiry. It makes possible and motivates the asking and answering of new questions. In this respect, Baron, Dobbin, and Jennings's research is clearly exemplary.

We see several aspects of their research process that deserve attention. First is the advantage of multiple authorship. This is a case in which the project benefited from a specialized division of labor. Dobbin developed a familiarity with the historical materials while Jennings buried himself in piles of statistical analyses. The interaction of these two types of data collection and analysis was essential to the insights the project produced. The second aspect is tenacity. The authors stuck with the project despite numerous dead ends, disappointments, and frustrations. Third is the willingness to let go. The authors dropped favored lines of inquiry, unconfirmed hypotheses, and the factor analysis results. This aspect is potentially in conflict with tenacity, thus a tension between the two will inevitably develop. It is not easy to drop lines of inquiry, pet hypotheses, and the products of hard work simply because they do not contribute to the final research outcome. We suspect that the ability to accept and live with this tension is a useful skill to have on the journey to exemplary research.

JOURNEY SIX

Making War and Peace

P. Devereaux Jennings

Frank R. Dobbin

James N. Baron

There is a temptation to depict the origins and evolution of our project as deliberate and well planned, but the making of "War and Peace" was neither. The beginning of the project was particularly serendipitous. Jim Baron was rummaging through old personnel documents in the library and happened across the data we eventually analyzed in the paper. Once under way, the project progressed through a series of seeming missteps and backward moves. Thinking we might perform elaborate econometric analyses, we coded dozens of industry-level variables, over time, and estimated scads of preliminary regression models. Thinking that we would focus on the professionalization of personnel administration, we scoured every article we could locate on the nature of personnel from the turn of the century through the 1950s. Ultimately, we abandoned these and various other approaches in favor of one that focused primarily on the impact of the state during World War II, documented by both qualitative and quantitative historical data.

In retrospect, this somewhat disorganized process of doing organizational research was actually critical for the end result. Perhaps the most important lesson we learned is that doing quantitative analysis with historical data must be a highly iterative process. Moving back and forth frequently between the Conference Board data and primary historical sources was indispensable. Doing so prevented us from developing ad hoc arguments about relationships we found in the quantitative data that were inconsistent with the historical record and, at the same time, prevented us from making arguments based on historical documents that were contradicted by the data.

❝ This paper charts the transformation of the employment relationship in different industries during the second quarter of this century and is based on a representative sampling of U.S. business organizations. The first section documents changes in the control systems that prevailed in the U.S. industries between the Depression and the end of World War II. The descriptive analyses generally corroborate portraits that have recently been provided by neo-Marxists of how and where technical and bureaucratic controls evolved. The second section sketches an explanation for the rapid diffusion of bureaucratic controls that apparently occurred between 1939 and 1946. It examines the role of three key constituencies in shaping modern systems of work force control: labor unions, personnel professionals, and the state. In particular, the analyses underscore the large role of government intervention in manpower activities during World War II in bureaucratizing employment. This effect of the state blurs the distinction between "efficiency" and "control" explanations of bureaucratic controls and internal labor markets, calling attention to institutional sources of change in organizations' employment structures. The concluding section highlights the implications of the findings for efforts to understand the employment relationship. **❞**

(Baron, Dobbin, & Jennings, 1986, p. 350)

Yet this research strategy was frustrating because it meant that we were continually disproving many of our pet hypotheses. Just when we had developed an elegant theory about something we found in the data, we discovered contradictory evidence in the extant historical materials. Just when we had crafted an interesting argument based on the historical materials, our Conference Board data failed to back it up. Had we stuck to one method or the other, our conclusions would doubtless have been very different, and we would probably have reached them considerably sooner than we did. On the whole, our experience showed us why "many quantitative analyses of historical series fail to realize their potential [by neglecting history]" (Isaac & Griffin, 1989, p. 873): It is much easier to neglect history. In the following paragraphs we offer some additional details and illustrative examples of the research process involved in the making of "War and Peace."

The Serendipitous Start

What led Baron to the particular section of the library where he found our data was a combination of foresight and luck. Baron was interested in assessing theories regarding the determinants of internal labor markets and other aspects of organizational personnel systems.

Baron thought that if he could locate historical data across a range of firms or industries, he could not only shed light on long-standing debates about the origins of internal labor markets, but perhaps also offer insights into recent trends *away* from reliance on internal labor markets and long-term employment relations (Pfeffer & Baron, 1988). So Baron began scavenging through the Stanford libraries, where, in late 1982, he happened upon a dusty volume containing the most recent (1946) of the Conference Board personnel surveys that we eventually analyzed in our paper. That report referred cryptically to three prior surveys that had been done on related topics, but it gave no references or titles; another six months of detective work had to be invested before we tracked them down. (No one at the Conference Board could recall such ancient history. Eventually, they produced a chronological listing for us of their publications since 1916, which helped us find the three other surveys. Perhaps unduly influenced by the Marxist literature on control systems, it never occurred to us, for instance, that the results of the 1936 personnel survey would have been published under a title like "What Employers Are Doing for Employees.") After repeated inquiries and efforts to track down Conference Board old-timers, we learned, unfortunately, that they had seen no reason to retain the original questionnaires, which prevented us from undertaking the organization-level analyses we had been shooting for.

> 66 The NICB members have traditionally had higher response rates than nonmembers, and "in any survey that is conducted solely through correspondence it seems justifiable to assume that it is the more progressive companies that will cooperate" (NICB 1947, p. 3). Yet despite these real and potential biases, the prevalence of the personnel practices that we examine is actually *lower* than in other surveys conducted during this period, which probably suffered from even more severe response and sample biases. For example, although the mean firm size in the 1935 NICB sample (1,836) was higher than the population mean for establishments, two other surveys done at that time reported mean firm sizes of 2,557 and 4,753 (Pierce School 1935; Parks 1936). In addition, three surveys from the early 1930s of personnel practices, all more limited in coverage, reported even greater prevalence of personnel departments, job analyses, rating systems, and employment tests than did the 1935 NICB survey, both in the aggregate and for specific industries (Pierce School 1935; Parks 1936; Timmons 1931). For instance, Pierce School (1935) reported that 43% of the 254 firms surveyed used job analysis, whereas 18% of firms in the NICB sample reported using job analysis (or 27% when NICB industry groups are weighted to reflect the industry mix in the Pierce School study). For those few industries represented by a relatively large number of cases in these smaller surveys, estimates of the prevalence of various personnel practices correspond more closely

to the NICB data. This, in turn, gives us some confidence in the NICB
data.

   In short, the NICB surveys apparently provide the most reliable and
comprehensive data available on personnel practices in the early decades of this century. One historian of the period refers to the NICB
studies as "excellent in every respect, . . . [they] offer the best statistical
evidence available on most aspects of welfare capitalism" (Brandes
1976, p. 193), and scholars have recently used these data in charting
the spread of personnel departments and internal labor markets (e.g.,
Jacoby 1983, 1984, 1985; Kochan and Cappelli 1984). Although the
samples are perhaps biased toward organizations that were likely to
adopt bureaucratic personnel practices, and thus may misrepresent
overall *levels* of usage, they portray employment practices across industries and over time more accurately and in greater detail than other
possible data sources.   **99**

(Baron, Dobbin, & Jennings, 1986, p. 359)

Baron was first intrigued by these data because they promised to
help adjudicate economic efficiency and neo-Marxist control arguments about why firms adopt personnel practices (e.g., Edwards,
1979). However, the data he uncovered helped frame the research
question at least as much as the research questions determined the
kinds of data he sought. This feature of the research process seems
worth emphasizing: Success in archival research depends not only on
the ability to find data that allow important questions to be addressed,
but also on divining the questions that can (and cannot) be illuminated
by data that happen to come your way. Baron had a similar experience
earlier in his career, when he came across a vast, rich archive of
information gathered by the U.S. Employment Service describing the
job and promotion structures among a large and diverse sample of
California firms (Baron & Bielby, 1980). His interest in structural bases
of inequality sent him looking for these kinds of data, but finding them
also steered him toward a whole new set of organizational concerns
that he might not otherwise have pursued.

   After locating the data, Baron began searching for research assistants
to help him realize the full potential of the project. He presented his
new ideas to Dobbin in a prearranged meeting to discuss Dobbin's
research on the origins of public policy and its effects on personnel
practices. Baron asked Dobbin if he knew any graduate students who
were interested: Dobbin was. Baron was introduced to Jennings by
Jennings' adviser, who worked next door to Baron and had heard he
was looking for research assistants. Jennings had been researching
various issues relating to organizational control and was interested in

supplementing his student stipend. Baron wanted a second research assistant, so he hired Jennings, at least for the summer of 1983.

A Series of Missteps

The threesome began with what seemed to be a very straightforward set of hypotheses about the determinants of organizational employment practices. These hypotheses were generated by a major debate among theorists of the employment relationship. Efficiency theorists argued that organizational size, turnover, and work force demographics were primarily responsible for the development of bureaucratic employment practices, while other theorists, especially neo-Marxists, argued that unionization, efforts to reduce worker autonomy, and increasing firm size led to the development of new methods of technical and bureaucratic control over labor. We sought to relate variations in control practices across industries to differences in these efficiency- and control-related imperatives.

After a year of collecting new variables, running exploratory regressions every which way, and playing with varieties of statistical methods to collapse the sets of personnel practices into coherent employment regimes, we came to a dead end: Our analyses did not explain much of the variance in practices across industries. The main reason was that the variation over time appeared greater than the variation across industries. There was an enormous growth across all industries in the use of "bureaucratic control" between 1939 and 1946, and less variation within each time period in the use of different control regimes by industries than we had anticipated. Moreover, some of the interindustry differences made little sense to us in terms of either efficiency or control imperatives.

At first we did not know exactly what to make of this. We were somewhat disappointed that interindustry variation in the cross section paled in comparison to variation over time by industry. Most historical studies and organizational theories highlighted the role of interindustry differences in firm-specific skills, firm size, work force race and gender, unionization, and the like. The data seemed somewhat inconsistent with all these accounts. Yet we soon realized that if the data could not help adjudicate among competing theories very well, perhaps it was because those theories were deficient, not because the data were flawed. We became excited by the prospect of sorting out why many features of bureaucratic control proliferated during World War II.

> 66 An employment-stabilization plan introduced in shipbuilding in 1941 illustrates how the state attempted to limit competition among firms for employees, which had been producing high turnover and wage inflation, by developing a bureaucratic model of personnel relations for an entire industry. In southern California, the creation of large shipbuilding and aerospace industries within the same labor market wreaked havoc on both industries (Gray 1943, p. 7). In April 1941, the National Defense Advisory Committee, predecessor of the WLB, organized a conference of management and labor representatives from the Pacific shipbuilding industry. Guidelines concerning wages, hours, shift work, strike avoidance, and apprentice training were adopted (U.S. Bureau of Labor Statistics 1941, p. 1162). These guidelines effectively standardized industry work arrangements and working conditions to prevent "pirating" of workers. Similarly, in June 1942, the building trades unions agreed to a WLB proposal to stabilize wage rates on all federal projects. Though less complex, this agreement had the same effect as the shipbuilding stabilization plan: drastically reducing turnover and wage competition by creating a standard model of employment relations within the industry. Jacoby has suggested that governmental intervention during World War I had a similar effect (1985, pp. 140-47). 99

(Baron, Dobbin, & Jennings, 1986, p. 369)

Dobbin began to research wartime federal policy. He examined a variety of sources, including the orders, directives, and reports of such agencies as the War Production Board and the War Labor Board. As it turned out, these and other agencies took direct and indirect steps that encouraged firms to use bureaucratic personnel practices and to develop other internal labor market mechanisms. Government boards and agencies assumed control of coal mines and railways during the war and intervened in labor negotiations in steel. The government also instructed the auto industry to retool to make tanks, and it pumped money into the airplane, explosives, and rubber industries. A review of wartime management publications found that managers responded to such changes by promoting the new employment practices in order to either cope with or circumvent federal control. We thought we had finally figured out what was going on: Our survey data should show exceptional rises in the use of bureaucratic practices in strategic, war-related industries, where federal intervention was greatest.

Yet when we returned to these data we found that the war-related industries showed only slightly higher than average increases in the use of bureaucratic personnel practices, compared with other manufacturing and nonmanufacturing industries. Still convinced that the war-related industry hypothesis was right, we tried analyzing the impact of the war differently, looking at industries that had the greatest problems with turnover, those that had the lion's share of war contracts, and those that saw the greatest production increases during the war. Again, war industries did not seem to differ much from other industries in the Conference Board data. We thought we had come to another dead end.

Our response—almost a reflex after a year and a half of work—was to return to the primary historical sources. According to federal documents and corporate histories, government policies affected not only industries that were directly involved in the war effort, but those that were not as well. For instance, federal hiring controls were often used to prevent the loss of munitions workers to other industries, which meant nonmunitions industries had at least as much need for personnel practices that might quell turnover as had munitions industries. The state appeared to be an important source of and stimulus for the development of the modern bureaucratic regime, which diffused through both obvious and subtle means, including coercive and mimetic pressures as well as personnel functionaries who were active in interpreting the institutional environment.

> **66** Firms were therefore compelled to initiate or expand personnel departments to document their needs. Because employees had to classify jobs by skill and wage categories to satisfy the new national stabilization plans, job analysis and evaluation flourished (Walters 1945, pp. 10-11), as documented in table 1. The government also required firms to file "manning tables" detailing skill and manpower needs and encouraged them to enumerate jobs in terms of new *Dictionary of Occupational Titles* (*DOT*) guidelines (U.S. Bureau of Labor Statistics 1945, pp. 419-20). Thus, the government encouraged the formalization of work roles and the diffusion of standard job definitions across firms by providing employers with a free and easily accessible job-analysis system. Other reporting requirements necessitated employment and turnover records, rating and salary classification systems, and promotion paths reflecting skill gradients among jobs—all designed to aid the war effort by ensuring maximum utilization of human resources within and among firms. Companies without competent personnel departments were hard-pressed to justify their staffing requirements, and firms that had not previously done so moved quickly to implement or augment personnel departments, job analysis and evaluation systems, wage surveys, and manpower analyses to substantiate their labor needs. **99**

(Baron, Dobbin, & Jennings, 1986, pp. 370-371)

Assembling the Article

Persistence, sometimes verging on desperation, was beginning to pay off. We felt that we had pinned down what was going on during the war; now we had to write up different sections of the project and try to assemble them into a coherent paper. Unwilling to give up our concern with control versus efficiency arguments, we relied on the original introduction that had focused on that debate. We incorporated sections on turnover and size, on unionization, and on federal intervention—each the length of a journal article. In addition, we had run hundreds of descriptive analyses of the data, using very imaginable data-reduction technique—from k-means clustering to multidimensional scaling to factor analysis—in order to group practices and industries. We decided to report only the results of our principal components analyses because the results were fairly similar using each technique. We also had dozens of quotes to back up every point we wanted to make. Here we ran up against one of the disadvantages of combining quantitative and historical methods: It is not easy to give up all of the evidentiary quotes and historical asides you amass, especially when each author feels somewhat committed to the specific prose he has penned. We felt we had enough material to write a book, and we even toyed with the idea of following up the paper with one. But we eventually managed to pare the paper down to a piece merely twice the length of an unusually verbose journal article. We presented the paper at a session of the American Sociological Association meetings, and after a few more rounds of revisions, submitted it to the *American Journal of Sociology.*

We received a "revise and resubmit." The editor said that reviewers found "substantial merit" in the manuscript, but that it was too long. Questions were raised about the factor analyses. One reviewer liked the analyses, but suggested that we had not fully mined the results we presented. Another reader of the paper had already proposed that we eliminate the factor analyses, since they were tangential to the central argument but might serve as the focus for a second paper. The somewhat contradictory nature of the reviews was frustrating, and we were all exasperated by the prospect of having to go through another round of revisions and rewrites. We let the paper sit—a case of "out of sight, out of mind." After calming down, we went back to work.

We had resisted removing the factor analyses before because of the time and effort we had spent generating them, but eliminating the six tables of factor loadings and factor scores now made sense: we could save space, avoid additional explanation, and put them in the pile of already omitted items to craft a sequel to "War and Peace" (Baron, Jennings, & Dobbin, 1988). In the fall of 1985, we submitted the final draft with only summary data on differences in practices across industries and over time and with fewer quotes and historical passages. The paper also had more on the representativeness of the data and a refocused introduction and conclusion. *AJS* accepted it. We were happy.

> 66 [8]These conclusions (and those that follow in this section) are buttressed by supplemental analyses of the 1935-46 data, including factor and cluster analyses of industries and personnel practices. Detailed results are available on request. 99
>
> (Baron, Dobbin, & Jennings, 1986, p. 361)

Learning from "War and Peace"

If "War and Peace" has any strengths, they are based on the way it tries to make sense of a complex set of theories about the employment relationship, using unique and varied data. The match of data, methods, and theory occurred only after a great deal of effort and debate. As it turned out, our aim was not simply to determine which theory explained more variance, but to develop a coherent explanation using a wide range of theories, methods, and data. We did not discard data along the way when they seemed to make no theoretical sense; nor did we ever completely falsify the different sets of hypotheses. We held them in reserve until we could use them to help assemble a more refined, complete picture of the evolution of modern employment relationships.

The connections among data, methods, and theory became apparent only through a long series of missteps, dead ends, and rewrites. At times it appeared to Jennings and Dobbin that they were running analyses aimlessly. Baron had the same view, but also felt pressured to preserve a sense of "progress." Ultimately, each set of analyses led to a set of provisional hypotheses, which, in turn, led to more analyses, often with different techniques, and further modification of the hypotheses. In this way, the analyses were strung together, even if their overall direction and pattern were clear to us only in retrospect. At the same time, we collected historical documents on whole topics, such as work force demographics, which we never really explored in the paper, but which helped give us a sense of context for interpreting those documents and analyses that we did use. Connections were made, in other words, through a halting process of exploration and iteration, guided by a great deal of thoughtful reflection and some luck.

Any strengths of "War and Peace" are also a result of our diverse talents and backgrounds. All three of us were interested in organizations, but we came to that interest in very different ways. Baron came to it from his work on structural causes of stratification and workplace discrimination; Dobbin, from his work on the institutional effects of public policy on personnel practices; Jennings, from his work on corporate control mechanisms. Given such different orientations and interests, we sometimes had difficulty coming to consensus, but the advantage of this diversity was that we gave full airing to a wide range of theories. In addition to our different theoretical orientations, we had somewhat different empirical and methodological orientations. Both Baron and Jennings had experience in amassing, manipulating, and analyzing large panel data sets, whereas Dobbin had more experience collecting survey data and applying historical research methods. Finally, we were also somewhat diverse (at least originally) in our standards of excellence and timetables for this project. Whether because of temperament or career stage, Baron was probably more focused on the costs of errors and adverse reviews, while Dobbin and Jennings were probably more focused on the returns of research and publication, impatient with the time the project was taking. The fact that the three of us liked one another and were quite similar in many respects generally helped ease these tensions and divergent interests, though on some occasions that may simply have made the role conflicts stickier.

The project had some impact on the work each author subsequently did. It sparked an interest in human resources management for Jennings, who is now pursuing a project on the professionalization of that field (Jennings & Moore, 1990). It fueled Dobbin's interest in the effects of public policy on organizational practices, and he is now using Conference Board data to look at the impact of the federal government on the development and diffusion of fringe benefits (Dobbin, 1988). And it strengthened Baron's interest in understanding how historical forces and different institutional environments help shape the employment arrangements that organizations adopt, interests he has since pursued in a number of different domains, including California's state civil service (Baron, Mittman, & Newman, 1991; Baron & Newman, 1990; Strang & Baron, 1990). The experience has convinced us of the usefulness of supplementing data analysis with primary historical research where possible, and vice versa.

The article also generated some debate—at least initially. After it appeared, the *American Journal of Sociology* published a comment by Charles Denk (1988), who was a year ahead of Jennings and Dobbin in the Stanford sociology doctoral program. The comment made some methodological suggestions concerning longitudinal analyses for the data. The suggestions made good sense, but we had not seen Denk's comment prior to its submission for publication and therefore had no chance to discuss with him our own explorations with dynamic analyses. So Jennings and Baron drafted a formal reply to Denk (Baron, Dobbin, & Jennings, 1988) with some help from Dobbin, who was en route to a new job. We acknowledged that Denk made useful suggestions, but pointed out that the limitations of our data had prevented us from carrying out suggestions such as his.

However, our sense is that "War and Peace" has had little impact on any of its intended audiences. This may have something to do with our effort to reach a number of different audiences, so that we succeeded in reaching none of them. Predictably, economists and historians told us we were reinventing wheels they had discovered long ago. Organization theorists do not seem to have found much of organizational interest in our analyses; many researchers interested in stratification and work no doubt see our work as far afield from their concerns; and historical sociologists typically pose different sorts of questions. Even when your work is cited, it is important to recognize that research articles, like all social phenomena, undergo a process of social construction and labeling. What inevitably seems like a rich, subtle, variegated, and complex argument or set of empirical results to the author gets defined in a pithy, stylized shorthand by scholars who subsequently cite—and thereby define—your contribution to a literature. (An example would be the following hypothetical citation of our paper: "Personnel activities flourished during World War II [Baron, Dobbin, & Jennings, 1986].") This sometimes is frustrating, but it can also be liberating: One's inability to control how the discipline will construe a given piece of research suggests the importance of satisfying internal standards, of writing for *yourself* as much as for any clearly defined reviewer or audience.

Commentary

Comments on "War and Peace"

Pamela S. Tolbert

In "War and Peace," Baron, Dobbin, and Jennings provide an integrative analysis of the role of internal organizational requirements and external environmental forces in structuring the personnel function in modern organizations. To appreciate fully the scope of this contribution to organizational theory and research, it is useful to consider briefly the general development of studies of formal organizations over the last four decades.

Although the historical origins of the sociological study of organizations as a distinctive academic subfield are usually traced to the early twentieth century, with Weber's (1946) classic analysis of the bureaucratic form of organization and Taylor's (1911) more pragmatically oriented studies of the structure of weak organizations, the central impetus behind the contemporary proliferation of systematic, comparative analyses of sources of formal organizational structure is probably most closely identified with Woodward's (1964) pioneering work on organizational structure and technology. Over the approximately 40-year span since Woodward began her research, some marked shifts have occurred in work on this problem.

Probably the most notable change has been a general shift from closed systems models of organizations, treating formal structure as the result of efforts to manage relations among individuals and groups within an organization (e.g., Blau, 1970; Pugh, Hickson, Hinings, & Turner, 1968; Woodward, 1964), to open systems models, premised on the assumption that formal structure is driven primarily by problems of changing resource flows and relationships with major actors in the organization's environment (e.g., Pfeffer & Salancik, 1978; Thompson & McEwen, 1958). Most empirical analyses and explanations of structural variation have focused primarily on either internal relations or

193

external relations; few have attempted to consider systematically both sets of relations or the interplay of internal needs and external demands in shaping structure.

Despite changes in dominant theoretical views of the primary locus of structural variation, a remarkably constant assumption that has underpinned the vast majority of post-World War II research on formal structure is that organizations can and do adapt their structures frequently in response to immediate problems they face. This implicit assumption is evidenced both by researchers' reliance on cross-sectional data in developing and documenting explanations of structure and by the notably ahistorical character of such explanations.

> **66** We do not mean to imply that such firm-level considerations as scale, turnover, and labor unrest were unimportant in shaping modern personnel systems; indeed, we have alluded to their effects throughout. Nor do we wish to suggest that management and labor were thoroughly passive recipients of edicts from above. We do, however, take issue with perspectives that trace changes in the employment relationship to ineluctable imperatives shaping organizational behavior, whether those perspectives refer to surplus-expropriating capitalists, profit-maximizing managers, or utility-maximizing laborers. Such accounts are reductionistic and overly simplistic. By sanctioning modern employment practices and by encouraging the diffusion of those practices throughout the economy, the state has played a major role in the spread of bureaucratic control and internal labor markets.   **99**
>
> (Baron, Dobbin, & Jennings, 1986, p. 379)

However, the notion of a normally high degree of flexibility and responsiveness in structural arrangements runs directly counter to the real-life experiences of most individuals in organizations. A common response to those who question apparently inefficient and ineffective organizational practices or policies is some variant of "This is the way we do it." Occasionally, such responses are elaborated by historical explanations of the origins of the arrangements. Hence, in sharp contrast to traditional organizational theory, everyday practical experience in organizations is likely to lead to the conclusion that structural arrangements often have more to do with historical problems and inertial forces in organizations than with current problems and conditions.

Major paradigms in organizational theory have begun only recently to direct attention to historical and inertial aspects of organizations in explaining structure (see, e.g., Hannan & Freeman, 1977; Meyer & Rowan, 1977). A central and very valuable contribution of the work of

Baron and his coauthors on structures for personnel management is the provision of a well-developed model of what such explanations might look like.

By examining historical data on the use of various personnel practices by firms in different industries over a lengthy period, they are able to trace the patterns of adoption of personnel structures in the context of a carefully developed historical account of critical national events, an account that considers a range of corporate actors and interests involved in such adoptions. Based on the quantitative data and the more qualitative historical record, they argue that the spread of personnel structures is not completely compatible with current class conflict explanations (which, like traditional closed systems models in organizational theory, typically emphasize organizational problems of internal coordination and control as the driving force behind structural arrangements). Their analysis suggests that in most cases the spread also reflects the progressive institutionalization of rationalized personnel systems; thus the role of environmental pressures on organizations, created both by increasing governmental regulation and proselytization by representatives of the new occupation of personnel management, is also taken into account in their explanation.

It is important to note that in developing this argument, they effectively deal with a central criticism of institutional theory: its frequent failure to specify the roles of particular agents and interests in instigating social change. The analysis carefully locates the source of the institutionalization of personnel structures in the interwoven interests of the state, industrial managers, unions, and an emergent occupational group.

I have used this article in courses on occupations, as a well-articulated case study of the role of organizations in generating new professional and managerial occupations, and in courses on organizations, as an important example of a well-crafted, contextualized analysis of sources of structure. As an incidental point, it is interesting to note that most graduate students in human resource management that I have taught are both fascinated with and generally convinced by this account of their occupational origins.

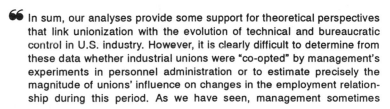

66 In sum, our analyses provide some support for theoretical perspectives that link unionization with the evolution of technical and bureaucratic control in U.S. industry. However, it is clearly difficult to determine from these data whether industrial unions were "co-opted" by management's experiments in personnel administration or to estimate precisely the magnitude of unions' influence on changes in the employment relationship during this period. As we have seen, management sometimes adopted and extended specialized personnel activities even in the absence of unions or proximate union threats, especially in the nonmanufacturing sector (see, e.g., banking, insurance, and trade in table 1). Also, unions genuinely perceived many of these innovations to be beneficial. The same seniority systems that provided firms with convenient bases for administering rewards also protected industrial workers from layoffs and capricious treatment. Thus, unions and bureaucratic arrangements may have been *complementary* means of controlling workers in many instances (particularly in CIO industries), rather than alternatives, as Pfeffer and Cohen (1984) have suggested. Increased accommodation between labor and management during this period aided the diffusion of modern personnel innovations.   **99**

(Baron, Dobbin, & Jennings, 1986, p. 368)

As a model for theoretically integrative research on organizational structure, this analysis has a number of implications for future work on this topic. First, although a variety of researchers have underscored the need to incorporate historical and social context into any explanation of organizational structure, strikingly few studies have heeded this injunction. "War and Peace" illustrates the theoretical richness that is gained when the historical contexts of structural analyses are explicitly taken into account. This work also demonstrates the importance of being sensitive to potential alliances of interests among various actors, both within and outside of the organization, in constructing historically grounded explanations of structure. Another way of putting this is that Baron, Dobbin, and Jennings's analysis highlights the frequent problems that beset accounts positing a single dominant interest as the driving force of organizational change. More often than not, "competing" explanations that point to different interests as the locus of structural change are not as competitive as they seem, but rather represent partial explanations.

This approach also points up the need for careful construction and mining of historical, archival sources of data on organizations. Because longitudinal data—specifically, data that extend over several generations—are usually necessary to observe changes in structural patterns among organizations, researchers need to develop the required methodological skills for locating and using historical sources of organizational data. It is clear that such data are not without serious problems and limitations. This is pointed up by Denk's (1988) criticism of Baron et al.'s failure to address directly the issue of sources of interorganizational variation in the adoption of personnel structures. The kinds of data needed to answer adequately the questions raised by Denk are quite different from the data that were available to the researchers. Hence the collection and use of archival material require not only considerable ingenuity on the part of researchers, but also careful recognition of the limitations posed by such data to the documentation of underlying theoretically causal mechanisms. In some cases, it is likely that such limitations could be overcome in part through more in-depth historical analyses of a subset of cases designed to supplement the analyses of the broader patterns of change.

Finally, although Baron et al. do not specifically raise the issue of processes of population-level change, their research underscores the need for empirical research addressing the current theoretical debate over respective roles of selection and adaptation in generating changes in organizational populations. Did the increasing prominence of formal personnel practices across industries occur primarily through the widespread adoption of such practices by extant organizations, or through environmental selection of organizations that resisted such change? This issue, which has important implications for the research agenda of organizational studies, requires the kind of broad-scale, longitudinal research exemplified in "War and Peace."

Commentary

The Proliferation of Modern Personnel Practices

Walter W. Powell

Over the last two decades a good deal of scholarly attention has been focused on the origins of modern personnel systems. When and where did personnel departments, job evaluations, and career ladders first appear? Two answers have been offered to account for the early development of personnel practices during the period from the 1920s to the 1940s. One line of thinking stresses the need for new forms of control in an environment where dramatic changes in organizational scale and scope rendered direct supervisory control impossible. This control perspective is at odds with an efficiency account, which highlights the need for employers to reduce costly turnover and to develop firm-specific skills in work settings where technology was becoming more complex.

Interestingly, these competing arguments share a good deal in the way of common assumptions. Both suggest that during this period of transformation, the work setting had become larger in scale and more bureaucratic with regard to rules and procedures. Both seem to agree that the technology of work was more demanding and more susceptible to disruption. Each argument, then, locates the development of internal labor markets in management's response to changes in the nature of work. The fundamental difference between control and efficiency perspectives is in the nature of management's motivation: greater control over workers versus "smoother," more efficient labor policies.

66 Efficiency and control theories, however, involve some similar explanations of the evolution of bureaucratic employment arrangements. Divergent theories sometimes point to the same causes but interpret the underlying mechanisms differently. For instance, Marxists highlight a "crisis of control" occasioned by increasing organizational scale in American enterprise (Gordon, Edwards, and Reich 1982, p. 175), whereas orthodox organization theorists stress the technical and administrative superiority of bureaucracy in large organizations (e.g., Blau and Schoenherr 1971). Gordon et al. also emphasize employers' attempts earlier this century to reduce turnover as technologies became more sophisticated, costly, and susceptible to disruption. This factor too is discussed by various efficiency theorists, who highlight the transaction costs associated with replacing workers who command firm-specific skills (Doeringer and Piore 1971; Williamson 1975). Finally, neo-Marxists have emphasized management's desire to forestall or weaken unionization by vesting control in impersonal technical and administrative arrangements. Here too their historical portrait overlaps with other accounts. For instance, institutionalists since Slichter (1919) have traced modern personnel practices to union avoidance efforts. However, these authors typically assert that bureaucratic practices were not forced on labor conspiratorially or malevolently; rather, "workers had strong interests in the characteristic bureaucratic features of the internal labor market" (Jacoby 1984, p. 57; also see Steiber 1959; Kahn 1976; Rubery 1978; Elbaum 1984). Consequently, it is not easy empirically to distinguish portraits of the employment relation that emphasize imperatives of social control from accounts emphasizing organizational efficiency and rationality.

In short, increased interest in the consequences of contemporary employment systems has renewed theoretical debates about their origins. As a result, there has been a recent flowering of historical research on the advent of modern personnel practices. This paper extends this research by charting the transformation of the employment relationship during the second quarter of this century. We first describe changes in the prevalence of personnel practices in U.S. business firms from the Depression to the years following World War II. Past historical studies have described changing employment systems in specific industries, such as iron and steel (Steiber 1959; Stone 1974; Elbaum 1984) or chronicled changes in the U.S. economy (or manufacturing sector) as a whole (e.g., Clawson 1980; Gordon et al. 1982; Lawrence 1984; Jacoby 1985). Our analyses, in contrast, are based on several large and comprehensive surveys of U.S. corporations across diverse industries. Our findings generally corroborate and extend the results of previous historical analyses and case studies of how and where "bureaucratic control" developed. **99**

(Baron, Dobbin, & Jennings, 1986, pp. 351-352)

But this debate is rather unsatisfying on two counts. First, without the appropriate historical materials, it is very hard to gauge management's motivations. Perhaps managers really felt that new personnel practices would reduce conflict, avoid unionization, and organize workers more efficiently. Disentangling motivations is difficult indeed. Second, were managers the sole driving force behind these fundamental changes in the workplace?

On this second point, Baron, Dobbin, and Jennings have made a critical contribution. They have traced the role of a different set of constituencies—personnel administration professionals, the federal government, and labor unions—in shaping the evolution of the modern workplace. To be sure, other scholars had previously pointed to key roles played by forces other than management (e.g., industrial relations researchers had emphasized the actions of unions, while Sanford Jacoby had highlighted the work of personnel administrators), but no one had previously looked across industries and offered a broad institutional account of the diffusion of modern bureaucratic labor practices. In my brief comment, I focus on several questions: How different is Baron, Dobbin, and Jennings's argument from the more dominant and well-developed literatures? What issues do these authors raise but leave unresolved? And, finally, how should future work build on their pioneering efforts?

Using data from National Industrial Conference Board studies in 1927, 1935, 1939, and 1946, Baron, Dobbin, and Jennings found that changes in employment practices generally spread in a series of stages. In 1935, several employment practices associated with scientific management were already present in a number of modern mass-production industries. Surprisingly, however, bureaucratic employment policies such as job analysis, job testing, and rating systems were also prevalent in such nonmanufacturing industries as insurance, banking, and transportation. Because the NICB studies gathered industry-level data, it is not possible to speculate about what kinds of imperatives shaped the strategies of these early-adopter companies. But by examining the pattern of adoption in later time periods, Baron et al. show how previous arguments that emphasize management prerogatives and firm-level considerations (size, technology, volume of turnover) fail to account for the widespread use of modern employment practices.

Several factors stand out in their analyses. First, while there is a correlation between average firm size in an industry and the prevalence of personnel practices, it is a modest relationship. Indeed, specialized personnel units and job evaluation systems spread rapidly to industries with a smaller average firm size. Second, turnover does not appear to have had a robust effect on the adoption of personnel practices. During the war, industries with the highest rates of turnover were no more likely than average to adopt new personnel practices. Third, during the war years, bureaucratic personnel policies spread rapidly, but this diffusion was not limited to firms involved in the war effort. These findings suggest a general proliferation of bureaucratic personnel procedures. To be sure, the pace of diffusion differed greatly across industries and by practice. Some practices, such as centralized personnel departments, were widely adopted, while other practices were more sporadically embraced.

> 66 Turnover is a second causal imperative emphasized by various perspectives on the employment relation. To be sure, turnover and labor scarcity increased during the war period, when many bureaucratic practices were adopted. Average monthly separation rates across all industries rose from 3.1 per 100 workers in 1939 to a peak of 7.3 in 1943. Quit rates rose from 0.8 to 5.2 per 100 workers during this same period (U.S. Bureau of Labor Statistics 1940, 1943). Table 3 lists turnover rates before and during the war (September 1, 1940, and 1943) for specific industries with data available. The table documents dramatic increases in turnover in this subsample of industries, including several essential to the war effort (e.g., shipbuilding, autos, and aircraft).
>
> In spite of this evidence, however, there are reasons to doubt that bureaucratic controls resulted directly or even principally from turnover per se. Essential industries varied considerably in their turnover rates, yet bureaucratic personnel practices flourished in most of those industries during the war. Moreover, some industries exhibiting the highest rates of turnover were no more likely than average to adopt personnel practices directly aimed at reducing turnover. Despite high turnover, for instance, firms in shipbuilding and glass apparently did not rely heavily on morale surveys, exit interviews, or service insignias (NICB 1947, p. 32). Rather, as we discuss below, the federal government selectively intervened in certain industries, including shipbuilding, to stabilize employment by mandating or encouraging the adoption of certain bureaucratic practices. In other words, government policies constrained firms' responses to turnover, and the politics of labor mobility, defined largely by the state, may have been more decisive than the economics of mobility during this period. Jacoby (1984) has made a similar point about World War I, namely, that the federal government fostered norms about "acceptable" turnover levels, which were couched in the rhetoric of national security interests. 99

(Baron, Dobbin, & Jennings, 1986, pp. 363-364)

Two agents, as it were, played critical sponsorship roles in the development of modern personnel administration. During World War II, the federal government intervened in employment policies in an unprecedented manner. In an effort to secure stable employment in defense-related industries, the federal government enacted policies with broad effects. Baron, Dobbin, and Jennings suggest that federal efforts had two general consequences: (a) the creation of a federally approved, easily recognizable model of state-of-the-art employment policies, one that greatly expanded the personnel function; and (b) new enthusiasm and/or willingness on the part of individual firms to develop their own idiosyncratic sets of personnel practices.

After the war, members of the personnel profession worked hard to ensure that the practices developed during wartime were not abandoned. The profession grew dramatically, suggesting that the personnel domain was enlarged and extended to new issues and expanded to more companies.

> 66 As personnel work became professionalized and personnel practices were institutionalized, the profession grew rapidly. The number of personnel and labor relations professionals in the United States increased from fewer than 30,000 in 1946 to 53,000 in 1950 and 93,000 in 1960; in comparison, the professional work force as a whole increased from 3,879,000 in 1940 to about 5,000,000 in 1950 to 7,336,000 in 1960 (U.S. Bureau of Labor Statistics 1949, p. 107; U.S. Bureau of the Census 1975, pp. 140-41). Thus, in percentage terms, the growth rate of the personnel profession far outstripped the growth rate of other professions (and of the U.S. labor force as a whole) during the postwar years.
>
> Once adopted, bureaucratic employment practices survived despite environmental changes, which is consistent with theories of organizational inertia (Stinchcombe 1965; Hannan and Freeman 1984). They also served as models for new or peripheral firms in an industry that were entreated through publications such as those of the NICB to adopt these state-of-the-art practices.   99
>
> (Baron, Dobbin, & Jennings, 1986, pp. 375-376)

Baron, Dobbin, and Jennings have done a marvelous job of using NICB data and historical materials to document the multiple origins of personnel policies and to highlight the critical role played by the state and the personnel profession in sponsoring and validating these forms of organizational practice. As is the case with any novel line of work, certain issues are not fully resolved. Let me mention several key questions for future research, then comment on the general line of inquiry pursued by Baron and his coauthors.

The authors speculate that crises, such as World War II, can be critical in triggering innovation. They argue persuasively that wartime needs led to unexpected changes in employment relations. But what of the government role in the postwar era? Did government involvement recede or continue but under a new agenda? We do not get a good sense of how the expanded role of government during the war may have fundamentally altered government policy regarding employment relations.

Baron, Dobbin, and Jennings are correctly equivocal about whether unions were co-opted by new employment policies or played a pivotal role in their adoption. This is an extremely complicated question. For their part, the authors are content to note that labor-management accommodation during wartime served to fan the diffusion of personnel innovations. Several critical questions remain, however. Once in place, do these innovations help cement that accommodation? Do subsequent labor-management conflicts erode or weaken personnel practices? Or does the institutionalization of the personnel function fundamentally alter the relationship between labor and management?

> 66 Tolbert and Zucker (1983) have argued that internal organizational imperatives such as size might predict adoption of bureaucratic innovations early in the diffusion process but not after the process is well under way. Table 2 suggests that this pattern pertains to the relationship between firm size and the adoption of employment innovations. The rank-order correlation between average firm size in an industry and the presence of two key bureaucratic controls—specialized personnel units and job evaluation systems—declined considerably in manufacturing between 1935 and 1946. This decline is consistent with the institutionalization process discussed by Tolbert and Zucker: "As an increasing number of organizations adopt a program or policy, it becomes progressively institutionalized, or widely understood to be a necessary component of rationalized organizational structure" (1983, p. 35). "Efficiency imperatives" became less imperative as modern personnel administration became standard operating procedure. 99

(Baron, Dobbin, & Jennings, 1986, pp. 362-363)

This paper makes a major contribution to the development of a more macro, or institutional, account of organizational change. But it also shares some of the limitations and present blind spots of this perspective (for a more detailed discussion of the current state of institutionalism, see DiMaggio & Powell, 1991). One liability of studies of the adoption of particular practices is that they do not (as Baron et al. note on p. 359) tell us much about the scope or consequences of adoption. Was the adoption merely "window dressing," a ceremonial signal of modernity, or does it have fundamental effects on how work was conducted? Research that adopts a broad comparative focus simply cannot provide answers to such fine-grained questions.

Finally, how durable are externally sponsored organizational innovations? The general issue of persistence, or reproduction, of institutional changes has not yet received sufficient attention. Once in place, how are personnel practices perpetuated over time? The answers to these questions will not be simple, as they undoubtedly involve a combination of psychological factors (cognitive understandings of what a modern workplace should look like), historical residues (path-dependent processes of evolution in which there are increasing returns to existing procedures), and political interests (the desire on the part of personnel professionals and the state to maintain their influence). It is a testament to the quality of Baron, Dobbin, and Jennings's fine work that it raises such fundamental questions about the sources and viability of organizational change. By opening the door to a new way of understanding the development of modern personnel practices, they also contribute to a deeper and fuller understanding of patterns of social change.

Journal of Management
1985, Vol. 11, No. 2, 67-80

"When the Sleeper Wakes"*: A Short Story Extending Themes in Radical Organization Theory

John M. Jermier
University of South Florida

This is a short story about the two minds of Mike Armstrong, Dialectical Marxist Theory's romantic "everyman" and Critical Theory's "anti-hero." The story contrasts day and night versions of Armstrong's worklife as a skilled operator in the control room of a large phosphate plant located in Tampa, Florida. The two versions are presented to illustrate theoretical descriptions of psychic processes engaged when human actors confront an alien world and make sense of it. Alternative forms of subjective alienation, reified consciousness (drawn from Critical Theory), and reflective militancy (drawn from Dialectical Marxism) are developed as deep psychic states through which meaning is constructed in the world. It is proposed that subjective alienation is shaped by mythical forces in the broader symbolic environment and that it profoundly conditions actions and attitudes. Its importance in understanding organizational behavior and the practice of humanistic management is discussed in terms of human meaning-making processes.

Within each of us there is another whom we do not know. He speaks to us in dreams and tells us how differently *he* sees us from how *we* see ourselves...

(Jung, 1970)

The Dream

5:28 a.m.
Thursday, May 2, 1985
Tampa, Florida

*Adapted for use in this paper from H.G. Wells' "When the Sleeper Wakes," in E.F. Bleiler (Ed.), *Three prophetic novels of H.G. Wells*. New York: Dover, 1960.

I am grateful to *Journal of Management* reviewers for their thoughtful comments on an earlier version of this paper. Special thanks to Tom Sanders and Jeannie Gaines for discussions about the story and Craig Jermier for adding his inspiration to it. They are not, of course, responsible for my use of their comments.

Address all correspondence to John M. Jermier, College of Business, University of South Florida, Tampa, FL 33620.

Introductory Remarks:
Journey 7

"I am most comfortable reflecting on it as a mixed-genre piece that anticipated devices helpful in representing this decade's bewildering human organizational realities." With this sentence, John Jermier concludes his commentary on his exemplary journal article, "'When the Sleeper Wakes': A Short Story Extending Themes in Radical Organization Theory." The particular organizational reality that he addresses in the article is the nature and meaning of alienation for the contemporary worker. The mixed genres to which Jermier refers are the journalistic, anthropological, and literary methods he employs to explore the phenomenological and theoretical meanings of worker alienation.

The need for new "devices to represent" our findings in organizational research is rooted in the emerging reconceptualization of what social science is (see Zald's commentary in this volume). The 1980s have seen the postpositivist consensus in the philosophy of science infiltrate the thinking of organizational scientists. Authors such as Burrell and Morgan (1979), Cooper and Burrell (1988), Hartman (1988), and Hassard and Pym (1990) have discussed the importance of the ideas of Kuhn, Popper, Pierce, and Derrida. However, most of the impact has been on conceptualization. A response that we have encountered frequently in discussion of these issues with colleagues and students is the plaintive question, Where do we go from here? We know how to do and how to judge research modeled on the natural sciences. We are not sure how to proceed empirically in a brave, new, pre-, multi-, or postparadigm organizational "science." Perhaps this explains why empirical work has continued to fit the natural science model (Podsakoff & Dalton, 1987).

Jermier's *Journal of Management* article stands out as a positive response to the uncertainty of our renewed intellectual world. Jermier explores the possibilities of the literary short story genre for communicating the essential features of three paradigms of alienation. Mike Armstrong's dream and nightmare portray the dry, abstract theorizing of critical theory and dialectical Marxism as fluid, concrete realities. The stories weave together Jermier's fieldwork in a phosphate manufacturing plant with his deep understanding of two important but underrepresented theoretical traditions.

The commentators, including Jermier himself, find it necessary to qualify their acceptance of this work as empirical. As Linda Smircich points out, the answer to this dilemma is not to search for some "overarching criterion—some metaparadigm standard—for judging one paradigm over another." Rather, it is a recognition that current perspectives on the meaning of empirical research need to be broadened. In broadening, we face the challenge to create new criteria for what is good work given the evolving meanings communities of scholars assign to the category "empirical." Smircich tackles this task in her commentary by providing parallel evaluations of Jermier's work using different criteria.

Joanne Martin illustrates the conservatism of traditional conceptions of empirical research with the cases of distributive justice research and feminist organizational research. She goes on to explore issues surrounding the possibilities that Jermier's example raises.

Our involvement with this exemplar goes back to Peter's role as editor of the special issue of the *Journal of Management* on organizational symbolism in which the article was published. He included it in the issue as an innovative and imaginative approach to symbolism. We expect it to be the controversial exemplar in this set. Jermier's novel representation of theory and data brings alive the meaning of alienation for human subjects. His comparative theoretical analysis focuses our own thinking about the phenomenon.

More broadly, in this text, Jermier's work serves as the stimulus for the valuable discussion of art, science, knowledge, and representation in this chapter. Jermier, Smircich, and Martin point forward to the needs and possibilities of research in the 1990s. Jermier's Mike Armstrong story is an exemplar of the possible, of innovation, of the experimenting that we need to do in presenting our empirical under-standings. Jermier's experiment is a beginning in our search for modes of research communication that capitalize on the opportunities open-ing up in the community of scholars.

Literary Methods and Organization Science: Reflection on "When the Sleeper Wakes"

John M. Jermier

Now and then, my review work, research, and writing are disturbed by the most important question in the field of organization science: Is there progress? For me, this entails the equally important question: Who is benefiting from the progress? It is difficult to answer these questions because the organizational social science literature has become *oppressive*—burdensome in sheer quantity, onerous in expense, overwhelming to catholic readers. Usually, I am able to think or converse with someone deeply enough to answer by identifying several domains of significant learning (cf. Webster & Starbuck, 1988). The rise of meta-analysis and metaethnography, annual reviews of focused topics, and handbooks and books of readings facilitate this accounting.

However, what seems to overshadow the accumulation of knowledge in any subfield of organization studies is the apparent truth that a greater diversity of viewpoints concerning life in contemporary organizations exists now than ever before. Moreover, many organizational researchers now accept alternative epistemologies that underwrite diverse viewpoints (e.g., positivist, phenomenological, critical; Habermas, 1971) and the unique standards each applies in judging contributions.

Gradual leveling of the open conceits of positivism during the last two decades enabled the editors of this volume to sample a wide variety of organizational research genres and celebrate the field's diversity. But it is important to note that the field's top refereed journals (assessed by citation impacts and prestige ratings) publish few studies grounded in counterpositivist epistemology. The journals'

editors complain that they do not receive many nontraditional manuscripts. Authors contend that the top journals' editors and reviewers
are biased against nontraditional manuscripts.

66 *When the Sleeper Wakes . . . The Dream*

5:28 a.m.
Thursday, May 2, 1985
Tampa, Florida

"I'll shut it off now," thought Mike, lying in the king-size waterbed of his
condominium at Palm Court Village. He could always wake up a few
minutes before the alarm rang, a command of time he considered
remarkable. He had so much confidence in it that he occasionally did not
set the alarm, challenging himself to get to the phosphate plant before
the 7 o'clock whistle. "I'm in touch with nature," Mike reasoned.

He got out of bed, shut off the cosmo-time clock, and thought, "No
chances today though—I have to meet with Phil and the guys and the
OSHA official about the new safety regulations."

As Mike stepped into the warm shower and adjusted the steam/mist
massager, he focused on last night's game. "A three-run triple in the
bottom of the thirteenth. Fantastic! That moves the Braves into first place.
Wish they had better relief pitching, but what power hitters. God, cable!
I can watch a different game every night!"

Mike realized it was approaching 6:40. He hurriedly dragged a comb
across his head, grabbed a high-protein, instant breakfast and mixed it
with low-fat milk. He had a great sense of well-being when he ate right.

The Z290 turned over right away. Mike adjusted the air conditioning
and eased the plush seat back. The thirteen-minute drive to work was
always soothing. Mike drowsily switched on the digital FM radio.

"That's 'Survivor' on 95 YNF, Tampa's home of rock 'n' roll. This is the
'Breakfast Flakes' bringing you the finest in rock programming in the Bay
area. It's 78 degrees under brilliant blue skies and there's no chance of
rain today."

On a dark desert highway . . .

" 'Hotel California'! What a classic! The guitars sound awesome
through these speakers." Mike drifted back to the song's lyrics:

Mirrors on the ceiling . . .

Immediately, the screaming guitars captured Mike's attention and
drove the lyrics from his mind. After a couple of minutes, he remembered
his destination: "Wow! I almost missed the turn."

In the distance was the small pond with palm trees and flowers
surrounding it and the attractive Thomas Industries sign. As Mike waved
to the security guard, he gazed at the gargantuan structure of brick and
steel, high voltage lines, cranes, railroad cars, machinery, storage bins,
smokestacks, and iron walkways, all semi-enclosed by a great wall of
gypsum. On the night shift, when the plant was well-lit, Mike likened it to

an alien spaceship, ready to take off, or just landing. Even by day, Mike thought the structure looked extraterrestrial. "Makes me feel kind of like I do when I'm in the St. Augustine Cathedral," he observed.

It was 6:59 a.m. when Mike punched the clock outside the sulphuric acid reactor complex. A few workers, gathered around Phil, the foreman, were talking about an article in the *Tribune* having to do with dangers to the ground water posed by phosphate plants. There was some concern that low-level radioactivity, often present in the gypsum byproduct, would transfer to rain water as it seeped into the aquifer. Mike heard one of the new employees say: "According to the article, the fluoride gas produced is a health hazard to us too."

Before he finished his sentence, Phil responded: "What we produce here isn't *really* hazardous. Why do you think we pay the lab group to work around the clock? They have to keep records for the county, the state and the feds. Remember in '79 when EPA was investigating us? They couldn't pin a *thing* on us. If you think that gypsum pile is contaminating the water in this area, how do you explain all the wildlife in the front pond? There's fish, frogs—why, even ducks . . . they're growing and multiplying faster than anywhere else in the county. No, sir! We can be proud of what we produce here! Without fertilizer, half the crops in this country wouldn't be harvested. If God intended us to live without fertilizer, he wouldn't have given us the brains to mine the wet rock and mix it with acid."

Mike responded: "I read that article. It wasn't a headline story or anything. I think it was one column in the Metro section—mostly positive stuff."

At that moment, the plant manager and a stranger wearing a blue suit and a visitor's tag walked by silently. The group began to move to the Personnel Auditorium, about 100 yards from the sulphuric acid reactor complex.

After a brief introduction, Byron Jöhannsen of OSHA said: "Good morning, gentlemen. I'll be brief and to the point. We've been spotchecking the plant and have noticed a couple of problems. Most of you aren't wearing hard hats and safety glasses. This is a must in all industrial plants and we need to bring this one up to standards. Second, the masks the company bought two years ago to protect you from dust in the dry-side storage areas and to prevent you from breathing fluoride gas don't fit properly over beards or long hair. So we're ordering management to begin enforcing the safety rules and see that the masks fit. We can't allow the plant to operate with these health risks."

"We're cooperating with OSHA 100% on this," the plant manager hastily added. "Any of you with beards or hair that keep those masks from fitting right have to clean up your act, right away. Any questions?"

Mike scanned the room and broke the lengthy silence: "Does that mean nothing can be done about the dust and vapors, or . . . "

Before he could finish, the manager began the answer Mike himself knew only too well: "My God, all phosphate plants have some dust and vapors because of the process we use. We can't tinker with the process—it's the most rational way to make triple, and it's the triple that keeps us in business. It's out of our hands here. Engineers have studied this and you know they have to design the process to run as efficiently as possible. There's a very delicate, natural balance among the parts of this plant. It's nothing personal—simply technical requirements and decisions."

Mike noticed himself nodding to the techno-logical tempo of the manager's speech, as were others in the room. While walking back to the reactor complex, Mike thought about shaving his beard: "Small thing, really. I'm still free to dress as I like . . . free to buy what I need . . . free to think."

The day passed quickly. According to Mike's digital wristwatch, it was 3:04 p.m. Phil's face looked strained as he approached Mike's station: "Bad news, Mike. I had to bust Larry Jones and Randy Markus in Granulating—walked in and caught them smoking dope. I guess it was hash. I had to call Security to have their stuff searched. They found more in Jones' car. We'll probably have to let them go—they're up in Personnel now." Phil anticipated Mike's question: "Mike, I *had* to do it. That drug rule has been on the books for years. It's there for a reason. We can't have *anybody* in this plant acting dreamy. It's full of hazards—heavy machinery, steam lines, acid lines, slurry lines. And you know how expensive the equipment is."

Although Mike appreciated the freedom drugs gave him, he tightened his lips, nodded slowly, and said: "It's not your fault, Phil. We knew the rule would have to be enforced sometime or it wouldn't be there. I know it's nothing personal—you're just doing your job. Rules are tools, like knives. They're not always razor sharp, but they serve a purpose. We need to stay in touch with what's real here." A state of calm engulfed Mike as he experienced what he thought was the reasonableness of his statements.

It was 3:50 p.m. as Mike walked into his living room and switched on the wide-screen television to watch the ballgame. His thoughts drifted to the workday: "I wonder why Randy was so careless at work? He was never in trouble in high school. He could have hidden it, like everyone else. Granulating work is . . . " Mike's attention was abruptly drawn back to the screen: "Stupid commercial," he muttered. "I buy light beer because I want to drink light beer. I don't care if it's less filling." He sprawled on the couch and was soon dozing.

Mike's nap was disturbed by the front door opening. It was Sarah. "Sell any houses?" he inquired groggily.

"Yes," Sarah replied.

Mike grabbed a light beer. As he began drinking it, he turned down the volume on the television and put a cassette in the remote-controlled tape deck. "Sarah, there's a song I'd like you to listen to," Mike said, replaying "Hotel California." He drew two lines of cocaine on the table. The world was soft and warm and distant and . . .

When the Sleeper Wakes . . . The Nightmare

6:15 a.m.
Thursday, May 2, 1985
Tampa, Florida

Sarah's grating voice heralded another dreary day: ". . . and grab your shirt. Mike! Mike! Rise and shine, Mike."

He rolled over, looked at her, and wished she were the dream mate her voice had just banished. He wiggled his shoulder to rearrange the pillow under his head.

"You're going to be late," she cautioned. "It's 6:15."

"Another minute," he pleaded. "I was dreaming . . . I was in tune and in time with life . . . everything went right . . . nothing bothered me . . . it was *so* smooth."

"That was a dream all right," Sarah said sarcastically. "Charlie called. He'll be here at 6:30. Why is he picking you up? I thought you weren't all that friendly with the people at work."

"The company's changing some rules . . . we heard they're going to try to make us shave every day and cut our hair. Charlie and Randy and I are talking it over before work."

Mike rolled out of bed and flipped on the stereo. On the way to the shower, he stumbled over Gypsum, his miniature silver poodle. "Dammit Gyp! One of these days you're going to kill me."

Brooding, he turned on the water and waited for it to warm up. "They can't make me shave," he muttered as he stepped into the shooting shower. "I've had my beard since I was 21. No company should be able to dictate that."

Mike realized it was getting late. "Hell-fire! Someone else's time is always on my mind. Whose life is this?"

A horn blasted outside the condominium as Mike rushed to get dressed. Climbing into Charlie's new Cutlass Supreme, he noticed Randy had on a gold chain heavy enough to anchor the *Queen Mary.*

"Morning, Mike," Charlie said grimly.

"Hi, Charlie, Randy. I've been thinking about the masks. We need to push Barkley to get us some that fit, if we have to wear them. It's the plant manager's decision."

"Mike, you know they aren't going to re-outfit the whole plant with new masks. They'll say it's too expensive," Randy said.

"Randy, let's not make it easy. . . . Make *them* say that. Let's not defeat ourselves," said Charlie.

Mike angrily agreed: "Right! Why do we have to work in dust and vapors in the first place? That's the *real* issue. Let's stick together on this. First, we tell them to get rid of the problems. If that fails, we push for better equipment. But, let's *not* let them tell us how to look!"

"Okay, okay," Randy responded. "Turn up the radio—I like this song." Charlie did so, and "Hotel California" briefly silenced the group.

On a dark desert highway . . . you can check out any time you like. . . .

"The perfect description of Thomas Industries," Mike exclaimed. "We help lay the traps. We punch out, but don't stop working. It shows on our faces. Our minds are *crippled!*" Charlie and Randy nodded. "The noise from the control room, that damn Thomas Industries sign, the gyp mountain, smokestacks . . . all of this is with me every night before I go to sleep." Charlie and Randy were silent.

They arrived just in time to punch in before the 7 o'clock whistle. "Goddamn whistles," Mike grumbled. "Remind me of grade school." As he grabbed his time card, he thought of the Woody Guthrie cartoon poster of the worker punching out, with a punishing right, the horrified face on a time clock. He smirked.

Ever since whistles were installed, Mike tried to avoid his work station until at least 7:15. As he entered the sulphuric acid reactor complex, he heard Phil say: ". . . if God intended us to live without fertilizer, he wouldn't have given us the brains and machinery to mine the wet rock and mix it with acid." Mike noticed Phil glancing at him disapprovingly.

Indignation always gripped Mike when Phil used religion to defend the industry. He thought: "Phil, you, I, Barkley, and every other employee here knows that gypsum pile is hot. Do we need a Karen Silkwood scene to get some attention? There's too much fluoride gas in the plant. There aren't enough safety checks made on the power and steam lines, heavy machinery, or storage bins. Every year there's less money for product testing, safety, and environmental stuff. Who do you think you're kidding?"

Mike knew it was a mistake to challenge Phil openly. He walked away resolutely. The group began moving toward the Personnel Auditorium. Mike motioned to his coworkers to pick up the slack while he was gone and followed the group.

Following a short speech by Byron Jöhannsen from OSHA on safety violations in the plant, Jack Barkley began talking: "We're cooperating with OSHA 100% on this. . . . Any of you with beards or hair that keep those masks from fitting right have to clean up your act, right away. Any questions?"

Mike probed: "Does that mean nothing can be done about the dust and vapors, or . . . " Before Mike could finish, Barkley began the answer Mike knew his question would provoke: ". . . We can't tinker with the process—it's the most rational way to make triple. . . . Engineers have studied this. . . . There's a very delicate natural balance among the parts."

Mike whispered acrimoniously to Charlie: "Why do *we* have to make all the adjustments? They should clean this toxic waste pit up—spray the dry-side more, get rid of the vapor leaks, check the uranium dumps! Man! We shouldn't have to take this."

Barkley looked directly at Mike and said calmly: "If you have a problem with that, it's because you're not thinking straight. Talk to a technician if I don't make sense to you. *All* this benefits *you!* Besides, it's OSHA that forced these issues. Ask Jöhannsen!"

"Men," said Jöhannsen reluctantly, as everyone's eyes turned toward him, "our job is to protect your health. At this point, we can't make the company eliminate dust and fumes. We know the face masks are uncomfortable, but they *will* fit. It's the best we can do, now. We think they will protect you."

Mike's sense of frustration multiplied as Jöhannsen spoke, but he knew it was unwise to provoke Barkley further. He nodded his head in mock acquiescence.

"Being rational doesn't just mean following *production* logic," thought Mike, as he walked back to his station. "These guys may *look* easy, but I bet they'll find a way to get back at the company for this. *I* sure have!"

Phil unexpectedly walked into the control room. Mike was beginning final checks before shift change. "Bad news, Mike, I had to bust Larry Jones and Randy Markus in Granulating. . . . We'll probably have to let them go."

Mike viewed drug-taking as a crutch, never accepting it as a liberating act, but was furious on principle: "Phil! That rule hasn't been enforced in over three years. Why the hell now? And why in Granulating? The work there is the worst in the plant—it's hot and dirty and *boring!* Everybody on nights is high or low. . . . The work gets done. You're trying to get back at Randy for filing against you!"

Phil stared mutely at Mike and then started to walk away. He turned, and angrily, but deliberately, responded: "Mike, if the rules are too tough here, I'm sure you can find other work."

Mike called the threat: "Don't push me, Phil. That's on my mind every day—and on everyone else's too."

Phil shouted as he left the room: "Let me know when!"

Mike recalled all the layoffs last year and thought: "I'm an idiot! I let him get to me. I should know better than to go one-on-one with a supervisor. There are so many other ways to fight back."

Mike left the control room to find Randy and met him and Charlie walking toward the time clock. Randy looked ragged and resigned. Mike embraced him compassionately and said: "The whole plant's in an uproar. We'll find a way for you to keep your job—you can count on that. Let's go to the Sunset and have a drink."

In the parking lot, Mike glanced back at the plant and thought resentfully: "You can check out any time you like, but . . ."   **99**

(Jermier, 1985, pp. 68-73)

The importance of this volume rests, I think, less on whether or not each piece of research selected can serve as an exemplar and more on the potential of the book to anticipate the nature of organizational research in the 1990s. During this period, I expect to see greater experimentation and eclecticism as paradigm wars subside and received philosophies become more suspect. In the absence of paradigmatic mandates, blurring and mixing of genres (Geertz, 1980) will make it more and more difficult to maintain firm boundaries between artistic representations of organizational life and the "science of organizations."

The inclusion of my experimental representation of a modern work day (Jermier, 1985) in this volume anticipates the potential of the humanities to inform understanding of organizational life. Also, it invites consideration of similarities and differences between literary texts and texts produced by empirical organizational researchers. That is, it provokes thinking about written representations of organizational life as a literary genre and raises questions about the writers' commitments, the purpose(s) of writing, and the relation of literature to society (see Eagleton, 1976; Williams, 1977).

Consistent with the editors' guidelines, this commentary will focus primarily on recounting the steps leading to publication of "When the Sleeper Wakes." It will also include a description of the publication aftermath and some reflections on the nature of representation in artistic and social science work.

Producing the Sleeper

GENESIS

From the point in 1969 when I consciously withdrew from competitive college athletics and began serious study of philosophy and economics, there existed an uneasy tension between my ordinary curricular studies and my pursuit of radical thought and discourse. The tension was amplified as I began formal graduate study in administrative theory. The formal curriculum was challenging, but neglected political economy, radical sociology, critical psychology, and administrative fiction (see Waldo, 1968) in favor of microeconomics, conventional organizational behavior, logical positivism, and statistics. Occasionally, I found an elective to indulge these interests, but most of my knowledge outside the mainstreams came from extensive reading on my own and developing colleagueships with authors whose work I was studying.

By 1979, I was ready to take my first academic position. I knew my strong interests in both conventional administrative studies and radical thought were unusual, but I was determined to forge a writing and teaching career in a college of business without abandoning radical humanistic inspirations. In 1983, I moved to my present position, having found a more politically serene and academically free employment setting. I began to bring even more Marxist humanism and literary verve into the classroom and found that both undergraduate and master's students were receptive. But, when asked by students for some of my writing developing these viewpoints, all I could produce were some highly academic, technical pieces I knew would not enrich their thinking. My colleagues' work presented similar problems, and I could not suggest that students spend 15 years reading classics and interpretations of classics as I had.

In May or June 1984, while teaching a course in organizational behavior, I was thinking seriously about critical theory (see Bronner & Kellner, 1989)—the amazing analytical scope, the wealth of critical insights, the radical fusion of the humanities and social sciences, the opaque prose. Once explained as a theory of consciousness, students related critical theory to things they knew best: popular culture (drugs, major league baseball), technoscientific domination and the destruction of reason (the rock-theatrical group *Devo*lution), compulsive consumerism (subliminal advertising, quick credit), ideology (Organizational America), and so on.

I wondered: Could I effectively illustrate critical theory with a short story? I knew I could write academic articles, but would fiction work as a method of exhibiting theory? Although a short story illustrating critical theory would have been useful in the classroom, I knew I would not write it for that purpose alone. I suppressed the idea temporarily because I was unsure about the connection between literary methods and theory development.

However, during that summer's Academy of Management meetings, my enthusiasm for the short story project resurfaced. First, it slipped out in conversations with friends, and I began to refine the idea by discussing varieties of fiction (naturalism, realism, symbolism, expressionism, and so on). Then, I tested it with collegial acquaintances. Eventually, I was discussing it with scholars I had not known before. No one discouraged it. The Academy is a very supportive intellectual forum. I assumed this accounted for the unanimous affirmations of my proposed fusion of critical theory, deep subjectivity, and literary form better than did a counterpositivist Zeitgeist.

In late August, I phoned Jerry Hunt, editor of the *Journal of Management*, to see if he would review a piece of part fiction, part theoretical analysis. Under Hunt's editorship, *JM* was advertising openness to consider papers written from a critical perspective and presented in alternative formats. Hunt said something profoundly clever about how much of the science he read and reviewed seemed like fiction anyway and told me he would have it reviewed. He also mentioned that Peter Frost was guest editing a special issue of *JM* on organizational symbolism and suggested that I contact Peter with my idea. I remember explaining to Peter that I thought I could illustrate the critical theory notion of reified consciousness in relation to mythical forces in the broader symbolic environment with a short story and a theoretical reprise. Because of his naturally uplifting manner, any skepticism Peter may have had beyond his request for a prospectus was not detectable. I wrote the prospectus. Based on it, Peter encouraged me to submit a finished article for formal review by January 31, 1985. I committed to the project—and the genre.

The genesis of this project differed from that of others I have undertaken in several ways. First, it arose from a strong desire to share difficult insights with a broad audience. Second, it emerged during a period of intellectual harmony for me as I was successfully integrating radical epistemology, theory, and method with practical discourse. Third, I solicited and received an unprecedented amount of collegial input prior to undertaking the project. This encouragement led me to believe that my colleagues wanted (and in some cases needed) the article. Fourth, from the beginning, I targeted a single publication outlet and had no alternatives in mind.

PROCESS

The research process was an exercise in eclecticism. I was aware that good fiction must inform and entertain. In order for the story to inform, it had to be more than a medium in which "stick" characters were pushed around by theoretical imperatives. This led me to the field. I contacted the director of the environmental impact group in a local phosphate manufacturing plant who had taken an M.B.A. course with me the previous semester. He said his bosses would not approve a university research study because too much controversy surrounded phosphate manufacturing. He said he could authorize an "extended plant tour" as part of their public relations program and arrange some opportunities to talk with employees. I knew this limited access would not enable me to write an ethnography, but I was fascinated by the conflict between the phosphate industry's supporters (Fertilizer is needed to produce food!) and critics (Phosphate manufacturing is hazardous!). After the first full day of field research, I had learned enough about the phosphate industry, the history of the local plant, the production process (including environmental impacts and health and safety hazards), the nature of the work, and key labor conflict issues to set the story at "Thomas Industries." I returned to the plant several times over the next two weeks, spending partial days in my limited role of visitor-critical theorist/researcher, talking with anyone who had a few minutes, joining meetings with my student informant or his designees, walking freely about behind the security clearance my visitor's badge provided, wearing a hard hat and safety glasses when instructed to do so, taking liberties no visitor had taken before, learning what it felt like to manufacture phosphate. When asked, I revealed my identity as a professor of industrial behavior (looking for case teaching material). I ended the observation period shortly before it appeared that my visa would expire and goodwill would be strained.

With my observations sloppily recorded in abbreviated form on loose sheets of paper (but vividly in memory), I began to think about producing the article. I reviewed some key pieces on subjectivist research methods and radical theories of worker consciousness (cited in the article). I read some of Jean-Paul Sartre's (1949/1966, 1972/1974) essays on writing. I reread some of Sartre's novels and plays, this time to learn how existentialist themes drove the stories. I read extensively about writing short stories.

Although the story could have been focused exclusively on an antihero (drawn from critical theory), I decided this would be too limiting. I knew of the rich history of American working-class resistance and learned about patterns of resistance by phosphate workers from my fieldwork. It seemed necessary to advance the image of the active, selectively militant worker who was neither a class-conscious revolutionary nor a passive, docile automaton.

The literary device that would allow me to contrast the two views of worker alienation sprung from the pages of *When the Sleeper Wakes*, H. G. Wells's anti-utopian novel. In a literature class many years ago, I slighted the assigned reading of *The Time Machine* because I was more engaged by the Sleeper's dream-entrancement method of transporting characters to alternative realities than by the technomechanistic time-travel method. (Edward Bellamy's *Looking Backward* provides a classic literary model of this, while Woody Allen's popular film *Sleeper* is one of its hyper-art transmogrification.) It occurred to me while paging through Wells's novels that, with a modification in the time-lapse device, I could present contrasting (night and day) versions of the work life of a skilled operator in the phosphate plant. Each reality could be plausible (and probably is in part), but I symbolized my sense of verisimilitude by labeling the awakened state of mind as a daytime "nightmare."

Another input to the research process was popular culture. I opened myself more to everyday life, especially to cultural practices I learned were part of the highly paid skilled operators' lives (e.g., television, sports, rock music, technogadgets, alcohol and other drugs). I chose to script drug usage as a central part of the story for three reasons: (a) three informants corroborated it as a typical practice in parts of the plant; (b) journalists were reporting that "drug use at the workplace [was] as common as the coffee break" (e.g., Brecher et al., 1983, p. 57); and (c) it was neglected in theories and studies of organizations. For largely the same reasons (and because critical theory images required it), relatively detailed representations of the operatives' nonwork lives were presented.

The synthesis of these research inputs was accomplished during my annual Christmas holiday with family in Wisconsin and Minnesota. The prominence in the story of Don Henley and the Eagles' "Hotel California" is the result of hearing the song at my youngest brother's house while thinking about the lives of Thomas Industries operatives, hotel imagery in Wells's novel, and Lukács' (1962/1971b) facetious contention that leading German intellectuals had taken up residence in "a beautiful hotel, equipped with every comfort, on the edge of an abyss, of nothingness, of absurdity" (p. 22). The nested symbolism was too good to pass up.

WRITING

The ease with which I was able to write the first draft of the story was surprising. I outlined the structure of events to unfold in two simple scenes, based on theoretical considerations and field observations. I completed the draft in about two days.

Most of the crucial decisions about the story's characteristics were determined prior to writing. Following Sartre (and my sense of intended realism), I revealed the story from the *point of view* of a selectively omniscient, nonparticipating narrator. The naturalistic *setting* was derived from field observations and conformed with neo-Marxist descriptions of the nature of society and work settings (see Jermier, 1985, Table 1). The story's main *character*, Mike Armstrong, was created carefully as an ideal type (cf. Van Maanen, 1988, p. 65). His dual states of mind and action dramatized the existential moments of personal alienation (Laing, 1965). They also symbolized the self-contradictory aspects of capitalist worlds. I sketched the dreaming Armstrong flatly, as antiheroes often are; Armstrong awake was rounded a bit to reflect his growing awareness. In both states of mind, Mike's last name reveals physical prowess, but lack of class consciousness, the dominant features of his character. The story's *tone* and *style* were chosen to convey radical viewpoints concerning the plight of working-class people and their ways of living. A deep *irony* underwrote the story, contrasting what working-class people deserve and what they get. I extended this to the theme of self-repression. As the song goes, "We are all just prisoners here of our own device." (Later, I discovered the theme expressed even more soulfully in Bob Marley's "Redemption Song": "Emancipate yourselves from mental slavery . . . . None but ourselves can free our minds.") Finally, I laced the story with *symbolism*, an important method of expressing deeper cultural forms compactly.

Writing the reprise and implications sections of the paper was difficult. A new semester had begun and northern visitors were finding their way to the Gulf Coast. But the real problem was that I lacked space to discuss the story's subtle points, its relationship to the theoretical positions, the epistemological underpinnings of "doing fiction," and (as mandated by the journal) ?managerial implications? Nevertheless, I completed the first draft nearly on deadline and awaited collegial input.

Part of the problem was alleviated when I received the reviews early in March 1985. My local colleague Jeannie Gaines (Management Department) provided some helpful ideas for shortening and increasing the impact of the story. I sought out Tom Sanders, a highly successful short story author (Creative Writing Department), and prevailed on him for advice. Tom detected some "overwriting," made a few technical suggestions, and was enthusiastic about the story's potential. (Later, he encouraged me to make one final revision and submit it to *Esquire* or the *Atlantic Monthly*. Other demands distracted me from Tom's kind ambition for me and I was never able to follow through.) Peter Frost suggested framing the theme more in the paper's abstract, as I had in the letter of submission to him, and artfully summarized reviewer comments. External reviewers Richard Boland and David Cray found some textual inconsistencies and challenged me to clarify further theoretical nuances. John Bryson, the third external reviewer, suggested adding a table. This was very important because it allowed me to clarify symbolism in the story, explain the reprise better, and spell out theoretical implications using little space.

The early feedback was positive and constructive. The exhilaration I felt was brief because revision deadlines pressed, but my gratitude for these mature reviews was lasting. I struggled with the final revision primarily because I was hoping to find a way, in the space available, to make the characters deeper and more appealing, to detail further the setting, and to enhance the dramatic qualities of the story's plot. I settled for providing better instruction in the theories. This deprived

JM readers of a scintillating literary experience, but did add columns of competing text to traditional organization theory's vision of humanistic management. The paper was accepted without further revision in late April 1985. It was published during July 1985, less than one year from the point of serious conception.

Aftermath and Reflections

In the more than five years since this article was published, it has become what people identify me with more than any other piece. To my knowledge, it was first put to use in a scholarly forum by Linda Smircich and Marta Calás, at the Standing Conference on Organizational Symbolism held in 1987 in Milan, Italy. Their essay, published shortly after the conference, used it to help develop a postmodernist critique of the organizational symbolism literature and to advance some creative suggestions on how to read organizational studies differently (Smircich & Calás, 1987). In their view, the article's most interesting features were that it presented and clarified theoretical perspectives in a novel way, using the short story format (p. 254), and that it emphasized the fictional (invented) "truths" in all organization theory and research texts (p. 255).

I have used the article in teaching students at all levels, but find it works best in doctoral and advanced graduate seminars. (I am aware of its use in several other Ph.D. programs, but have not discussed its effects on students with anyone.) Research colleagues in the United States and abroad have been generous in acknowledging the study as a "creative" and "provocative" piece of work, even when they were less complimentary about an aspect of its execution. Some wondered why I undertook such a "risky" project, but seemed to respect my exercise of a writer's freedom and *JM*'s boldness in publishing the piece. (Perhaps I should have considered this project risky, despite Sartre's [1949/1966] notion that people appreciate an author's appeal to *their* freedom as *readers* who interpret and thereby coproduce the work. The fact that I did not consider it risky may mean I made too many compromises.)

In my mind, this piece made two contributions to the organization science literature. First, it complemented radical structuralist models of work organization by bringing the human mind into analytical focus. In contrasting radical views of subjective alienation, alternatives to objectivist labor process analysis (e.g., Braverman, 1974) and to more orthodox models of class-conscious workers (e.g., Lefebvre,

1970) were illustrated. Second, by implying that literary methods could play a role in developing organization science, it invited *JM* readers to consider similarities and differences between artistic and scientific representations of the social world. It should be noted that "When the Sleeper Wakes" was derived from theoretical considerations and qualitative data, but that an ethnographic analysis was not conducted. The observation and interview period was too short to accomplish the goals typical in ethnographic research. However, the use of the short story format to illustrate (exhibit) theory anticipated the introduction of the formalist genre in organizational ethnography (Van Maanen, 1988). And the use of literary methods to present field data paralleled (blindly), in style if not in substance, developments in literary journalism (Sims, 1984), "experimental" anthropology (Marcus & Fischer, 1986), and impressionist organizational ethnography (Van Maanen, 1988).

However, writing free of the traditional distinction between science and creative expression did lead to some unexpected difficulties. In the final stages of production of the story for this book, a member of the publisher's staff called me with a copyright problem. Two of the three companies controlling permissions on the Eagles' "Hotel California" refused to allow the song's lyrics to be reprinted as I had used them in the original article. Thus, the story published in this volume had to be purged of the Eagles' lyrics. Removal of all the direct quotations from the song had three effects: (a) it made the story less coherent; (b) it satisfied the copyright police; and (c) it served as a reminder that scientific norms allowing free use of words published in the public domain (assuming proper citation) do not hold in the world of literary expression.

A more significant problem is that the epistemology underwriting the study was not explicitly stated. I think this has led to some confusion. The most complicated aspect of the article is that it is a work of "science-fiction." It confounds the positivist/realist/naturalist dichotomy between fact and fiction.

Some readers may interpret the article to mean that any given description of organizational life is but one of an infinite number that could have been presented, all of which are equally plausible. Others may interpret this to mean that field research does not improve our understanding of organizational life beyond that of armchair theorizing or literary imagination. Still others may interpret this to mean that art and science applied to organizational life are identical in purpose, consequences, and method.

Given the article's treatment of field data and its sketchy methods section, I understand how a reader might take my theme in any of these ways. Let me comment briefly on each of these interpretations and then set out a more defensible view of the relationship between literary and organization science texts.

Concerning the first interpretation, it is true that scientific descriptions are somewhat arbitrary, but not all descriptions are equally plausible. The reason I had Armstrong experience dual realities was because well-developed, competing theoretical descriptions existed and because I knew some evidence supported both. Multiple representations usually add insight, but some hold more descriptive power than others.

The second interpretation equates the truth value of field research data with completely fabricated descriptions. Good fiction writers conduct rigorous research and create a story to inform as well as entertain. The credibility of a story, even an impressionist tale, is related to the veracity of factual detail and inferences made from that detail. The fiction writer seeking to inform in an entertaining way (and not shock to promote understanding, as in expressionism or surrealism) has freedom in depicting, but must not invent description. The organizational scientist using literary methods to inform is constrained in the same way unless he or she reveals a primary purpose of evocation. "The Sleeper" is not a complete fabrication. Its form and characters flowed from my imagination, but the content of the story was based in theory and concrete field data. Had I relied more on field data and less on theory in scripting the story, the contribution would have been enhanced. But the original purpose of the study was to exhibit theory through fiction, not to produce a literary journalistic or impressionist tale (cf. Van Maanen, 1988).

In the third interpretation, we confront the idea that all representations (artistic/literary, scientific) are constructed by social producers and consumers. Therefore, all forms of representation are, in part, rhetorical devices promoting the interests of their class of creators.

This last interpretation corresponds more closely to my view of the relationship between art and science, but glosses some important distinctions. Obviously, art and positivistic social science differ in surface form of expression. However, at an abstract level, all forms of representation of the social world, whether artistic or scientific in nature, are aimed at making the world more meaningful by deepening understanding of the human condition. Art and science share this purpose. And all representations have descriptive *and* normative (political) content. They claim to apprehend faithfully some domain of human experience *and* they either assist in the process of social reproduction or are subversive to it (see Horkheimer, 1937/1972). Both art and science have political consequences.

The key difference between artistic (and literary) representations and scientific representations of the social world is in method. Scientists *must* anchor their knowledge claims in empirical and theoretical evidence produced by systematic research. The artist *may* create representations with this method, but is free to use imagination, fantasy, dream states, altered consciousness, or any other method to produce humanistic insight.

Thus art and science do not differ in *purpose*: Both seek to enlighten understanding. And it is not the value content and political *consequences* of the image produced that separate art from science: Neither artistic representation nor scientific representation is value neutral. The primary epistemological difference between art and science is in *method*. Claims of scientific understanding must be defended with evidence, while artistic insight may spring from sources other than qualitative and quantitative data gathered through systematic research.

Having stated this, I must emphasize that scientific methods do not guarantee apprehension of deep reality. Naive empiricism can lead to representations that are markedly inferior to those strictly imagined. Van Maanen's (1979a) distinction between presentational (shielded) and operational (revealed) data illustrates this well.

Looking backward to 1984-1985 leaves me willing to surrender the critical-formal-literary-impressionist method of "The Sleeper" in favor of a more epistemologically streamlined method I am now calling *critical ethnographic fiction* (cf. Scholte, 1987). But that is a story for another time.

As a piece of fiction, "When the Sleeper Wakes" lacks literary distinction. As a piece of positivist social science, it violates ordinary conceptions of realism. As a piece of "science-fiction," it resembles literary journalism, impressionist ethnography, and "experimental" anthropology, but is light on data. I am most comfortable reflecting on it as a mixed-genre piece that anticipated methods helpful in representing this decade's bewildering human organizational realities.

Commentary

Stories of Mike Armstrong and the Idea of Exemplary Research

Linda Smircich

Reading 1: A Positivist View

It is odd to appreciate " 'When the Sleeper Wakes': A Short Story Extending Themes in Radical Organizational Theory" as an exemplary piece of empirical organizational research when it does not look like "research" at all and its status as "empirical" is questionable. If you expect to see a methods section, information about the sample, testimony about the validity of measures, and comments about prediction, you'll be disappointed.

And, although this paper claims that "the characters' lives are created from actual field work" (p. 74), no other comments are offered by Jermier to place him on the scene to have witnessed such goings on. Despite his disclaimers (e.g., "This study . . . uses typical cases" and "The method . . . differs from purely fictional expression"; p. 74), the paper looks suspiciously like an invention—an interpretation given more strength by Jermier's own choice of subtitle: "A Short Story . . ."

> 66 This study is primarily a theoretical analysis which uses typical cases to illustrate positions. The method is subjectivist (Morgan & Smircich, 1980; Poole, 1972) because the realities probed are psychic, and differs from purely fictional expression in that the characters' lives are created from actual field work and theoretical description. 99

(Jermier, 1985, p. 74)

> 66 In this study, class-based workplace dynamics have been dramatized in relation to divergent forms of alienated consciousness to illustrate the importance of human meaning-making processes in understanding organizational behavior. Further theoretical analysis and research will clarify and assess the realism of these alternative viewpoints on the meaning of alienation in work.   99

(Jermier, 1985, p. 79)

More disturbing, the paper ends with statements that this study has "dramatized" workplace dynamics—bringing to mind those television programs now popular, in which murders and abductions drawn from the news are dramatically reenacted. "Dramatized" suggests some playing with the "truth" for effect. But in the final sentence Jermier seems to admit to doubts, and perhaps to reassure us that he hasn't gone completely off the deep end, he closes the paper by saying, "Further theoretical analysis and research will clarify and assess the *realism* of these alternative viewpoints on the meaning of alienation in work" (p. 79; emphasis added).

Overall one could say that Jermier's paper stands in an ambiguous place with respect to our expectations for realism and authenticity in research. From the standpoints of empirical research based on positivist philosophy of science assumptions, this paper is an aberration. I wonder why such a paper was published?

Reading 2: A Multiparadigm View

By the late 1970s the hegemony of the positivist approach and the accompanying vision of what an organizational science would look like came into question from a number of directions. Some scholars noted the tension between the norms of detached scientific inquiry and the desire for useful practical research (Susman & Evered, 1978; Thomas & Tymon, 1980). Other scholars argued that organization theory was too identified with managerial interests and underplayed inherent conflicts in organizations (e.g., Benson, 1977; Clegg & Dunkerley, 1980; Frost, 1980). They argued for more dialectic- and power-focused analyses of organizations, analyses that would be critical of current organizational arrangements. Still others wrote about the absence of attention to mindfulness and meaning in organizational research (e.g., Evered & Louis, 1981; McCall & Lombardo, 1978; Pondy & Boje, 1975; Pondy & Mitroff, 1979; Van Maanen, 1979b; Weick, 1979). There were calls for more subjectivist, social definitionist, and cultural work (Pondy & Mitroff, 1979). By 1979, Burrell and Morgan's book *Sociological Paradigms and Organizational Analysis* had both observed and legitimated the multiparadigm status of the field.

> **66** The divergent states of mind of Mike Armstrong illustrate the psychic processes engaged as human actors confront an alien world and make sense of it. The meaning experienced is a creative product of the properties of the alien world and the actor's psychic processes.   **99**
>
> (Jermier, 1985, p. 78)

All of these happenings made a difference. Under the editorship of Jerry Hunt, the *Journal of Management* revised its editorial policy and included the statement, "In addition to more traditional work, the *Journal* welcomes submissions that expand the study of management and organizations from a critical theory or 'radical' perspective; use qualitative methods; or address issues such as organizational culture, symbolism, rituals or legends, etc." (*JM*, Spring/Summer 1983). Stepping outside the boundaries of the positivist empiricist perspective and acknowledging the multiparadigm status of organizational analysis meant redrawing the standards for judging the "goodness" of scholarly research and "accepting" different forms of research.

Against this context, the special issue on organizational symbolism, and publication of Jermier's paper as part of it, makes sense. That is, alternative paradigms are based on different assumptions about the nature of reality and knowledge. They open up different ways of seeing—that is their main contribution. As Jermier illustrates so well, the story of a life would be told differently from the standpoints of different paradigms.

Jermier's work acknowledges the existence of multiple paradigms, in fact he portrays the various perspectives side by side in Table 1. But he writes as an advocate of radical views. His paper questions the traditional humanistic approaches so much a part of the organizational literature. He juxtaposes the much less well known critical/radical visions of work life against the more familiar vision implicit in "liberal" organization theory. His paper proposes political interpretations of reality over more traditional "humanistic" ones.

From a multiparadigmatic standpoint, Jermier deserves our appreciation. He ventured outside mainstream views to question the theoretical perspectives that dominate the field. His work contains criticisms of both organizational practices and the practices of organizational theory. And so it is "true" to a radical spirit.

❝ The psychic processes explored in this study differ from current approaches to conceptualizing characteristics of workers in several ways: (1) they are viewed as developing within objectively alienating and exploitative work settings and societal arrangements; (2) they may be isomorphic with or partially reflective of mythical forces in society; (3) they are deeply subjective, cognitive substances through which meaning is imposed upon the world; (4) they map domains of societal processes and represent collective phenomena in mental time and space; and (5) they are more fundamental and powerful mental forces than are expectations, beliefs, or even values, and profoundly condition actions and attitudes.

The theoretical viewpoints on alienated consciousness illustrated here depict the effects of problematical organizational events on workers quite differently (Table 1). The anesthetized Critical Theory worker is so skilled at programmed rationalization and diversionary consumption that he or she barely notices the recurring surgery that separates and subjugates true self (cf. Laing, 1965). There is no counterforce or retaliation since this worker mistakes even capricious and surplus repression as natural and inevitable; there is no noticeable injury, hence no reprisal. The effects on the reflectively militant worker are poignant and potentially explosive. This worker cannot live at the level of ideology and therefore openly experiences the "buried features of working class life" (Matza & Wellman, 1980, p. 1). This creates feelings of incredulity, indignation, anger, horror, dread, fear, and loathing. The injuries are usually internalized, but their comprehension in a broader system of meaning creates an unexpected resiliency. It is the carefully timed and varied reprisals which generate managerial transformations and crises (cf. Morgan, 1984).

As Table 1 shows, concepts of humanistic management that are radically different from traditional organization theory derive from Critical Theory and Dialectical Marxism. They emphasize the importance of the political-economic context in analyzing subjective states and propose macrolevel change strategies to eliminate alienation and humanize work (e.g., Jacoby, 1975; Nord, 1977).   ❞

(Jermier, 1985, pp. 78-79)

Nonetheless, even from a paradigms view, judging the goodness of this paper is problematic. It doesn't fit the mold of either a theoretical argument (e.g., Benson, 1977) or an empirical one (e.g., Stone, 1974). Other advocates of alternative paradigms—for instance, Michael Rosen, in "Breakfast at Spiro's" (1985) in the same volume as Jermier's paper—ground their work in lengthy ethnographic experiences. Their writing works to convince us of the validity of their portrayals even if from alternative perspectives. Jermier's doesn't. On what grounds could we call this strange paper "good"?

Reading 3: A Literary View

Our evaluations of research typically focus on methods, on matters of reliability and validity, on questions of dependability of measures and the generalizability of findings, and whether the findings are consistent with a particular theoretical position. But these questions obscure the extent to which *all* research is a kind of writing (Lyotard, 1984). Acknowledging that our research is *literature* (don't we call it that all the time?) gives us another way of assessing our work.

Empirical researchers—whatever their paradigmatic persuasions—attempt to translate a reality "outside" to the "inside" of a text. They fashion symbols on a page for a reader, who through the activity of reading makes "reality" present again. This view of the nature of research points to the ways we construct knowledge in texts—and to the unspoken agreements between writers and readers about what will "pass" as knowledge. This view suggests that the credibility and "goodness" of a piece of empirical research depend not only on the activities of writers, as some observe (Van Maanen, 1988), but on the activities of readers as well (Calas & Smircich, 1988).

From the standpoint of reader-response criticism, a school of thought in literary theory, standards of judgment cannot be applied separate from the subjective experience of reading (R. C. Davis, 1986; Iser, 1978; Tompkins, 1980). Thus when we read an article we should pay attention to what "effects" it has on readers. What feelings are evoked? What kind of thinking does it encourage? How provocative? Pleasurable? Unsettling? And how does it accomplish these effects?

It is from this perspective that I most appreciate Jermier's paper and believe that he deserves our compliments. His work may defy our expectations and cause us to ask questions about how we see and about how we judge knowledge, but in so doing he helps us learn about ourselves as a community of readers and writers.

I've used Jermier's paper in an OT doctoral seminar for several years, and have witnessed how profoundly a/effective it is. Presenting theory in the form of short stories is "novel" and immediately engaging. The detailed comparisons of the different theories (Table 1) make it much easier to grasp their nuances. Contrasted against the dream and the nightmare, the assumptive bases of traditional theories are much clearer to see. This graphic comparison combined with memorable stories frequently has a consciousness-raising effect for students as they gain more diverse perspectives on the "same" circumstances. But Jermier's text is not equally a/effective for all readers. After all, it is Mike Armstrong's story, not Sarah's.

On another level, Jermier's paper is a/effective because it confounds our usual criteria of judgment. It blurs the distinction between one institution, research/truth, and another, literature/fiction. It plays with the conventions of organizational science writing by mixing stories and theoretical arguments. It pushes our community's limits of acceptability by not playing by the rules of what is "normal." On one hand, it offers verisimilitude; on the other, it offers no means through which we feel we can authenticate the "actuality" of what is portrayed. Perhaps it makes us uncomfortable because we don't know what to take it *as*.

But does it move anyone to revolution or to join in a class struggle? Not that I've observed. But would we expect it to? How much "radicalness" would we expect to see in a school of management—or in the *Journal of Management,* for that matter? Reading Jermier puts us into contact with the limits and constraints of our institutions in more than one way.

For instance, Jermier's stories are provocative, raising a question for us: Is Mike Armstrong self-actualizing, a dope fiend, a victim, or a soon-to-be revolutionary leader? When Jermier calls for "further research" to "assess the realism of these alternative viewpoints," he seems to undermine his own position, suggesting that there is some overarching criterion—some metaparadigm standard—for judging one paradigm (one Mike Armstrong) over another. Why, after pointing out that there are multiple stories, does Jermier have to end by saying "further research" will tell us which is the real one? Apparently stories alone are not enough; some form of postscript is needed to permit these stories to exist inside the *Journal of Management* because this is an institution of science, not fiction.

But from a literary point of view Jermier's paper is an intriguing fiction—and so is *every other* exemplary article, qualitative and quantitative, in this volume. All of the exemplars are using representational strategies to achieve the "effect" that they should be constituted "as knowledge" by the reader, but most of them obscure their textual nature. Jermier's paper "hides" its textual nature less. If, by so doing, his work encounters institutional constraints, the encounters are enlightening ones for us, for they help us to understand better the limits we have established for our community.

Commentary

Escaping the Inherent Conservatism of Empirical Organizational Research

Joanne Martin

Those of us who have unconservative political convictions and a commitment to doing empirical organizational research have a problem: Empirical research in our field tends to be inherently conservative. Presuming that we confine our data collection to Western, noncommunist, industrial societies, we must study organizational systems that have been shaped by conservative economic ideologies and dominated by a predominantly white male managerial class.

Below, I illustrate these assertions regarding the inherent conservatism of empirical research (using examples from distributive justice and feminist studies of organizations). Next I discuss how Jermier's 1985 paper, " 'When the Sleeper Wakes': A Short Story Extending Themes in Radical Organizational Theory," offers a solution to these difficulties.

Justifying the Status Quo

Most theories of distributive justice are based on an equity or exchange model that postulates that people, even those who have

Author's Note: I am grateful to the organizational behavior faculty at the Australian Graduate School of Management, University of New South Wales, and the faculty of the Psychology Department, Sydney University, for their assistance during the sabbatical year this paper was written. I also would like to thank Peter Frost, Thomas Pettigrew, Shelley Taylor, Marta Calás, and Linda Smircich for helping me to think in new ways about the issues discussed in these pages.

relatively low incomes, will restrict their social comparisons to similar others and will be satisfied as long as similar inputs yield similar reward levels. Thus people at the bottom of an income distribution should be content as long as similar others are equally poor (e.g., Homans, 1961; Walster, Walster, & Berscheid, 1978). In effect, equity theories argue that the economic inequalities characteristic of capitalist societies are considered just, even by those who have the least.

In contrast, other distributive justice theories argue that a different pattern of response is possible. For example, relative deprivation research has shown that, if the magnitude of pay inequality between the prosperous and the disadvantaged is unusually large, some disadvantaged people will make upward dissimilar comparisons to more prosperous people and will find those comparisons unjust (e.g., Martin, 1981; Runciman, 1966).

However, even relative deprivation researchers admit that this pattern of reaction is relatively rare; most low-income people, under most conditions, will say that the status quo system of income inequality is expected, reasonably satisfying, and moderately just (e.g., Cook & Hegtvedt, 1983; Crosby, 1976). Must we conclude that equity theory's predictions, which so effectively support current patterns of inequality and domination, are congruent with most people's beliefs?

It may be misleading to conclude that disadvantaged people accept economic inequality with equanimity. Their responses may be influenced by false consciousness and/or social desirability biases. Most people in our society, including the disadvantaged, have been taught a meritocratic ideology that implies that if a person earns relatively little, it is that person's own fault. For many poor and low-income people, this self-critical attribution is inappropriate. In addition, research results may be affected by social desirability biases. Subjects in studies may offer answers that conform to what they think their bosses, teachers, or researchers expect to hear.

This analysis raises a series of empirical questions: Would these same subjects voice support for radically different systems of reward distribution if they felt they could speak freely? Can false consciousness be empirically examined? Could people somehow be made aware of the effects of false consciousness? Distributive justice researchers have found it very difficult to address these questions in an empirically grounded way.

 Worker Consciousness and Organization Theory

With the emergence of Radical Organization Theory, many traditional and neo-Marxist concepts have been applied in studies of workplace dynamics (see Goldman, 1985, for review). However, a specific type of schema, studied extensively in Marxist analyses of the worker, remains unfamiliar to most organization theorists. One of the purposes of this study was to integrate concepts of class consciousness, defined as the extent of workers' awareness of their emancipatory role in history (cf. Mann, 1973), into the writings on organizations. These concepts are developed in terms of the subjective alienation literature and are proposed as active, psychic forces which serve the worker in selecting, organizing, and making meaning from impressions associated with capitalist power dynamics.

Moments of Subjective Alienation

In Marx's (1932/1964) early philosophical writing, worker alienation is presented as an historically necessary result of the tension generated between the contradictory social forces of production and the private appropriation of capital. Workers are legally separated from ownership of the means and product of their labor (objective alienation) and comprehend, in a shared way, their position in oppressive, class-based production systems (cf. Bramel & Friend, 1981; Nord, 1977). Thus, while objectively alienated, awareness of class oppression and the transformative historical mission prevents separation from true self.

Neo-Marxist formulations of alienation, originating with Lukács' (1923/ 1971a) classic essay, attempted to describe and explain the lack of awareness of class-based oppression on the part of workers. Concepts of subjective alienation were developed to represent mystified psychic states where workers misconstrue the reality of class-based oppression for freedom (Jermier, 1982).

Table 1 presents elements of two prominent humanistic Marxist theories of subjective alienation, Critical Theory and Dialectical Marxism, and contrasts these with humanistic organization theory's self-actualizing worker. The table was constructed to summarize differences in perspectives on subjective alienation illustrated in the story and discussed below.

Central to Critical Theory formulations of worker consciousness and alienation (represented in "The Dream") is the concept of reification. In capitalist market systems, workers must sell their labor power and thus become semi-human objects of exchange, commodities, things (Israel, 1975). Reification is the "moment in the process of alienation in which the characteristic of thinghood becomes the standard of objective reality" (Berger & Pullman, 1965, p. 198). Reified consciousness is characterized by a *deprivation of awareness* which prevents realization that the world is socially constructed and can be remade. There is a concretizing and *naturalizing* (or *supernaturalizing*) of existing technical processes, social relations, concepts of reason, meanings of time, and definitions of adjustment (see Horkheimer, 1947/1974; Horkheimer & Adorno, 1944/ 1972). Only those momentarily not under "the spell" (Adorno, 1966/1973, p. 312) resist absolute integration or reject the benefits of the status quo.

The power of reification in rationalizing existing conditions of employment for workers is supplemented by the "culture industry" (Horkheimer & Adorno, 1944/1972) which is at once ideological and diversionary. Marx used the term "camera obscura" in *The German Ideology* to refer to the process whereby a distorted, upside-down version of the world (propagated by the privileged classes) becomes the standard of objective reality. The major institutions in society (schools, churches, the family, advertising and entertainment, etc.) act in harmony to present a version of the worker in society which denies oppressive realities. Cultural domination is completed when consumption is manipulated so thoroughly that consumers feel compelled to frenetically buy and use the culture industry's latest products, even though they see through them (Horkheimer & Adorno, 1944/1972). Workers are anesthetized by the persuasive rationalizations readily accessible in mythical structures and by manipulated, diversionary consumption, such that the injuries of class are neither perceived nor felt. Workers are viewed as eternal dreamers. Partly due to their programmed atomization, they are unable to transcend their entrancement.

(Jermier, 1985, pp. 74-75)

Studying Feminist Alternatives That Do Not Yet Exist

Empirical difficulties are even more acute in feminist organizational research. Most organizational hierarchies are controlled by white men, with women relegated to lower positions with less power and less pay (e.g., Bielby & Baron, 1986). Must feminist researchers restrict attention to the few innovative organizational forms that are congruent with feminist ideologies. By definition, these organizations are atypical and rare. Furthermore, most do not survive long in a competitive, efficiency-oriented, male-dominated environment.

If feminist researchers want to go beyond the study of "outlier" feminist organizations, then we must cope with the empirical difficulties inherent in studying contexts where formal structures and informal norms have been created and controlled predominantly by white men. In such organizations, which are the norm in industrial societies, women's behavior at work is tightly constrained. To the extent that feminist alternatives are even considered in such contexts, these alternatives may surface only as hard-to-study thoughts and feelings, not visible behaviors. In addition, as in the justice area, social desirability biases may affect what people are willing to express and false consciousness may influence what they experience internally.

How then can organizational researchers do empirical feminist work? Critiques of previous studies are certainly possible. Gender-based inequalities can be documented, as in studies of occupational segregation or pay discrimination. Innovative feminist organizational forms can be studied. Individual-level studies of feminists within patriarchal organizations can be done, although these have to focus primarily on cognitions and attitudes, rather than on behavior. Other, less limited, forms of feminist organizational research seemed to me, before I read Jermier's paper, to be virtually impossible: How can a researcher study a feminist alternative that does not yet exist?

Jermier's Resolution

Jermier offers a solution to these difficulties. His "short story" describes a day in the life of a blue-collar worker. The first version of the story portrays the day's events from the perspective of false consciousness and the second version describes the same events with an "awakened" sense of alienation. Although Jermier's paper is not empirical research, as it is normally practiced, it does offer a vivid and richly detailed portrait of the thoughts, feelings, and behaviors of a person experiencing what critical theorists and dialectical Marxists refer to as organizational oppression.

❝ REPRISE

> Like Graham, the central character in H. G. Wells' anti-utopian novel, *When the Sleeper Wakes*, this story's main figure, Mike Armstrong, encountered a nightmare world upon awakening from a deep sleep. However, it was not the dramatically inhuman, mechanical-urban world of the 22nd century which Armstrong encountered. This was not a story about dark, dusty, subterranean factories, blue-uniformed workers pale and disfigured from their labor but automatonically punctual, or brutal state police who coerce laborers. Instead, it was a story about alienated life in and around a modern, urban factory where the mechanisms of administrative control are subtle, complicated, and not encompassed by the plant gates.
>
> Armstrong experienced these events first during a dream state and then again while awake. This literary device was used to compare and contrast two radical descriptions of subjective alienation, reified consciousness, and reflective militancy, and to illustrate the power of mythical forces in organizational settings. The main character's dual states of mind and action dramatize the existential moments of personal alienation (Laing, 1965) and symbolize the self-contradictory aspects of capitalist systems. ❞

(Jermier, 1985, pp. 73-74)

Jermier's work can be criticized because he describes the protagonist of his story as a "typical case," drawn from his field research; he does not present evidence supporting this contention. To a limited extent, I think it would be valid to push Jermier a bit in the direction of science, for example by requesting some documentation of the "typicality" of his protagonist and the frequency of the patterns of reaction he describes. However, it is important to recognize that even a study of a single, atypical individual can be of interest, particularly for radical theorists interested in exploring the limits of the possible.

Rather than pushing Jermier further in the direction of science, it is important to appreciate that fiction is more like science, and science more like fiction, than most of us would like to admit. There is a growing body of work that provides support for Jermier's use of fictional devices in his research (e.g., Krieger, 1979). For example, Clifford and Marcus (1986) and Van Maanen (1988) have argued that deindividualized, highly abstract language makes the authors of scientific texts invisible. By eschewing the use of personal pronouns and using passive verb constructions, scientific authors seek to replace the individual narrator, with all his or her idiosyncratic biases, with the impersonal authority of an apparently objective truth teller. Geertz (1988) also shows how scientific authors use writing style to enhance their authority. For example, the introductory paragraphs of anthropological texts often describe the ethnographer's reaction to his or her first sight of the people to be studied, with responses (for example, of "otherness" and distaste) that the reader might be expected to share. Through stylistic devices such as these, scientific authors, like some fiction writers, present themselves as omniscient, enhance rapport with the reader through tacit assumptions of similarity, and draw attention away from what they do not or cannot know.

Jermier, in contrast to most social scientists, largely refrains from using stylistic devices that lend an undeserved aura of unquestionable, deindividualized, objective truth to his writing. In "When the Sleeper Awakes," Jermier focuses on an individual, semifictional protagonist who describes his perceptions and feelings in personal terms. Jermier makes his own and his protagonist's political perspectives explicit, acknowledging that which is ambiguous and unknown.

In this exploration of the elusive boundaries between science and fiction, Jermier retains the vividness and concrete detail that are the hallmarks of solid empirical work, while freeing himself from traditional ways of reporting empirical observations. In addition, through his willingness to consider fictional approaches, he enables the reader to imagine alternatives that might not yet exist, except in the mind of the protagonist/author. In both these ways, Jermier escapes the inherent conservatism of empirical research.

Although his is not empirical research in the sense that term is usually understood, his brave "experiment" encourages all of us to invent our own experiments, unconstrained by the usual ways of thinking and writing about empirical work. For example, we could examine how people think about distributive justice and economic inequality in an ideal world where merit, productivity, and prosperity might be differently linked. Now, perhaps, we can think about new ways of organizing that might become possible if gender were decoupled from status and if feminist values—for example, concerning the debilitating effects of hierarchy—were taken seriously. Jermier's example enables all of us, no matter what topic we study, to write more openly about what we think we do and do not know and why we think we can or cannot know it.

The Hopi Migration Symbol. From their point of emergence to the fourth world, the Hopi clans made a four-directional spiral migration throughout the whole of America, as a purification and weeding-out of the evil brought from the previous world. These signs on rocks, pottery, and altar boards show the patterns made by the individual clans as they spiraled in again upon their center to be reunited at their permanent home. (Drawing by Oswald White Bear Fredericks, © 1963 by Frank Waters, from Frank Waters, *The Book of the Hopi*, Viking Press, New York, 1969. Used by permission of Viking Penguin, a division of Penguin Books USA, Inc.)

PART II

Lessons from the Journeys

Themes and Variations:
An Examination of the Exemplars

Peter J. Frost

Ralph E. Stablein

In this essay we share the results of our reflections on the common themes that appear to us as significant. The themes we discuss are based on our immersion in the seven cases provided in Part I of this volume. We attempt to make our analysis transparent by relying heavily on quotation from the authors' accounts and the commentaries. The themes we choose to emphasize reflect both the reports of the authors and commentators and our responses to those reports. The themes discussed here are surely not the only ones available in these cases. We encourage our readers to examine the cases for additional themes that may be relevant to their own experiences and quests.

Persistence

Each of the studies in its own way is a story of persistence, of staying the course. That persistence shows up in various ways. Researchers (and commentators familiar with their studies) report the importance of taking the time and expending the energy necessary to get the work done, to follow leads, to stay with the data and the research questions long enough to begin to see patterns, relationships, and flaws. Examples of this kind of persistence can be seen in several of the reports. Hackman observes on Gersick:

> After Connie Gersick finished her dissertation research . . . she returned to me the tape recorder she had borrowed to use in the research. I thanked her for remembering to give it back, but then did a double take:

Something was not right about that machine, it did not look quite the same as the others we had in the supply closet at the Yale doctoral program in organizational behavior.

Closer inspection revealed that the function keys on the recorder were different colors. The record, stop, and fast-forward keys were black, as they always had been. But the play and rewind keys were bright silver. The mystery was quickly solved: Connie had hit play-rewind, play-rewind, play-rewind so many times in analyzing the team meetings she had recorded that the paint on those keys had been worn away, exposing and putting a sheen on the original aluminum.

Sutton and Rafaeli comment on the failure of their initial hypothesis:

We checked the way in which we had constructed the scales and the raw data that Larry had sent us dozens of times, but could find no errors. Anat also tried again and again to run slightly different regressions in the desperate hope that "maybe this one variable will save our paper."

Later, they essentially went back to the beginning of their study, searching inductively for clues by conducting a series of qualitative studies involving extensive time in the field.

Meyer, Barley, and Gash reflect on their data collection:

By March 1985, with the survey in the mail, the authors began the initial phase of what would ultimately become a grueling two years of reading and coding approximately 200 articles. . . .

. . . Every two weeks, the authors would read and code a set of 20 articles individually. Gash would calculate interrater reliabilities, and the three would then meet for three to five hours on one or two evenings to discuss variables on which agreement was low. The meetings, which rarely began until Barley and Meyer had put their kids to bed and Gash had returned from her nightly dance class, typically ran late and were both physically and emotionally draining.

For Meyer, Barley, and Gash, persistence required hard decisions with time-consuming consequences. The development of their coding scheme provides an example:

The authors split a variable measuring social integration into two separate indicators: one measuring references to individual integration into the organization and the other integration at the level of the social system. The move required that all previously coded papers be recoded.

Jennings, Dobbin, and Baron describe the experience of their data analyses:

> After a year of collecting new variables, running exploratory regressions every which way, and playing with varieties of statistical methods to collapse the sets of personnel practices into coherent employment regimes, we came to a dead end: Our analyses did not explain much of the variance in practices across industries.

After some confusion and downtime, the investigators regrouped and went back to a search for new data, which they analyzed, but once again they drew a blank:

> Again, war industries did not seem to differ much from other industries in the Conference Board data. We thought we had come to another dead end.
> Our response—almost a reflex after a year and a half of work—was to return to the primary historical sources. . . .
> Persistence, sometimes verging on desperation, was beginning to pay off.

Meyer describes how his data collection on hospitals was almost complete when he realized a natural intervention in the form of a doctor's strike might shed interesting new light on the functioning of hospitals. He decided to take advantage of the opportunity, urged on by colleagues Ray Miles and Jeff Pfeffer:

> I'm thinking of mailing questionnaires to hospitals' chief executives, because the 25 field interviews I've just conducted have worn me out.
> But when I tell Bob Biller I intend to use this method, he offers an analogy: "Sending questionnaires to CEOs would be about as likely to produce valid data as writing to the Romanoffs in 1918 and asking them, 'What happened last year?' " Instead, Biller urges me to study one or two hospitals intensively. When the strike begins I opt for three, expecting to spend an additional week in the field, two tops. But the strike lasts for a month.

Jermier talks about doing fieldwork for his short story, visiting a phosphate manufacturing plant to interview employees and observe interactions. This part of the process took two weeks. Persistence in this case is revealed in his search for a literary form to present his ideas:

I reviewed some key pieces on subjectivist research methods and radical theories of worker consciousness (cited in the article). I read some of Jean-Paul Sartre's (1949/1966, 1972/1974) essays on writing. I reread some of Sartre's novels and plays, this time to learn how existentialist themes drove the stories. I read extensively about writing short stories.

Although the story could have been focused exclusively on an anti-hero (drawn from critical theory), I decided this would be too limiting.

Locke's initial offer to act as mediator in the Latham and Erez dispute was rooted in the persistence of the two antagonists. They had individually produced a series of studies investigating the participation issue. The process of identifying their differences and then designing critical experiments required further persistence. As Latham says, "The process was painstakingly slow in that every word that would be uttered by the experimenter had to be written down in script form." Later, on discovering that the two initial experiments did not resolve the conflict between Erez's and Latham's results, the authors had to return to the drawing board. Reading the scripts for the first two studies provided clues that led to the design and implementation of two more crucial experiments.

It is, perhaps, not surprising that the authors report that exemplary research requires persistent, hard work. We note that persistence, while generally a virtue, can become stubbornness, even closed-mindedness. Thus Alan Meyer struggled with letting go of his persistent pursuit of operational definitions for coupling concepts. Similarly, Jennings, Dobbin, and Baron report their reluctant abandonment of favored hypotheses regarding the practices of war-related industries. However, in ending this section, we think it is important to acknowledge that persistence is a seemingly necessary, though certainly not a sufficient, condition for good research practice.

Handling Your Own Rat

In each of the studies in our set, the researchers immersed themselves in the work needed to understand what was going on. One way or another they got their hands dirty. As Hackman notes in his commentary on Gersick, "If you aspire to breakthrough research, stay insistently close to your phenomena." He credits Bob Grice, an experimental psychologist at the University of Illinois, with the phrase "Always handle your own rat."

Gersick did this through her observing, recording, and seemingly endless playing and replaying of the recordings until she understood what was going on. Sutton and Rafaeli eventually learned the lesson of the importance of immersion. Initially they inherited a data set that they worked on and analyzed intensively. However, it was only when they encountered road blocks, when they couldn't make sense of their findings, that they took the next step of "handling their own rat" by going into the field to see, experience, and discover for themselves the meaning of the data.

Baron literally dirtied his hands in a dusty archive to rediscover the old Conference Board surveys that provided the quantitative data for the "War and Peace" exemplar. Jennings, Dobbin, and Baron describe the ensuing immersion, in survey material and in historical documents, and the value of the back-and-forth iterations they made until they could make sense of the phenomena they studied.

Barley, Meyer, and Gash classified and coded an entire population of articles on organizational culture and lived with that material week in and week out until they felt they had a process that was "as impervious to methodological criticism as possible." Hours of detailed clarification, recoding, and seemingly endless argument yielded a startlingly reliable set of 22 indicators, all exceeding an alpha of .80 (Barley, Meyer, & Gash, 1988, p. 39).

Deep involvement in a study was one of the keys to the way Latham, Erez, and Locke were able to solve the puzzle of differing results in Latham's and Erez's goal-setting studies. (The other was the development of an effective mediation process.) Even within a research paradigm as well established as the laboratory method and in a program of research as well developed as goal setting, there were surprises that, when carefully examined, yielded new insights. Locke notes:

> From the viewpoint of the experiments themselves, what struck me most was the number of differences in procedure and design that can occur when two people are allegedly studying the same phenomenon. In this case there were at least nine differences in procedures or designs of the Erez and Latham studies. Some of these were quite subtle (e.g., self-efficacy instructions). Many were not evident from reading the printed versions of the studies (e.g., differences between tell and tell-and-sell instructions; telling subjects to reject disliked goals). (Latham, Erez, & Locke, 1988, p. 769)

Therefore, it took careful, painstaking detective work by Latham, Erez, and Locke, looking at old experimental protocols, searching through their own recollections of how they did their research and tapping recollections of an ex-student to identify possible causes of the Latham-Erez dispute.

Meyer's experience is also interesting. His initial close attention to the hospital data led him to a conceptual model that he felt emotionally comfortable with but that did not meet with acceptance in the journal to which he submitted the work. It took a jolt from the associate editor of *ASQ* to stimulate him to let go of the loose coupling idea, to return to the data and additional data collection for clues on the meaning of his results. Out of this iteration, probably building on the earlier images and patterns in his mind about the data, he experienced a breakthrough that allowed him to make sense of his study in ways that were acceptable to him as well as to the editor and reviewers at *ASQ*. While we might raise the issue of whether the original conceptual map of his findings might have been valid but simply unacceptable to one set of scholars, there is sense in Meyer's own positive experience of the transformation:

> Accepting this conceptual reorientation was hard, but the benefits are immediate and unmistakable: ideas jell, the writing flows, solutions to logical dilemmas present themselves, and new data sources materialize.

The article itself has proved to be durable. Weick, who did not rule on it while editor of *ASQ*, describes it as one of three articles he would consider rich enough to devote an entire semester of study to in a research methodology course.

Jermier collected his data on life in a phosphate manufacturing plant in two weeks. He devoted a great deal of time to a search for the right form to present his ideas and arguments. He read intensively Jean-Paul Sartre's essays on writing as well as his novels and plays. He read Wells's *The Time Machine* and *When the Sleeper Wakes*, which gave him the idea for the form and structure of his paper.

In general, it appears that the way the process of "rat handling" took place was different for all of the various researchers in our set. This was in part a function of the kinds of questions they asked and the nature of the research settings they chose. They learned different lessons and achieved different objectives as a result of their immersion. Rat handling allowed Barley, Meyer, and Gash to clarify and construct a robust data set. Gersick, Meyer, and Sutton and Rafaeli came to understand the meaning of their data; Gersick and Meyer were able to build their respective theories and Sutton and Rafaeli to test their theory. Latham, Erez, and Locke discovered the importance of carefully articulated experimental procedures. Jermier was able to identify and use an effective form for communicating his ideas.

We think that in all these cases, "getting their hands dirty" served to draw the researchers closer to the phenomena they were studying. It served to create as well as to stimulate patterns of thinking in the minds of the researchers that in turn may have triggered understandings and insights grounded in a deep familiarity with the matter of interest. We are struck by the demonstration that attention to detail, whether minor methodological distinctions or subtle theoretical nuances, plays a key role in the production of these exemplars. The back-and-forth iterations between "mind and matter" that we observe in the reports of these studies may be essential to the creation of interesting and important research.

The Emotional Side of Research

One stereotype of research is that it is a dispassionate process. The investigator is depicted as detached from the ideas, the methods, and the findings of the study he or she is conducting, as a neutral, unemotional actor in the scientific enterprise. We think the original dictum that gave rise to this distortion was intended to help minimize bias in the way a study was run, to steer the researcher away from forcing data to go the way he or she felt they should go to fulfill a preference. We believe that, over time, this has been translated, in some research method texts, seminars, and symposia, into an admonition against feelings as a component of the mature researcher's repertoire. If this were true, research would be a rather mechanistic and unimaginative endeavor. There would be no recognition or legitimation of the roles of hunches and intuition, of exhilaration and disappointment, of passion in the way a research project is carried out. The reports in this monograph suggest that doing research is a human endeavor, that those who do it—at least those who do it well—care deeply about ideas, procedures, results, and how others view their work. Taken to one extreme, strong emotional connections to one's research might create conditions in which faulty thinking is not recognized, procedures become ends rather than means to discovery, results are seen as malleable, to be changed to suit a bias. Taken to the other extreme, stifling one's emotional feelings about the research one does might cut one off from creative insights about the way the phenomenon being studied is functioning, might stifle the passion to persist, to stay with a finding or an idea even when feedback seems to discount it.

In the Barley, Meyer, and Gash study, it was the passion that Gash has for precision and clarity that forced the group to improve in a significant way the working definitions they used in the study. The "razzing" that went on among the researchers served to keep the members of the group from getting too self-important, and it strengthened the team:

> No one, including Barley, was spared the pain of verbal digs and epithets. Gash often had occasion to remind Barley that he was once again "foaming at the mouth" and that he was far too stubborn for his own good. Meyer was repeatedly told that he was in danger of becoming even "more of an ideologue than Barley."

Aggression seemed to release tension and cement the relationships among the three authors. The razzing also served to improve their performance as researchers, for example:

> Meyer and Barley quickly labeled Gash the team's "psychologist," which, roughly translated, meant that of the three she was the most concerned with parsimony and that she was less willing to conceptualize phenomena as social structural in nature. The label (hotly contested by Gash) became a leitmotif that stood in good currency for two years. For instance, it was ultimately at Gash's instigation that the authors split a variable measuring social integration into two separate indicators.

Later, Meyer, Barley, and Gash observe that

> without Gash's insistent emphasis on the techniques that won her the label of "psychologist," Barley and Meyer may have succumbed to a "true believer" syndrome, which might have resulted in findings more open to criticism.

Sutton and Rafaeli's account vibrates with the emotional energy that the authors brought to their work on emotion. (Is it accidental or incidental that as people who appear to revel in emotional interactions, they came to study the phenomenon of emotion?) The title of their commentary itself includes the subtitle, "A Tale of Bickering and Optimism." For these two authors, one role of arguing is to keep their relationship from becoming complacent, which they fear will lead them to become "overconfident, or lazy, or—worst of all—to stop arguing." They end their commentary with the thought, expressed as a concern, that "we believe that the *quality* of our work will suffer if we stop bickering and are left with only our optimism" (emphasis added).

Researchers have feelings about their ideas. For Sutton and Rafaeli, working on emotions was "fun stuff." Latham expresses the excitement and irritation he felt when Locke proposed at a dinner that he mediate a series of experiments to test Latham's and Erez's competing explanations:

> I felt both excitement and irritation. I was excited on two accounts. First, Ed is a stickler for detail. I knew with his assistance that we would discover the reasons for the discrepancy in findings. He would force us to make explicit every detail of our research. Since both Miriam and I trusted Ed, and since both of us respected his research skills, I knew that what I would be asked to do would be fair. Second, I was excited because, to my knowledge, the idea of using a mediator to design studies to resolve a scientific dispute had never been proposed previously. This unique aspect in itself all but guaranteed an interesting project regardless of the outcome of the research. . . .
>
> I was also irritated at two levels. First, I felt that I would be "nitpicked" by Ed and Miriam to do "this and that" when there was other unrelated research I had planned for that year. Further, at the risk of sounding arrogant to the reader, I was confident that my findings would be replicated because they were based on both laboratory and field experiments. The laboratory experiments had been conducted by people other than me, thus eliminating the possibility of experimenter bias; further, some of these laboratory experiments had been conducted by "blind" experimenters. Finally, the field experiments had been conducted by disinterested parties who were interested only in the outcome—productivity. Thus the feeling conflicting with excitement was despair. There was no face-saving way of avoiding a situation that I believed should never have come to pass. On the whole, however, my feeling of excitement in attempting to solve a mystery outweighed any feelings of irritation.

Erez, the other protagonist in the mediated goal-setting study, expresses her excitement at the unique opportunity to work with Latham and Locke on this project. She also admits to some doubts about the wisdom of joining the project:

> I must admit that when I told my colleagues that I was going to work on this joint project, some of them discouraged me and advised me to withdraw from it. They argued that the project was of a zero-sum game, and they worried that we could end up fighting each other rather than resolving the scientific dispute.

Given such advice, she found herself assessing "my own feelings and thoughts, because there was no precedent from which I could learn."

Gersick, in the very first paragraph of her commentary, conveys a sense of excitement about her work on group development. She focused her attention on what intrigued her and the study that unfolded was a reflection in part of the excitement and curiosity engendered in her by what she was observing. She notes a little later in her commentary that she had become so absorbed by what she was encountering in her early work with groups that she forgot to carry out the assignment that took her into the groups in the first place:

> In my initial attempt to make conceptual sense of my observations, I was earnest and enthusiastic, but not very successful. I prepared a report to tell Richard how the project was going, with conclusions about how teams made progress. I even had a series of sketches of products taking shape, which looked a little like a stop-action film of toast popping out of a toaster. Richard's reaction to this was not what I expected. Instead of being captivated by my fledgling theories, he wondered what this had to do with his model. I had gotten so wrapped up in what I was doing that I had forgotten about it!

Jermier, in his commentary, conveys a sense of his strong interest in both conventional administrative studies and radical thought, and his determination to write and teach in a College of Business and to retain his humanistic roots and aspirations. He describes the birth of his idea of illustrating critical theory, how it stayed in his mind and would not go away:

> Although a short story illustrating critical theory would have been useful in the classroom, I knew I would not write it for that purpose alone. I suppressed the idea temporarily because I was unsure about the connection between literary methods and theory development.
>
> However, during that summer's Academy of Management meetings, my enthusiasm for the short story project resurfaced. First it slipped out in conversations with friends, and I began to refine the idea by discussing varieties of fiction (naturalism, realism, symbolism, expressionism, and so on). Then, I tested it with collegial acquaintances. Eventually, I was discussing it with scholars I had not known before. No one discouraged it.

Emotions, typically painful ones, accompany criticisms of authors' work. Conversely, acceptance of work by peers generates strong positive responses in authors. Sutton and Rafaeli, for example, were

ecstatic "when Pettigrew said that our paper was 'the top of the pops.'"
Each of the project descriptions in this monograph contains statements
that capture moments of frustration. Some authors even admit to
despair when they encounter obstacles or receive discouraging feedback from results or from peers.

None of these feelings is out of place in a research endeavor. In fact,
we think such emotions celebrate the intensely human nature of the
research process, particularly when it is undertaken in a spirit of
enthusiasm and optimism, when researchers tackle questions that
ensure a degree of risk. Questions asked may be wrong, procedures
may be flawed, the data may prove daunting to analyze and understand or might confound one's pet theories. Colleagues and critics
might discount one's work. All the energy and effort might come to
nothing. The human reality of research work makes personal identification and commitment almost compulsory. Celebration of success
and consolation in failure in such circumstances is appropriate. Research endeavors are undertakings that engage the intellects and the
hearts of those who create and produce them.

Collaboration

Persistence, immersion, and emotional involvement are potentially
individual qualities. In this section, we explicitly explore the social
nature of the research process. What becomes clear from reading these
commentaries is that no research project is completely done by a single
individual. Researchers require the collaboration of others to make
their projects work, to get them to completion. The collaboration takes
many forms. Identifying the authors of a research project appropri-
ately credits those who took many of the risks, stayed with the investigation for its duration, and likely endured the pain and enjoyed the
pleasures that were associated with the journey of the study. However,
there are many other actors involved in a given research venture, some
more evident than others.

Every study has been preceded by the investigations of other scholars. They have contributed thought and knowledge that sparks new
studies. Testing Richard Hackman's team effectiveness model (or,
more accurately, not testing it) got Gersick started on her research.
Meyer's initial theorizing was based on Karl Weick's notion of loosely
coupled systems. Sutton and Rafaeli became interested in research on
emotions after reading Arlie Hochschild's *The Managed Heart*. Latham
and Erez were stimulated initially by the goal-setting model

expounded and researched by Edwin Locke. In formulating goal-setting theory, Locke was reacting strongly against the work of the radical behaviorists, who dominated psychology, by emphasizing the importance of conscious intentions. Meyer, Barley, and Gash acknowledge that the intellectual seeds of their work were sown in the seminars on culture held in the late 1970s and early 1980s at MIT. Ed Schein and John Van Maanen were among the idea generators at those seminars, and they in turn were interpreting other scholars in anthropology. Baron, Dobbin, and Jennings were prompted into their research by long-standing published debates about the origins of internal labor markets. Jermier drew on the writings of the critical theorists, other radical thinkers, and H. G. Wells and his anti-utopian novel, *When the Sleeper Wakes*.

There are important intellectual lines from the past into each of the studies reported in this book. Other collaboration available to authors comes from advisers and mentors, especially when the work is a dissertation; from colleagues and peers in the employing institution and in the profession; and from gatekeepers, most notably editors and reviewers. The roles of colleagues as supporters, constructive critics, mentors, and interpreters loom large in almost every report by the authors as they reflect on their experiences with their projects. Informal contacts are also an important source of information. Not only did colleagues appear to play important roles, but the timing of their interventions appears to make a difference. Alan Meyer recounts the interventions of senior colleagues Ray Miles, Jeff Pfeffer, and Bob Biller when he was deciding whether and how to tackle the unexpected change in the hospital situation he was studying. Meyer's initial request for comments on his first draft, at that time titled "Patterns of Organizational Adoption," was met by an extraordinarily detailed response from Bill Starbuck:

> Bill Starbuck, whose office is next door to mine, has sent me a three-page letter. It warns that he will soon be giving me detailed editorial comments on my manuscript. Bill describes the philosophies, priorities, and procedures he is using in editing my paper, says that he is spending an average of two hours per manuscript page, and explains that he hopes the letter will keep me from becoming "irate or demoralized" when I see what he has to say about my creative product. It does.
>
> Instead, I'm astonished. Bill has completely reworked the paper's first 10 pages—cutting and pasting sections of my original text to organize the argument logically, writing out by hand proposed new sections, inserting transitional paragraphs and sentences to link it all together. Appended to the refurbished manuscript are an additional 14 pages

containing literally hundreds of explanations, comments, questions, and suggestions. A couple of weeks later, after the shock has worn off, I begin a major revision.

Meyer realized that clear writing is an essential part of communicating that one understands one's own work. He took to heart "invaluable lessons about writing logically, clearly, concisely, and grammatically."

Throughout the process of writing and finally getting journal acceptance of the manuscript, Meyer reports benefiting from the advice and counsel of many colleagues, as well as from the guidance and challenge that came from the editor and reviewers of *ASQ*. Meyer is able to quantify one aspect of collegial interaction: Over the term of the project, he collected a total of 29 pages of comments from 12 colleagues. In summarizing the collaborative nature of his research experience, Meyer writes: "Thinking and writing are solitary processes, but clarifying one's thinking and improving one's writing are social processes."

Gersick points out that the shaping role of her adviser, Richard Hackman, as well as the emotional support she received from Alderfer and from her husband were crucial to the completion and publication of her work. A social conversation with Warren Bennis led to the discovery of Stephen Jay Gould's work and an important stimulus for the conceptual framework for her study. Like Meyer, she had the benefit of her senior colleagues, Barbara Lawrence and Bill McKelvey, who interpreted editor and reviewer comments on her manuscript. Sutton, another author in our set, provided advice on an appropriate journal for her work.

Jermier credits *Journal of Management* editors with encouraging him to develop his ideas for the article he subsequently published in that journal. He also acknowledges Tom Sanders, a colleague in a different discipline, creative writing, for his guidance in writing the short story that was the form for the presentation of his ideas.

Sutton and Rafaeli benefited enormously from the generosity of Sutton's friend and former fellow student, Larry Ford, who gave them the "perfect" data set to work on in their study. A colleague, Jim Tucker, helped them make sense of unexpected and confusing results and in the process lifted them from depression. Staw, a senior colleague, provided useful interpretations of editorial responses.

Meyer, Barley, and Gash do not identify such contributions in their commentary, but in the paper itself they do acknowledge the insights, criticisms, and support of friends and colleagues across the time of the manuscript preparation. In a similar vein, Jennings, Dobbins, and

Baron do not identify any role of colleagues in their commentary. There is, however, a process of collegial influence that takes place inside the group itself that is evident in both these teams.

Coauthored research creates a special case of collaboration. There are some aspects of research that may make working in a team more advantageous than working alone. First, teamwork helps when there is a large task to be undertaken. It is difficult to imagine, for example, one individual successfully completing the coding tasks that Barley, Meyer, and Gash undertook in their study. At least, this would have been an even more time-consuming effort than it was when these researchers were involved in the coding of some 200 articles. This observation is valid also when we examine the project undertaken by Baron, Dobbin, and Jennings. The huge data collection and extensive analysis carried out in their investigation would have been very difficult to do if they were the responsibility of one individual. Second, the teams in this volume provided compensating skills and temperaments that allowed complex and varied issues to be resolved and tasks to be effectively accomplished. "Psychologist" Gash counterbalanced "sociologists" Barley and Meyer. Their razzing behavior, as noted earlier, contributed to a more open research process.

Jennings, Dobbin, and Baron note the same positive effects of collaboration in their commentary:

> Any strengths of "War and Peace" are also a result of our diverse talents and backgrounds. All three of us were interested in organizations, but we came to that interest in very different ways. Baron came to it from his work on structural causes of stratification and workplace discrimination; Dobbin, from his work on the institutional effects of public policy on personnel practices; Jennings, from his work on corporate control mechanisms. Given such different orientations and interests, we sometimes had difficulty coming to consensus, but the advantage of this diversity was that we gave full airing to a wide range of theories. In addition to our different theoretical orientations, we had somewhat different empirical and methodological orientations. Both Baron and Jennings had experience in amassing, manipulating, and analyzing large panel data sets, whereas Dobbin had more experience collecting survey data and applying historical research methods.

Another aspect of complementary balance in research teams is the relationship between senior and junior authors. Jennings and Dobbin benefited from the need Baron, a senior person in their professional lives, had to hire graduate students to work with him on a major study. They were hired to be collaborators and shared in the authorship of the study. The same process and outcome was true for Meyer and Gash, who as doctoral students were invited to join Barley, a newly hired assistant professor, as partners on the culture study. Erez likewise gained a valuable research opportunity from the proposal by Locke, a senior colleague, that a joint study exploring Latham's and Erez's divergent research findings be conducted.

The senior members of each of these research teams gained benefits from the energy, ideas, talent, and familiarity with literatures that the junior partners brought to the projects. The junior partners gained the learning experience of working closely with accomplished researchers and the opportunity to enter the job market with publications.

A final advantage of team research is the self-refereeing that goes on within the team. Thus, for example, Sutton and Rafaeli report, "We spent hours sitting in front of a Macintosh computer, fighting for physical control over the mouse while we struggled to craft sentences and paragraphs." Barley summarizes the process as being "marked by frequent arguments, endless clarification, and constant negotiation and renegotiation." Jennings, Dobbin, and Baron report that they "were constantly disproving many of our pet hypotheses." In more extreme form, the Latham, Erez, and Locke goal-setting research is actually designed around the self-refereeing dynamics of two antagonists.

Of course, this sort of process can produce its share of tension and conflict. These are outcomes noted in all the coauthored research projects in this monograph. Meyer, Barley, and Gash note:

> The meetings, which rarely began until Barley and Meyer had put their kids to bed and Gash had returned from her nightly dance class, typically ran late and were both physically and emotionally draining. Because all of the authors are reasonably stubborn and because all assumed that they had been extremely careful and thoughtful in their initial coding, the meetings generated heated intellectual debates and, occasionally, interpersonal conflict.

Sutton and Rafaeli engaged in bickering and arguments throughout the course of their project. This is a standard feature of their working relationship. Latham and Erez anticipated tension and conflict as they entered their series of laboratory studies. Tensions in the Baron, Dobbin, and Jennings project were partly about differing career pressures, standards of excellence, and timetables for the project.

In most of the cases in this book, the teams appear to have developed mechanisms for making tensions and conflicts productive. One device invented by Barley, Meyer, and Gash was "razzing." Sutton and Rafaeli made arguing a way to focus their energies and to ward off complacency and arrogance. Latham, Erez, and Locke created a formal mediation process for their project. Baron, Dobbin, and Jennings relied on mutual likings and similarities among the members to ease tensions. They observe, however, that sometimes similarity and likings may have "made the role conflicts stickier."

When the conflicts and tensions that arise in team projects are focused on solving research issues or are dissipated by formal or informal means or are accepted as part of the culture of the group, there is a sense implicit in all these commentaries that working together on research can be personally fulfilling. It can even be fun.

In many ways and at several junctures in the progress of a research process, it can be characterized as an intensely social, collaborative process. The case studies in this book illustrate the varieties of ways in which researchers collaborate. The almost ritualistic citations to the work of our intellectual forebears may be a modern form of ancestor worship, but it is also an explicit recognition that today's original research contributions are enabled by earlier contributions. Authors are also in debt to the mentors, friends, and colleagues who trained, supported, advised, and critiqued them. Finally, we acknowledge the intensely collaborative nature of jointly authored research studies.

Conferences as Catalysts

We are struck by the fact that several authors identify interactions within their professional associations as crucial to the development of their ideas and to the progress of their manuscripts. Academic conferences were settings in which "things happened" that served to renew authors' faith in their work and/or to help them rethink their ideas and writings. The activity around conferences is a reminder of the human element in the research process. Despite the increasing effectiveness of modern electronic communication media, many significant research moments continue to be grounded in real time, face-to-face interactions. Latham, Erez, and Locke devised their innovative research strategy over a dinner table at a Society of Organizational Behavior meeting. Jermier used the social settings of an Academy of Management conference to informally try out ideas he feared were too unconventional. Alan Meyer notes in his commentary the positive emotional and intellectual effects of presenting his ideas at the Academy of Management meetings in Detroit immediately following the emotional letdown of critical *ASQ* reviews on his first submission. He received timely support and constructive advice from Jan Beyer following his talk.

Meyer also mentions the importance to him of the smaller, more intimate Alta Conference on interpretive approaches to studying organizations. Participants at this conference appear to have made crucial interventions and suggestions on his work at a time when he was struggling to rethink the ideas for his paper and their presentation. Sutton and Rafaeli were persuaded of the value of their decision to study emotion when they presented a paper on emotion at the Academy of Management meetings in 1985 in San Diego to an enthusiastic audience.

Meyer, Barley, and Gash tested first the theory, and later preliminary data, at a total of three conference venues. They share with us another role of conferences for them: motivation. The approach of a scheduled presentation of preliminary findings to the Standing Conference on Organizational Symbolism generated an internal memo titled "Putting Nose to Grindstone." Jennings, Dobbin, and Baron experimented with the ideas and structure of their paper at a session of the American Sociological Association. Latham, Erez, and Locke presented their findings at the International Congress of Applied Psychology and the Society of Industrial-Organizational Psychology meeting. Their final article reflects inputs from audience feedback at those presentations.

The availability of forums in which ideas can be explored, tested, and presented is clearly important for the development of exemplary research. There is also an important role served by the presence at such conferences of colleagues, fellow professionals who act to provide emotional and intellectual support and guidance to those presenting their ideas. This function and these roles may be particularly important when the ideas are unorthodox or when researchers are trying to break new ground. They are also important supports for presenters who are new to the field and/or come from schools that do not have the resources to provide intellectual mentorship and critique as effectively as do some other schools.

Getting Published

The research process is not complete without the communication of the contribution to the rest of the research community. When research occurs in an academic setting, this usually involves questions of where and how to get it published. Various aspects of this broad process are addressed in *Publishing in the Organizational Sciences* (Cummings & Frost, 1985). In the cases described in this book, the focus of the researchers' efforts was on getting published in journals.

For some authors in the set, communication is not a simple, routine task. This process is reported as being lengthy and sometimes painful. It is also acknowledged to be a learning process. The communication process actually contributes to the quality of the research communicated. The experiences of the authors, particularly Alan Meyer, Connie Gersick, and Bob Sutton and Anat Rafaeli, are instructive in this regard.

As a rule, the first step in the publication process is not submission of the manuscript to a journal editor. Sutton and Rafaeli are the exception. They submitted their manuscript to *ASQ*. The first presentation by Gersick was on her job interviews. Meyer shared his manuscript with Bill Starbuck, a new colleague at his first job site. Jermier negotiated the appropriateness of submission with the editors of *Journal of Management* before undertaking the research. The remaining authors presented their work at a variety of conferences prior to journal submission.

Eventual submission of the manuscript is inevitably met with criticism (Schneider, 1985). Every journal required revision. Gersick and Sutton and Rafaeli experienced rejection of their manuscripts by the first journals to which they submitted. Meyer perceived and felt the feedback from the associate editor and reviewers of *ASQ* as rejection of his work. In his commentary, he writes:

> The reviewers' reactions to what I consider the paper's most seminal and well-articulated arguments sting, but their repudiation of the concept of coupling hurts even more.
>
> If *ASQ* rebuffs loose coupling—the notion championed by its own editor, Karl Weick—then my paper's chances don't look very good. Thoroughly discouraged, I leave for the airport to fly to Detroit, where I am scheduled to present the paper at the annual meeting of the Academy of Management.

Meyer was on the verge of sending the paper elsewhere when, fortunately, Paul Nystrom, a senior colleague, made a crucial interpretation of the *ASQ* editorial feedback for Meyer: "Congratulations! You've cleared the highest hurdle." Meyer continues:

> He points out to me that Jerry Salancik wrote "the manuscript suggests a potential contribution," that Jerry invited me to "revise it for further consideration," and that Jerry has gone to the considerable trouble of writing a long letter spelling out specific goals for a revision. Paul goes

on to convince me that each of the reviewers has given constructive suggestions for improving the manuscript, that their comments include praise as well as criticism, and that the changes requested by the different reviewers are not contradictory. All in all, he says, this adds up to about the most favorable outcome I have a right to expect.

Meyer responded to this more hopeful interpretation of the reviews with a proposed plan for revision, which he sent to Jerry Salancik. In a follow-up phone call to Salancik, he heard again that "coupling may not be the most crucial explanatory variable at work here." Reluctantly, Meyer conceded: "Accepting this conceptual reorientation is hard, but the benefits are immediate and unmistakable."

A year of theoretical reorientation, additional data collection, and reorganization of the article around the chronological sequence of his research process resulted in the final version of "Environmental Jolts." Seven years had passed since the doctors' protest over raised malpractice insurance fees.

Gersick began the process of making her work public with the presentation of her findings at recruiting interviews, with mixed results. She describes the pain she experienced when attacked at one interview, apparently because of the exploratory nature of her study. One challenge she faced that is common to many scholars was to reduce a lengthy product (hers was a dissertation) to an article suitable for journal submission. Her first reviews were mixed. As in Meyer's case, Gersick relied on more experienced colleagues to help her "understand what the journal editor was saying." Her responses to the requests for revisions were not accepted by the editor and the manuscript was rejected. This revised manuscript had, in Gersick's judgment, "significant substantive improvements" due to the reviews. When she sent the work to a second journal, *AMJ*, the response and Gersick's experience were more positive. Gersick acknowledges the importance of Jan Beyer, the editor, who served as a coach and constructive critic of her work as it moved through the *AMJ* review process. Several revisions led to final acceptance of the manuscript seven years after Gersick's first group observations.

Sutton and Rafaeli describe the work they did to create the first submissible manuscript. It was rejected by *ASQ*. Their response to that result was emotional: "It has been more than three years since *ASQ* rejected the paper, but it is still painful to read the associate editor's opinion that 'the point is that this seemingly simple situation is rich and complicated and that your theorizing does not even address it seriously.' " They interpreted the editor's reaction as based on the structure rather than the content of their manuscript, thus they chose not to heed the editor's comments. Nevertheless, their reactions to the "11 pages of careful comments" from the *ASQ* reviewers were incorporated into the manuscript sent to the *AMJ*. The paper was finally published after revisions that reflected the influence of editors Beyer and Mowday, who had "hounded us about the nuances of the paper [and] . . . had offered hundreds of suggestions and comments aimed at refining every paragraph, and nearly every sentence."

Other authors in the set talk less about the process of getting published. Jennings, Dobbin, and Baron "were all exasperated by the prospect of having to go through another round of revisions and rewrites. We let the paper sit—a case of 'out of sight, out of mind.' After calming down, we went back to work." Jermier acknowledges the helpful challenges and suggestions of the reviewers at *Journal of Management*. He credits the editor with "artfully summarizing the reviewers' comments." Latham attributes the relative ease of acceptance of the Latham, Erez, and Locke manuscript to the years of experience that Locke and he had as editorial board members.

We think it is significant that the less experienced scholars write more and struggle more with the publication process. In particular, we note the emotional impact of the review process, the improvements in revised manuscripts, and the need to interpret the meaning of editorial comments.

The wide range of emotions experienced in the research process is described in an earlier section of this essay. The emotions experienced in the journal review process are decidedly negative. These negative emotions are reported by the junior authors. Graham and Stablein (1985) have focused on the beginner's perspective in greater depth. One helpful suggestion made by several of the authors in the cases presented here is to delay judgment on the value of reviewer comments so that their contributions are not lost in the initial sting of the feedback.

A number of the authors have reported that the review process contributed positively to their manuscripts. Not surprisingly, reviewers report that they emphasize this aspect of the review process (Jauch & Wall, 1989). Other commentators have emphasized the arbitrary, biased, and destructive nature of the review process (Crandall, 1986; Spencer, Harnett, & Mahoney, 1986). This is clearly an area that could use additional research attention.

There is an element of luck that strikes us as important in the gatekeeping process. If editors do not communicate effectively the status of papers and the meanings of reviews in writing and in other interactions with authors, then the authors may lose heart and with-draw—an outcome not intended by editors but one that can cost the field potentially valuable knowledge in the long run. In some cases, it would appear that the additional effort and attention given by editors may be influenced by their own commitments. Thus, fortuitously, Gersick's article arrived at *AMJ* at a time when Beyer was actively seeking and wishing to promote new research directions and qualita-tive approaches. Withdrawal from active scholarship may also result if authors do not have experienced interpreters around to help explain and even reframe what they see in the feedback they get from journals. From the reports here, we would conclude that there will be more problems for inexperienced authors. We would speculate that authors at smaller and less elite institutions than those represented here would be even more likely to suffer from the unavailability of interpreters. In addition, the more unorthodox the work, the more innovative it is, the more it may need champions, sponsors and supporters to get it into print in the influential journals.

At the End of the Day . . .

What is the impact of an exemplary study on the researcher who creates and produces it? On the field in which it is embedded? We asked the researchers to think about these questions and to respond as they saw fit. Their replies are both varied and interesting. Some have positive feelings about the outcome. Gersick notes:

> The article has been out for a while now, and the response has been gratifying. Over the years, the work has put me in contact with people who became valued colleagues and friends. It has given me a lot to think about.

The article won an award for excellence. It sparked a second study by Gersick, a laboratory investigation of project groups that as a formal article in the *Academy of Management Journal* was named "Best Paper of 1989" by that journal (Gersick, 1989a). The concept of "punctuated equilibrium," which she borrowed from paleontology to help her explain group processes, became the core of a theoretical piece she sub-sequently wrote and published in the *Academy of Management Review* (1991).

Commenting from his perspective on the Latham, Erez, and Locke article, Latham writes:

In the time since the paper's publication, the feedback has been very positive in terms of requests for reprints. More significantly, in August 1989 we were informed that our article had won the award for best paper in the Organizational Behavior Division of the Academy of Management.

The importance of the manuscript, in my opinion, is twofold. First, it suggests a relatively sane way of resolving a scientific dispute. Picking a mediator that the antagonists trust is far more productive for them and the field than carping back and forth in the literature about who is right. The answer is unlikely to emerge unless the combatants are willing to discuss their "honest differences." Second, the monograph lays to rest, or should lay to rest, the debate on the motivational effects of assigned versus participatively set goals. When supportiveness, goal difficulty, and self-efficacy instructions are held constant, and when the goal is assigned with a rationale so that it is not viewed as capricious, assigned goals are as effective in increasing performance as are participatively set goals. At best, when the goal is extremely difficult, participatively set goals may influence a self-report of goal commitment favorably relative to an assigned goal.

Latham notes that he is continuing to focus on participation in the goal setting process in his research.

Erez, commenting on the same work, notes in her section headed "Aftermath and Reflections" that the joint studies produced a convergence between Latham and herself on some aspects of participation and performance: first, that the tell-and-sell style of communication is as effective as the participation approach in "enhancing goal commitment and its consequent performance," and, second, that Latham had recognized "the theoretical importance of the two-step model, and the role that goal commitment plays in the relationship between participation and performance." She adds that they disagree on the practical implications of the two-step model. While not specifying it as her own next step, Erez suggests that future research ought to examine participation under a more wide-ranging set of conditions than were available in the studies she and Latham conducted.

Locke, who mediated the studies done by Latham and Erez, declares himself satisfied and pleased with the outcome of the experiment:

Since I did not see pdm as a moral issue, I welcomed the opportunity to help Erez and Latham discover the reasons for the disagreements in their findings. I think we did this pretty successfully. Latham, like myself, was interested in pdm as a paradigmatic issue—that is, does it work? Erez, I believe, based on her cultural background, perceived participation in a favorable way, but I give her credit for being a good scientist. I give both of them credit for being willing to put their ideas on the line in a high-risk venture. Both they and science are the better for it.

Locke, while not talking about his next steps as a researcher, argues that past work on participation has been on the wrong track, that the phenomenon will more likely yield to a cognitive than to a motivational explanation. He would like to see researchers study the phenomenon without the "ideological blinders" that close ideas and avenues for inquiry in advance.

A sense of positive outcomes coupled with a sense of incompleteness, even unease, is revealed in the reflections of Sutton and Rafaeli:

The aftermath has also included some sweet extrinsic rewards. The paper was published as lead article in the September issue, a sign that the *AMJ* editors thought that it was important. Both of us have since been promoted to associate professors with tenure, and several of the people who wrote letters evaluating our work have reported to us that their letters focused special attention on the quality of this paper. We were absolutely ecstatic about receiving the award for the best paper published in *AMJ* in 1988. And we are very pleased to have our paper be included in this book on exemplary research.

However, they express some doubts:

Yet, despite all of these lovely rewards, we still are plagued by lingering doubts about this paper and its subsequent effects on our research. We both still worry that the relationship between store sales and expressed emotions is a trivial topic. We worry that by focusing on four simple behaviors—smiling, greeting, establishing eye contact, and offering thanks—we offered an oversimplified view of expressed positive emotions. We also worry that we have focused too much on the expression of good cheer in our empirical work and not enough on the expression of unpleasant emotions.

This unease about drawbacks in their study has sparked each of them to conduct some further studies on the expression on negative emotion: "Anat studied interrogators who are paid to gain confessions from suspected criminals, and Bob studied bill collectors who are paid for getting payments from debtors."

Jermier, looking back at his paper, sees its flaws: It "lacks literary distinction . . . violates ordinary conceptions of realism . . . is light on data." However, he is comfortable with it as "a mixed-genre piece that anticipated devices helpful in representing this decade's bewildering human organizational realities."

Disappointment and some disillusionment can accompany good work. In both the works by Barley et al. and Baron et al., this theme is apparent. Barley et al. hoped that this article would stimulate debate on the social forces that impinge on the field of organizational behavior. However, as Meyer, Barley, and Gash note:

> As of the winter of 1990, response to the article has been disappointing. Although there have been occasional requests for reprints, and although Meyer and Gash have both been invited to review manuscripts that they would otherwise not likely have received, with Frost and Stablein's choice to include the paper in this volume, few efforts have been made to engage the authors in a substantive dialogue regarding the study's findings or the authors' concerns for the field. While it is probably too early to expect such discourse to appear in print, the authors regret the absence of debate in less formal contexts. Exchanges that follow the publication of research typically take one of three forms. Authors receive brief verbal congratulations, requests for reprints, or citations in later publications. Unfortunately, each form of feedback is devoid of interaction and fails to engage the field directly in a substantive exchange regarding a work's content or its implications for the field.

Jennings, Dobbin, and Baron report a similar kind of letdown feeling. The reception of the paper by the field was not as strong as they had hoped:

> The article also generated some debate—at least initially. After it appeared, the *American Journal of Sociology* published a comment by Charles Denk (1988), who was a year ahead of Jennings and Dobbin in the Stanford sociology doctoral program. The comment made some methodological suggestions concerning longitudinal analyses for the data. The suggestions made good sense, but we had not seen Denk's comment prior to its submission for publication and therefore had no chance to discuss with him our own explorations with dynamic analyses. So Jennings and Baron drafted a formal reply to Denk (Baron, Dobbin, & Jennings, 1988) with some help from Dobbin, who was en route to a new job. We acknowledged that Denk made useful suggestions, but pointed out that the limitations of our data had prevented us from carrying out suggestions such as his.
>
> However, our sense is that "War and Peace" has had little impact on any of its intended audiences. This may have something to do with our effort to reach a number of different audiences, so that we succeeded in reaching none of them. Predictably, economists and historians told us

we were reinventing wheels they had discovered long ago. Organization theorists do not seem to have found much of organizational interest in our analyses; many researchers interested in stratification and work no doubt see our work as far afield from their concerns; and historical sociologists typically pose different sorts of questions. Even when your work is cited, it is important to recognize that research articles, like all social phenomena, undergo a process of social construction and labeling. What inevitably seems like a rich, subtle, variegated, and complex argument or set of empirical results to the author gets defined in a pithy, stylized shorthand by scholars who subsequently cite—and thereby define—your contribution to a literature. (An example would be the following hypothetical citation of our paper: "Personnel activities flourished during World War II [Baron, Dobbin, & Jennings, 1986].")

The research done by Baron, Dobbin, and Jennings did have an influence on their subsequent work. Jennings became interested in human resource management and is studying the professionalization of that field. Dobbin continued to work with Conference Board data to investigate the effects of public policies on organizational practices. Baron became even more committed to the line of research developed in this study and is investigating, in several different domains, possible linkages among historical forces, institutional environments, and employment arrangements adopted by organizations.

One gains a sense from all these reports that doing research is work that is never really complete. What has been done may resolve some issues, ease some inner itches, but it also tends to raise fresh issues, to cast a new or different light on the phenomenon of interest. It may also leave an emotional residual or create new "fire in the belly" that sparks renewed research activity. Perhaps most interesting and not typically noted in discussions on method and the research process, investigators may grow in wisdom and understanding that illuminates their own fundamental stance toward work.

Sutton and Rafaeli, for example, ask themselves if "our best work together has already been done." They add:

> During these moments of uneasiness, we wonder if all of those lovely extrinsic rewards will cause us to become arrogant, overconfident, or lazy, or—worst of all—to stop arguing. We believe that the quality of our work will suffer if we stop bickering and are left with only our optimism.

Meyer, Barley, and Gash ask a larger question. Given the work they have done and its lack of impact, as they see it, they return to many of the questions that stimulated their research in the first place:

The authors are collectively left posing again a number of the questions that stimulated the research. Can the field of organizational behavior sustain a serious stream of basic research over an extended period of time without being influenced by the social forces that seem to have affected discourse on organizational culture? If not, why not? Are students of organizations simply unwilling to think critically about why they do research or about the uses to which their research is put? What social forces influence the topics that researchers pursue and the directions in which the research develops? Which forces are external to the research community and which do we, wittingly or unwittingly, create for ourselves? Finally, there is a normative question: Should we allow the patterns of influence documented in "Cultures of Culture" to occur and, if so, under what conditions?

Perhaps the matter of what impact research can have is out of the hands of researchers. At least this may be so in a system in which there is no systematic attention given to packaging and marketing one's ideas for audiences beyond the readers of academic journals. We are not arguing for or against the present way ideas prepared for journals are disseminated. We simply note that, at least in the short run, it may be unreasonable to expect much more than passing commentary within the field, occasionally an award that focuses attention on a product, and some citations in other people's work. There is so much information, in so many areas, coming out in fairly prosaic outlets, and frequently open to many different interpretations, that it is difficult for ideas in research journals to stand out and to have a high impact in a short space of time.

There may, of course, be ideological resistance or indifference to some ideas rather than others. There may also be circumstances in the context of work being done that will bring it to more particular notice than might otherwise be the case. Sutton and Rafaeli's paper may not have received as much attention, may not even have been published, had the editors of *AMJ* not been interested in work that used multiple methods competently. Similarly, Jan Beyer was particularly interested in qualitative research when Gersick's manuscript arrived at *AMJ*. The same can be said for the Jermier piece. It was written in an era when the editors of the *Journal of Management* were looking for material that would encourage work that addressed issues such as organizational symbolism and culture and would present critical as well as more traditional perspectives on the field. These manuscripts may have been submitted when the editors wanted to signal to readers and researchers trends in acceptable research methods and product they considered worthy of promotion in the field.

At the end of the day, perhaps the most useful thing researchers can do is to take their eyes off the intended positive impact of their work, at least initially, and do work because it is intrinsically interesting and important to themselves and their vision of the field. Such research could address any of a wide number of organizational issues. The relationship between self and research work has been discussed elsewhere (Berg & Smith, 1988; Sjoberg, 1989; Wildavsky, 1989). Jennings, Dobbin, and Baron put this perspective rather well. After lamenting the small impact of their article, they comment: "This sometimes is frustrating, but it can also be liberating: One's inability to control how the discipline will construe a given piece of research suggests the importance of satisfying internal standards, of writing for *yourself* as much as for any clearly defined reviewer or audience."

Beyond Exemplars: Some Reflections on the Meaning and Practice of Research in the 1990s

Peter J. Frost

Ralph E. Stablein

Empirical research that gains recognition beyond the fact of publication invariably has an interesting story to tell and provides insights on topics of theoretical and practical significance. In addition, it has something to teach us about the research process and how our own work might be improved. (Mowday, this volume)

In this monograph we have presented the recorded thoughts, reflections, and emotions of researchers engaged in the process of doing exemplary research. The actual work about which they reflect is published elsewhere. We have presented excerpts that capture the flavor of that work. Commentators have provided their own informed opinions on the quality of the works of these researchers. We have abstracted some of the themes and variations that appear to reside in the authors' ruminations. Are there broader lessons about doing exemplary research? We believe there are some implications from the cases presented here for the way research is organized, taught, and practiced. Our thoughts on these matters form the concluding commentary of the book.

The Tyranny of Time

One feature of the research process that unites several themes described by authors in this volume is that researchers need to have available large amounts of *time* that can be devoted to their work so that they are able to stay with the phenomenon until they understand it sufficiently well to talk about it with some confidence. In the present era, most organizational research is done in institutions that for various reasons put a premium on time. Doctoral students are perhaps the most fortunate group of researchers, although we suspect they would deny this, in that their professional lives can be organized around research projects, the deadlines of which they have minimal accountability for, and a dissertation process that is expected to take a year or two to complete. Of course, there are pressures on doctoral students to graduate as soon as possible so that they can meet financial and personal responsibilities and "start their careers."

Researchers who are junior faculty in universities in North America face a tenure clock that ticks incessantly. They are under enormous pressure to publish or perish, while also establishing their teaching, collegial relationships, and personal lives, often in new communities. Ironically, this external pressure to publish comes at a time when the junior faculty member is intrinsically motivated to do the same. At the extreme, researchers in this category live in a culture that encourages quantity over quality in research products. This is a context that perpetuates the illusion that if one concentrates on tackling safe projects and getting work done, thereby increasing the chances of gaining tenure, one will then subsequently have the time and opportunity to be creative, to do the research one really cares about. In our judgment, this is an illusion, because this careerist approach to research ensures that behind each hurdle lurks another one. Sacrificing one's creative urges to the tyranny of a tenure clock is likely to be followed by the tyranny of promotions, to associate, to full, and ultimately to chaired professorship. While we do not wish to deny the reality of tenure and promotion decisions, nor do we suggest that they be ignored by researchers, we believe that uncritical attention to these pressures can contribute to a learned, trained incapacity to engage in the persistent and creative efforts that characterize exemplary research.

Senior researchers face other time constraints. Simply being visible as a successful scholar in the profession ensures a multiplicity of demands on that scholar. These demands include invitations to review manuscripts for colleagues, to serve on review boards of journals, to edit monographs, to adjudicate for and even to coordinate academic conferences. Senior researchers more frequently than junior researchers serve as advisers of doctoral students, write for and review grant proposals, and serve on faculty, university, and professional committees. The list goes on. These are all important functions of being a researcher-in-a-community. In fact, as we noted in the previous essay, these activities (especially those in which scholars, as colleagues and peers, review and interpret the creative work of others) form the basis of a positive, important invisible college (Ben-David & Sullivan, 1975). However, when these sets of activities dominate the lives of researchers, it is likely that the time they need to be creative and persistent investigators is extremely limited. We note that most of the authors in this book were junior researchers when they did the work discussed here. Many of them were doctoral students and untenured professors. While this may be in part an artifact of the sampling we did for this project, and we know that senior researchers often publish much of their work in books (Perrow, 1985), we think this fragmentation and consequent scarcity of time are concerns that many senior scholars will acknowledge with some feelings of frustration.

Barriers to Immersion

A significant feature of the studies in this monograph was the value to researchers of becoming deeply immersed in their work. We think there are many forces that can direct researchers away from a willingness or even an ability to handle their own rats. One of these forces is the scarcity of time, as noted above. Another influence away from immersion is the uncritical use of previously developed research instruments, secondary data sources, canned programs for analysis of data, and tightly prescribed formats for presenting the findings of studies. These are useful or relevant components for doing research. We think, however, that any programmed facet of research also has the potential to distance the investigator from the actual phenomenon he or she wishes to study.

To illustrate, we raise the issue of construct validity measurement (Schwab, 1980). The emphasis on using existing, validated measures in our research may be a false economy. The pursuit of efficiency limits the constructs that are employed and thus theoretical creativity in specifying the nomological net. Unfettered theorizing will create a need for the arduous task of developing new validated measures. But this "extra" effort will yield better specification for the researcher and a richer array of constructs for the community of researchers to employ.

Another barrier to immersion is the delegation of research tasks. Taylorization of research projects may allow the delegation of subtasks to relatively unskilled workers, but it also reduces the researcher's familiarity with the phenomenon. Substantively important findings may be overlooked by less skilled assistants; substantively important decisions may be made innocently and unconsciously.

The Financial Underpinnings of Research

None of the authors in this set of exemplars mentions funding as an important ingredient of research. In a sense, it would seem that each of the projects described was a low-budget production with an impact emphasis given to bootlegging of either time or money by authors, to get the job done. One positive message that can be taken from this aspect of the research reported here is that it doesn't take a large amount of money to do interesting, creative, and important work. We think this is a valid point. However, it would be naive to suggest that good research does not need substantial funding (e.g., the expensive data set Ford gave to Sutton and Rafaeli). Much of the financial resource base of the studies reported here is implicit. All of the authors worked at universities and institutions that provide funds for research. The funding is often provided through low teaching loads, grants for research and conference attendance, and subsidization of research equipment and services. The strong research reputations of such institutions serves in part to attract funds or to make it easier for scholars who apply for financial support to get receptive attention from granting agencies. The same prestige can facilitate access to research locations. Scholars, particularly junior scholars, who are not in institutions or settings that provide direct or indirect avenues for research funds are likely to find it difficult to get even the most promising ideas off the ground.

Roadblocks to Publication

We were impressed by the degree to which authors attribute the success they had in getting published to the supportive, constructive feedback of colleagues, editors, and reviewers and to the interpretive skills of others who framed feedback from editors so that the authors were mobilized and directed toward constructive action in their responses to journals. As we noted earlier in this book, we have some concerns about the extent to which the positive outcomes described by authors here is open to chance. We refer to chance in two senses. First, there is the good fortune of a Nystrom interpreting editorial feedback for Alan Meyer, the encouragement of a Beyer and a Mowday to retrieve manuscripts by Gersick and by Sutton and Rafaeli after they had been rejected by another journal. So, even within an invisible college, there may be some serendipity in the rehabilitation and progress of research. Second, there is the good fortune of being within the walls of the invisible college itself. We do not quarrel with the existence of such a college; indeed, it appears to be a crucial underpinning of research as an enterprise within a community of scholars. However, we worry about the size of the college and the paths available for joining and benefiting from the college. Perhaps partly by accident, an artifact of our selection of articles, the invisible college seems rather small. The cast of characters who feature in our stories as colleagues, peers, and gatekeepers is rather limited. Several individuals appear on more than one occasion in different stories as champions and nurturers. Sutton and Barley feature as authors and, in other accounts, as advisers. We think their cases are typical. In a community of scholars this is as it should be—authors serve also as reviewers, as counselors, as champions.

One of our concerns is that if the invisible college is too small, then the diversity of research that gets noticed, nurtured, and even promoted may be too narrow. The skills within the community may be too few to meet the needs of its members. Another of our concerns is that to the extent that the college is in fact invisible, researchers with much talent who do not have ways to join may be lost as players who enrich the field as well as develop themselves.

Creating Contexts for Exemplary Research

TAMING TIME

There are some things that the field can do and that individual scholars can do to improve the quality of the systems we have that form the contexts for doing exemplary research. The scarcity of time to do good research and the importance of having time to do it need to be acknowledged explicitly in the system and by researchers. At the doctoral level of research, we suggest that the fairly lengthy period that students have to do dissertation research be celebrated in the system rather than ignored or seen as a cost or as dysfunctional. Students need to recognize and be helped to recognize the creative opportunities that the dissertation period offers for doing research. At the same time, we acknowledge that a relatively open horizon for doing research can immobilize the individual, so that such a celebration needs to be buttressed by other factors, such as the mentoring role of advisers and other researchers at appropriate stages along the way. The experiences of Connie Gersick and of Alan Meyer reported in this book are instructive in this regard.

Junior researchers who face a tenure clock need to be allocated responsibilities in their institutions that allow them to concentrate on their research. At the same time, the culture within which the researcher works needs to value the creativity, tastes, and ability of the individual and the importance of the quality rather than the quantity of work accomplished. Another value we consider important in this regard is that which permits a maturation process of researchers. Scholars at the beginning of their research careers typically develop products that emerge slowly, as they learn the ropes in their careers, begin to teach, establish collegial relationships, nurture their often turbulent personal lives, and so on. We suspect that the payoff of early research investments by scholars comes several years after the initial start-ups. It may be a process that is on an exponential curve, slow initially and fast later in the sequence. If one thinks about the length of time (measured in years) it took for Gersick, Meyer, Barley et al., Baron et al., and Sutton and Rafaeli to get one exemplary project into print, then our typical current systems of performance evaluation, which force a decision on a researcher's fitness for tenure after six or seven years, may allow too little time.

On the other hand, few would want to wait a decade to be judged for tenure. Yet this seems to be a reality for junior scholars today. We do not have the data, but one suspects that many junior faculty must make lateral or downward moves, enduring two tenure processes, before achieving tenured status. Others temporarily stretch the time available for tenure at their home institutions by taking leaves of absence. If these strategies have become the norm, perhaps an expansion of postdoctoral arrangements would acknowledge this reality, provide more time to develop research programs, and carry less stigma. Another alternative that may prove workable is a tenure process that emphasizes high quality on fewer products and on products that are not yet published. Some institutions do make decisions in this way. We recognize that decisions about tenure in organizational studies have to stand up against those that are made in the physical sciences and in other areas where a high quantity of publications is possible and valued, so that there are competing pressures on the way this decision is made.

The decisions made by junior researchers themselves are important. We have argued, from the data in this book, that attention to the challenge of a research question ought to take precedence over concerns of career, personal recognition, and so on. The latter concerns are not trivial. Sutton and Rafaeli, Gordon Meyer and Gash, Jennings and Dobbin, and Latham acknowledge and make explicit that extrinsic factors play an important role in their motivations to do the work they do. Intellectual merit and personal commitment enter the equation, as well. We think it is a question of priority and emphasis when exemplary research is involved. We believe that junior researchers—indeed, all researchers—need to be clear about the costs and benefits of doing research that is challenging and risky and be willing to pay the price as well as collect the plaudits when they do choose to undertake research projects.

Researchers who choose to do work that is close to their hearts face certain risks. One of these is that the project may not produce significant findings. Even if it does, the research might not be recognized by significant others in the field, affecting the chances for tenure. We think that being willing to acknowledge these possibilities at the start of a project is crucial. It enables the researcher to embrace the research as an inquiry of interest and promise, and will likely free the individual to tackle the work realistically. The research may not secure tenure for the individual at a given institution, but if it is exemplary and the researcher thinks in terms of a community of scholars beyond the walls of his or her own institution, and engages that community over time, we think the work done will enhance the lifelong career of the individual. Junior researchers who work in cultures that support this ethic, in which senior colleagues act as champions and sponsors who create and maintain space for good work to be done, are likely to find the choice to do what is interesting a relatively straightforward decision— as did those in this volume.

We have recommended that junior researchers be given more time to do their work. We realize that this suggestion then shifts the burden of carrying out institutional duties to senior scholars, whom we identified earlier as being already overloaded and having to cope with the fragmentation of their time. Perhaps the most important consideration that must be addressed systemically in universities that desire exemplary research from more established scholars is the way they draw on the time resources of these investigators. It is not clear that much thought is given by those who administer university systems to the best use of the time of senior researchers. They are often seen as a sunk cost, a resource to be used indiscriminately across the activities that must be done for an organization to function. In these situations faculty are expected to serve on too many committees, are asked to administer too many programs, and are expected to meet the needs of too many different constituents for any serious time to be allocated to exemplary research. Granted, some of the more resource-rich universities do not use their faculties in this way. Also, where they are provided frequently and with funding, sabbatical leaves create space and time for scholars to work on their research. It should be remembered, however, that exemplary research, as we have found in the cases presented here, takes long blocks of time and involves persistence, concentration, and immersion. If university systems face the reality of such requirements and acknowledge the range and diversity of the demands placed on senior faculty, there may be opportunities to give more systematic and enlightened attention to the use of faculty time.

We are not in a position to suggest what specifically might be done at given universities. We believe a survey of how different universities deal with the matter is perhaps timely. Senior scholars themselves face the hard task of "herding their horses," of focusing and concentrating and managing the activities they undertake if they wish to create conditions for doing exemplary research. They also need to influence the system to take the matter seriously.

In general, we expect the time pressures to grow more acute before they are brought under control (if they ever are). We worry about what these time constraints do to the quality of research in the field as well as the quality of the lives of the researchers themselves. We worry about increasing amounts of research done mindlessly and frantically, as researchers find themselves in an activity trap, chasing knowledge to meet extrinsic pressures. We worry about what the emphasis on research does to attention to teaching, to the balance between generation and communication of knowledge. We have little to say about teaching here, except in a later section when we talk about the apprenticeship aspect of research. However, we believe that teaching is a vital part of the role of the researcher. It is a deserving topic for another book.

We think that the way the various researchers in this volume appear to have created time for themselves, and the way they appear to have worked as if time were not a major constraint, provides some encouragement for those who wish to do good research work.

REMOVING THE BARRIERS TO IMMERSION

In our opinion, one way to increase the attention researchers give to the importance of getting their hands dirty when conducting their studies is to make it a valued and practical feature of the training we give to those who are learning the craft. All research students need to make incursions into the laboratory, into the field, into the literature, as well as into instrument construction and data analysis. They need to develop themselves as instruments of research so as to be open to observation and discovery of unexpected or novel occurrences in themselves and in the data. They need to learn that interaction with the phenomenon of interest is a blend of inner intuitions and outer contacts with whatever is being treated as data and that iterations between themselves and data lead to insight and understanding. Only with the experience of "doing it" will the lessons of the classroom truly make sense.

In various ways the researchers in this book model these aspects of immersion. Gersick temporarily forgot about the model she was to use in the project for Hackman and made her initial breakthroughs on group development. Sutton and Rafaeli went beyond the inherited data set to get at the relationship between emotion and performance. Latham, Erez, and Locke painstakingly reconstructed the scripts used by investigators to study goal setting and discovered the root of some differences in the behavior of subjects. Baron, Dobbin, and Jennings extensively worked and reworked the secondary data in their study to understand internal labor market relationships. Barley, Meyer, and Gash started from scratch and constructed their own coding system. Meyer resisted the temptation to use survey questionnaires on subjects who had information best revealed through interviews. Jermier wrestled with words to form affective and authentic representations of worker alienation.

THE CONTRIBUTIONS OF MENTORS
TO EXEMPLARY RESEARCH

Teaching students to do exemplary research goes well beyond formal courses. It is a craft that must be learned through doing. It is an apprenticeship, and those who teach the craft play a vital role in the system. We think more attention should be given to developing "doing" experiences throughout the research curriculum, for both undergraduate and graduate students.

An example or two from teaching decisions we have made in response to the material in this book will illustrate what we mean. In the past, we taught research by starting with the philosophy of science, moving to critique of the literature, and ending with an empirical project. Now the order is reversed. To supplement the scant research experience of undergraduates we have found the case section of this book valuable, as well. Students who have already grappled with data and computers are no longer fazed by novel statistical techniques in reading the literature. By the time we start to discuss research from a sociological and philosophical perspective, they have begun to develop for themselves some notions of the research enterprise. While they still object to Lakatos's (1970) vocabulary, there are fewer uncomprehending glares and challenges of "What's the point?" A second change, sparked by the junior author accounts of their publication experiences, has been the incorporation of a review process of research student assignments with an expectation to revise based on our editorial comments.

Currently, most students experience mentorship in the formal dissertation adviser relationship. Gersick expresses gratitude for the way Hackman helped her create and produce her study:

From the start, Richard had treated me as a skilled colleague. Being his research assistant did not mean making photocopies or executing detailed instructions. I had lots of room to find my own way and develop my own ideas. This did take me, temporarily, "off the track" for purposes of his research. However, I had plenty of good data to use for the observational tool (I did eventually come up with something Richard liked), and the independence I had been given allowed me to make some unexpected discoveries. I was also fortunate to have—after a short delay—Richard's support and interest in my ideas. With his encouragement, I decided to pursue my vague findings, study two more teams on my own, and write a technical report on the four observations.

Later, Hackman became more involved in her work:

Three years after my first group observation, I was ready to pull all eight case studies together and develop my ideas about the midpoint transition—which I had made the focus of the dissertation. At this stage, meetings with Richard became especially important. He had warned me at the start that he wasn't one who believed "it's only a dissertation, just get it done," and that he had come to expect to clash with students, sooner or later, over how much was "enough." I thought this was fine. I was obsessed with the work, and sufficiently idealistic to assume that my chairman should take it seriously.

Given this combination of perfectionists, my dissertation ended up taking a lot of Richard's time. I would draft a chapter, and we would talk about it. He shared my enthusiasm, asked excellent questions, and was especially good at catching "sloppy thinking." His criticisms and questions almost always looked *right* to me—one reason the work was so much fun despite its difficulty. (I think some students feel they have to struggle with their advisers—I felt my adviser was helping me struggle with the material.) Another reason was that Richard was much more likely to ask questions than to suggest answers. He didn't take over.

One way that he did exert strong influence was in his effort to persuade me to get "conceptual." He would ask me why some group behaved as it had, and I would start describing the specifics of what happened, for example, between Sandra and Bernard at the first meeting. "But you've got to go *beyond* that!" he would say. I didn't know what he was getting at, and he, meanwhile, expressed doubts about pushing me to do something I hadn't automatically chosen myself. After a while, I finally understood, and it was an invaluable lesson in how to build abstract theory—not just interesting stories—from qualitative data.

Other researchers in this book received direct mentoring from senior colleagues at their first jobs, as Alan Meyer did from Bill Starbuck. We would argue that, in part, Locke was mentoring when he mediated the study done by Latham and Erez.

The essence of this relationship between mentor and student is caught very well by Stephen Jay Gould (1989) in his book *Wonderful Life*:

> At some point, you just can't proceed any further with courses and books; you have to hang around someone who is doing research well. (And you need to be on hand, and ready to assimilate, all the time, every day; you just can't show up on Thursday afternoon at two for a lesson in separating parts from counterparts.) The system does produce its horrors—exploitive professors who divert the flow of youthful brilliance and enthusiasm into their own dry wells, and provide nothing in return. But when it works (as it does more often than a cynic might expect, given the lack of checks and balances), I cannot imagine a better training. (p. 139)

Doing Research Ethically

Inevitably, there are issues of conscience that researchers must face, as they initiate and proceed with their work. Matters of ethics are discussed in most contemporary research methods texts. However, it is rare that one has the opportunity to share with researchers the emotional and intellectual unfolding of researchers' experiences as they wrestle with the question of what is the right thing to do at different junctures of their work. While ethical issues are raised directly in only one of the reflections in our set, that by Sutton and

Rafaeli, their story is illuminating in what it suggests to us about the way to do research ethically.

Their confrontation with ethical issues came when their study was fairly far advanced. They had established the hypothesis they wished to test about emotion in the workplace, "collected" their data (a data set already compiled by their colleague Larry), and run their analyses. The dilemma surfaced for them when the results of their analysis produced the exact opposite finding to what they had hypothesized. They report having several reactions to this result. Initially, there seems to have been a stage of denial. They avoided each other, atypical behavior for them. In a mood of denial, they went back to scale construction, to the raw data, to different regressions, to try to get the result they sought, in search of one variable that might save the paper. Later, they became angry, Bob accusing Larry of sending them data that were reverse scored as a result of a coding error. Depression seemed to follow denial and anger. There is something in their progression of the apparently typical cycle of responses that people experience in the face of trauma (Kübler-Ross, 1970):

> We were soon convinced that the data were right and that our hypothesis was wrong. We began to talk seriously about giving up the paper, and were so depressed that we talked a bit about abandoning future research on expressed emotion. Anat even had private thoughts about turning motherhood into a full-time career.

Thus far, the researchers' experience had not involved explicit ethical decisions. However, the strong emotional responses a researcher experiences when faced with findings that can make or break a product may provide a condition in which he or she is tempted to tamper with findings or research questions initially asked in a study. After all, in the life of professional researchers, empirical studies serve not only to create knowledge. They are also the hard currency with which researchers negotiate their careers, and often play an important role in the construction of personal identity and self-esteem. Sutton and Rafaeli make the ethical issue explicit:

> Our initial inclination was to change the introduction so that it proposed new hypotheses that fit the data. We were disturbed by the prospect of writing a paper that did not reflect the process by which we had conducted our research, but we also had begun to learn an unstated, but powerful, occupational norm: When your hypotheses aren't confirmed, you don't admit it, you change the hypotheses in your introduction to fit the data. We had learned this lesson from conversations with more

experienced colleagues and from suggestions made by anonymous reviewers of our papers. We also learned that this practice is not limited
to the so-called soft sciences. When Bob described it to a friend who was
a genetics researcher, he replied "Of course, we always write our hypotheses after we get our results. It is more efficient that way!"

Sutton and Rafaeli resolved the ethical dilemma in favor of staying
with their initial premise. They give two reasons for doing so. One is
pragmatic: They did not want to look foolish. To change their hypotheses would be to deny the authenticity of their previous work on
emotion. The second reason they call "noble": "We wanted to write a
paper that reflected the process by which we had actually learned
about expressed emotions."

It is interesting to note that their decision apparently served to
transform their thinking about the research topic. It seemed also to
regenerate their creativity with respect to ways to proceed with the
study. In a sense, the cost of being ethical *in this case* was minimal. The
benefits to the researchers of the decision were considerable.

If we examine the research endeavors of the other authors in our set,
we see that in several cases, the work done involved immersion in the
data in ways that involved rethinking, reworking, and essentially
changing hypotheses about the phenomena under investigation. This
was the case in the Gersick study, in Alan Meyer's work, and very
explicitly in the Baron, Dobbin, and Jennings investigation. Were these
research projects then conducted unethically? The answer, in our
opinion, is an unequivocal no. The reason we raise the question here
is twofold. First, much of what is written about as research methods
in texts (and perhaps as they are taught in seminars on the topic) seems
to emphasize a strictly linear, "normal science" sequence of hypothesis
statement, data collection, data analysis, refutation or support of initial
hypotheses, and, finally, report and discussion of findings. What we
infer from all the studies in our set is that research rarely if ever plays
out in this straightforward way. It is a much messier process requiring multiple interventions and difficult decisions by the researchers.
Whether, as a researcher, one treats the hypotheses as the reference
point around which to make decisions to collect more data or one opts
to restate the original questions or propositions is a decision, or a series
of decisions, that has to be made on both practical and ethical grounds.

The ethical question to be answered here by the researchers is, Why
are you changing direction? If the reason given is that it is to increase
the probability of publication, to gain visibility, to win a prize or a
research contract or some other recognition, then the choice to proceed

in this way runs the risk of being unethical. The attention to extrinsic factors may (not must) lead to an attempt to fake the data, to distort the question, or to create a misleading presentation of the research that has been conducted.

Practically, the interaction of hypothesis and data leaves the researcher with interpretations and decisions to make about the meaning of the configurations he or she encounters. Deciding to change the question or to search for new data is then guided by a desire to know more about the phenomenon of interest. In this context, changing direction is a faithful adherence to the research process, not unethical behavior.

There are other ethical issues that are raised when one considers the way research is done in the organizational sciences. One pervasive issue is that of the rights of subjects in the studies being conducted. Most projects carried out in university settings (as well as through other organizational agencies) now require scrutiny of proposed techniques and instruments of research by ethics committees. To some extent such procedures can act to protect individuals from unnecessary intrusion on their privacy and on their rights as human beings. However, even with the existence of ethics screening committees, there remain major responsibilities on the shoulders of investigators when it comes to consideration of the kinds of research questions and practices that will be used in a given study.

When we are conducting research in organizations, it is usual that we study some stakeholders rather than every constituent group. Further, the findings of the research we do tend to benefit some stakeholders but may not benefit and may even harm other groups. What precautions might researchers need to think about that will protect subjects, and those in the larger context of society who are represented by the subjects, when the findings of their studies could be used by one group to control the lives of another? For example, manipulating the emotions of salesclerks may benefit managers; it may not benefit the clerks.

The more general issue is perhaps one that asks whether or not it is ethical to do research that might lead to a technology that alters people's emotions and/or their behavior in fundamental ways. We know there are no easy answers to this question. We believe that some acknowledgment is needed that there are costs as well as benefits to society when behavior in organizations is studied. Different stakeholders in organizations and in society may benefit or suffer differently as a result of the findings about behavior in and around organizations. Some accounting of the costs and benefits, in human terms, of such studies needs to be attempted and the reckonings ideally should be estimated before a study is launched, checked while the study is in progress, and assessed after it is over.

Given the differential distribution of resources and skills in society, some groups are in a better position to exploit research findings to forward their own positions vis-à-vis other groups (Lynd, 1939; Mills, 1959). Thus research produced with the purest of intentions may unintentionally serve powerful interests. This is a reality that every researcher, especially applied researchers, must take seriously. It is naive to dismiss these outcomes as unintended. They may be unintended, but they are predictable, even though the exact nature and extent of the appropriations is unknown in advance.

The implications of this research reality differ depending on the group membership and personal commitments of the researcher (Gouldner, 1979; Gramsci, 1971). For a researcher allied with the powerful, there is no problem. Others have adopted a variety of strategies to cope. In the extreme, we know individuals who have chosen not to pursue, or have discontinued, particular research activities. We know others who refuse to accept research consultations funded by organizations, based on the belief that such sponsors expect to gain advantage in one way or another. Some make sure that their findings and ideas are made accessible to less powerful groups. Some choose their research problems and projects carefully while acknowledging that there are no completely "safe" studies. Ultimately, this is a sensitive matter that the reflective researcher must address. There is also a role for the community of scholars in supporting the academic freedom of individuals who pursue unpopular research agendas.

One partial solution to the dilemma is for researchers to vary the focus they give to the groups of stakeholders and stakeholder perspectives relevant to their studies. Sutton and Rafaeli, for example, after completing their salesclerk study, began to ask themselves whether they had focused too much in their empirical work on expressed positive emotions and had neglected to attend to unpleasant emotions. For them, the question was one of incomplete coverage of emotions in their research. Sutton has since studied emotional issues connected with collecting bills from debtors. Rafaeli has studied emotions in the arena of paid interrogations and the extraction of confessions. Future research might consider more fully the costs and possible benefits of emotional displays by subordinates that accrue to the subordinates.

Several groups appear to be neglected in our research enterprises, including women (Tuma, 1989), nonwhites (Bell, 1989), and non-

Americans (Inkson, 1988). These and other less powerful groups, perspectives, and issues warrant our research attention.

In closing this section, we advocate that ethical questions be included in the routine repertoire of research questions investigators think about when initiating, conducting, and evaluating their studies. For example:

- Will this study harm any person or group of persons directly or indirectly?
- Who benefits and who does not benefit from this study?
- Does this study serve as a basis for empowering people and, if so, who benefits and who does not?

In addition, many professional associations provide their members with valuable ethical guidance (Academy of Management, 1990; American Anthropological Association, 1971; American Psychological Association, 1982; American Sociological Association, 1982).

We have used the Sutton and Rafaeli study to focus the discussion on ethical aspects of research. However, the points we are making are general ones. They apply to all the studies reported in this book, to the study of groups (Gersick), of doctors and hospital administrators (Meyer), of people's responses to goals (Latham, Erez, & Locke), of management consultants and academics (Barley, Meyer, & Gash), of personnel administrators and government agents (Baron, Dobbin, & Jennings), and of the thoughts and feelings of industrial workers (Jermier). They apply to all empirical research.

When Is Enough Enough?

We have celebrated the qualities of persistence, enthusiasm, and willingness to immerse themselves of all of the authors in this volume. Each in his or her own way overcame difficulties, discovered interesting things about the phenomena he or she was studying, and could sign off on projects that were quite successful. However, as one of our colleagues observed at a seminar in which we presented the ideas for this book, there may be a time when all the effort, desire, and familiarity with the subject matter fail to produce any significant insights or findings. Is there a point at which one should, in effect, throw in the towel—abandon the research and move on to something else? And if so, how does one know when to do this?

We think it likely that every researcher has had one or a number of projects that did not work out. In fact, to the extent that exemplary research is an entrepreneurial activity, one would expect the number of successful ventures by any one individual or team to be balanced or outweighed by the unsuccessful ones. In some cases, this means that nothing of significance emerged from the study. In other cases, it means that the study was never completed. We have no mechanisms in our research systems for recording the misses as it does the hits. Hits tend to be identified as published material. Misses rarely make it to publication. We might benefit as a scientific community if we had some way to know who else had tried to crack a particular question and why it did not work out. While we are already overwhelmed with information about the phenomena we study, there might well be benefits to future researchers of a repository, perhaps a computerized archive, of uncompleted or "failed" work that is organized so that we might learn from the efforts and contributions of others.

How does one know when to quit, to "fold the cards and walk away"? We know that there is no easy answer. Based on the ways researchers in this volume have described their experiences, we think that it is very difficult for anyone who cares about an idea and has invested large amounts of energy to let it go. The phenomenon of escalation of commitment to a project is probably very salient in research enterprises (Staw, 1981). The judgment comes down to the specifics of individual researchers and situations. Candid feedback from colleagues and gatekeepers can be helpful. It can also produce hurt feelings and a determination by the researcher to redouble efforts. Researchers might develop a checklist of indicators to test their lack of progress, for example:

- Is this project still fun to do?
- How much time have I actually invested in this project?
- Is this the best use of my time?
- Am I staying with this project out of a need to save face, through personal pride, or do I believe there is something here to pursue?

Perhaps the answer lies in having researchers pull back at different times during a project and ask not only the "should I continue?" question, but also, Have I become too narrow and fixed in the way I am pursuing this question? Stalled or failed research may be a function of a lack of creativity and flexibility in the way it is being conducted rather than an absence of substance in the topic being investigated. In turn, the inflexibility may be due to framing the unexpected in the research process as a threat that motivates a threat-rigidity cycle (Staw, Sandelands, & Dutton, 1981). Instead, the researcher may be able to reframe it as an opportunity that opens up inquiry. In such circumstances, the "small wins" strategy advocated by Weick (1984) may provide a fruitful avenue for incrementally applying renewed energy to the research.

The Sutton and Rafaeli study provides an example. Initially, the failure of the original hypothesis was viewed as a threat, yielding denial and repeated applications of the same response, as the researchers "tried again and again to run slightly different regressions." Reframing the unexpected finding as an opportunity to be explained opened Sutton and Rafaeli to a more sophisticated understanding of the research issue. A strategy of numerous small-scale attacks on the problem paid off.

When Gersick was stalled in getting her article accepted by a journal (it was "hanging by a thread"), she recalled the advice of Warren Bennis, to read Stephen Jay Gould's work. Openness to new inputs led her to the concept of "punctuated equilibrium" and an elegant theoretical explanation of her findings. This was an important influence on the later acceptance of her work at *AMJ*.

Meyer, similarly, was stimulated by feedback by Salancik at *ASQ* to reconsider the way he was conceptualizing his research findings. He was able to resolve difficulties others had pointed out in his work and to move the project to a successful conclusion. Baron, Dobbin, and Jennings's study and Latham, Erez, and Locke's study contain examples of stages in the research where the act of stepping back and reconsidering the methods, concepts, and/or findings provided fresh ways to tackle problems and enabled the investigators to complete their work.

The Impact of Research

We have identified seven studies in this volume as examples of good research. We have focused on the process of research rather than the products. However, the commentators have identified the individual contributions of each product. Our exemplars are limited to seven empirical organizational research articles published in journals in the decade of the 1980s. Clearly this is a small, biased sample. We think it is useful, nevertheless, to use this sample to ponder the kinds of contributions to scholarship such research makes.

Research, in our opinion, is only possible insofar as it builds on, or responds to, the existing body of research. Research is exemplary only insofar as it motivates further building, or reaction. Elegant methodology alone cannot qualify work as exemplary. In a letter to us in December 1988, John Van Maanen made similar observations about exemplary research. He expressed this view:

> I simply don't believe that there is any such notion of the crucial experiment or pathbreaking study in the social sciences—each work is connected to a larger body (both the authors and the fields) and the cumulative effect of a stream of work, or development of a theory circle influences the field, not a single work and certainly not the single article.

We should not be loading too many expectations onto any one research study.

One might distinguish the contribution of an individual research article on several, overlapping dimensions by identifying the study's relationship to the literature. The contribution can be the extent to which the study sheds light on a focused question related to an established theoretical domain. The Latham, Erez, and Locke study falls into this category. It addresses the matter of what kind of goal setting leads individuals to commit to a task and to perform at a high level. Similarly, the Sutton and Rafaeli investigation asks whether positive emotions lead to higher sales in convenience stores.

Second, contribution might mean the way in which research adds to the development of new theory in a particular area of the field. Gersick's model of group development is one such study. Meyer's study of hospitals is another in this vein. It contributes to our understanding of organizational functioning under the strain of environmental shock.

A third dimension of contribution is the degree to which a study helps illuminate or resolve debates between two or more theories or approaches to explaining phenomena. The Baron, Dobbin, and Jennings investigation of the evolution of modern personnel administration in U.S. industry fits into this category. The authors compare and test competing Marxist and bureaucratic interpretations of the development of modern organizations. Jermier uses three different conceptions of work in organizations—traditional organizational theory, critical theory, and dialectical Marxist theory—to explore workers' consciousness. Barley, Meyer, and Gash also fit in this category. They were interested in the ideologies behind management and academic discussions of corporate culture and investigated the direction of influences between the two groups' intellectual effort devoted to the topic.

A different notion of contribution is the degree to which a study has an impact on the human condition. Do the findings of the study lead significantly toward ideas, movements, or practices that make the world a safer, more emancipated, qualitatively better place in which to live? We do not believe that any of the studies in this volume belong in this category, in the sense that their results are sufficiently significant theoretically or practically to allow them to qualify. We think it is rare that any *one* research study has this kind of impact. It is usually through a series of studies by one or more investigators that such an outcome may eventuate. Moreover, work that in its reporting is confined to the page limits of a journal is unlikely to give authors the scope to convey ideas and findings on the scale we are talking about here.

Nevertheless, we do believe that the research programs to which these studies relate have the potential to help or harm the human condition. As discussed in the section on ethics above, we think that it is appropriate for researchers to include evaluation of a project's impact on this criterion in allocating their research time.

Our general discussion of impact has been brief because the contribution of an individual study happens mostly through its influence within a stream of research. The commentators have discussed this contribution for each case in Part I. A final evaluation of impact will require a longer time frame to allow the findings and ideas of these authors to be assimilated, interpreted, and critiqued within the overall development of the relevant research programs.

At the End of the Journey

We started out with some vague hunches and enthusiasms about doing a book on research in organizational studies. We initially thought about examining the latest methods used in empirical research. We changed our focus to the process through which empirical research is done. The body of work we have presented here is about doing research, not about particular studies and their findings. We repeat a statement we made earlier in the book: These are not necessarily the best research products of the 1980s. We do not know how one can categorically make the call that a particular piece of work is the best of its time, given the diversity of perspectives and practices that characterize a field and the uncertainty of a study's influence over time.

What we have tried to present to the reader is a series of case studies, stories, and interpretations of good research process, as told by the authors themselves. With the appropriate cautions about selective memories, social reconstructions, and so on, we think the result is interesting, provocative, and sometimes surprising. Textbooks tend to stereotype or idealize the research process. Novice researchers can blindly adopt this model and wonder at the demands it makes on their capacity and foresight. Even experienced researchers sometimes adopt this idealization if they do not think carefully about how they and their colleagues actually do research. The reports in this book tend to contradict the ideal, in the sense that they reveal the process as a human one. The research process characterized here is subject to serendipity as well as to plans. It is an imprecise, creative craft that takes time and requires perseverance. Researchers muck about in the ideas, methods, and data; they handle their own rats; they make tough decisions. They must communicate clearly and write well. Research harnesses and stimulates a range of responses and energies, blurring the boundaries of the emotional and the intellectual. The research process is social. It requires the collaboration, supportiveness, and discipline of a community of scholars and friends to whom researchers can and should turn for guidance and feedback. The research process is physical. It is embodied in personal careers and lives, conference interactions, telephone calls, and journal pages. It is our hope that the lessons these authors have shared with us will help demystify some of the activities in the research process and will stimulate readers in their own work.

One of our colleagues who received a Ph.D. a few years ago recently read some of the cases in this volume. She commented that what she had thought was her unique experience of frustration, pain, and delay, as well as of the joys of research, seemed to be more a shared experience inherent in the research process underlying the events described in these accounts. She expressed a feeling of relief. She observed that if this is the way good research can be done, then one can be freed from the tyranny of having to match the ideal image of research as an orderly, trouble-free, and unemotional undertaking.

We began the case section of this book with an exemplar that studied social and political influences on the way organizational researchers frame their models and their studies. We ended with an exemplar that used a short story to convey the meaning of ideas and data. Both approaches take seriously the social construction of knowledge in research communities. This understanding of knowledge building underpins our approach to research. Thus when trying to understand the process of producing good research, we looked to the social consensus of scholars, especially that of established, influential scholars. We consulted journals known for their rigorousness of peer review and a nominator panel of gatekeepers when identifying the exemplary cases featured here. We asked established scholars to comment on these papers.

Clearly, this strategy has a conservative bias. It favors the opinions of those who have succeeded in the past, those who have a vested interest in the existing body of knowledge. This bias reflects our understanding of the nature of the research enterprise. Contributions to knowledge can be identified only in reference to the existing knowledge base. Those who claim to produce new knowledge must gain the acceptance of the scholarly community for their claims.

It is to be hoped that the scholarly community is committed to a developing and increasing knowledge base, but this commitment is conservatively biased. The community is not motivated to accept novel understandings for their own sake, but it is motivated to seek and recognize *better* understandings.

How do the scholars recognize the difference between better and simply different? The answer centers on the credibility of the new offering, which brings us back to the conservative bias. Credibility is established by reference to the "conventional wisdom" as embodied in either the existing literature base of theory and results or the use of established methods that are presumed to contain built-in protection from faulty findings, but deciding on "better" is never just a rational, intellectual judgment by the community. Ideas, movements, and groups with power tend to shape what is constructed as the conventional realities in which research efforts are embedded.

As the exemplars in this book demonstrate, the scholarly community and the conventional wisdom are not static and unyielding. In fact, we believe that most scholars welcome challenges. But it is probably true that it is more difficult for those who challenge entrenched interests, established theories, textbook methods, or standard presentations to gain acceptance for their contributions.

We have ended the exemplars section with the piece by Jermier because, more clearly than any of the others, his publication confronts the idea that research, as Smircich puts it, is *literature*. We argue that it is useful to think about all research reports as literature. We think that the exemplars and the commentaries by the authors of the exemplars are literature, are stories, are fiction (Latour & Woolgar, 1979). This is not a criticism. Nor is it praise. It is simply a way of recognizing and representing the work that they and we do. Smircich observes:

Empirical researchers—whatever their paradigmatic persuasions—
attempt to translate a reality "outside" to the "inside" of a text. They
fashion symbols on a page for a reader, who through the activity of
reading makes "reality" present again. This view of the nature of research points to the ways we construct knowledge in texts—and to the
unspoken agreements between writers and readers about what will
"pass" as knowledge. This view suggests that the credibility and "goodness" of a piece of empirical research depend not only on the activities
of writers, as some observe (Van Maanen, 1988), but on the activities of
readers as well (Calas & Smircich, 1988).

Our earlier cautions about taking into account that the commentaries are retrospective reconstructions are meaningful in the sense that
they alert us to watch for statements that might "idealize" the research
process when it is recalled. Similarly, we have criticized traditional
descriptions of the research process as idealizations. Surely, in this final
chapter we have idealized the research process, too. If we take seriously the notion that researchers are constructing a fiction, whether it
be according to predetermined scripts set by the profession and produced between the covers of a journal or, according to more flexible
frameworks, such as happens in books, then we are more easily able
to see the interaction we, as researchers, have with the work we create
and do. We can more easily ask questions "about how we see and about
how we judge knowledge [and] in so doing . . . learn about ourselves
as a community of readers and writers" (Smircich, this volume).

Our hope is that this journey we have undertaken, with the authors
and commentators whom you have read here as our guides, serves as
a stimulus for you the reader to enrich your own journey, whether it
be in your role as researcher, as teacher, or as evaluator or in some other
role that is available to you as a member of the community of scholars.

We end with an image, one that evokes more than we can say about
the research process. It captures the simultaneous funneling inward to
the world of ideas and feelings and opening outward into the world
of "facts." The research journey is a spiral dance that constitutes both
the research and the researcher. Let us dance together, doing exemplary research.

Drawing by Johannes Richter.

Appendix: Exemplars of Organizational Research— Nominations

Barley, S. R. (1983). Semiotics and the study of occupational and organizational cultures. *Administrative Science Quarterly, 28,* 393-414.

Barley, S. R. (1986). Technology as an occasion for structuring: Evidence from observations of CT scanners and the social order of radiology departments. *Administrative Science Quarterly, 31,* 78-108.

Barley, S. R., Meyer, G. W., & Gash, D. C. (1988). Cultures of culture: Academics, practitioners and the pragmatics of normative control. *Administrative Science Quarterly, 33,* 24-60.

Baron, J. N., & Bielby, W. T. (1984). The organization of work in a segmented economy. *American Sociological Review, 49,* 454-473.

Baron, J. N., Dobbin, F. R., & Jennings, P. D. (1986). War and peace: The evolution of modern personnel administration in U.S. industry. *American Journal of Sociology, 92,* 350-383.

Bartunek, J. M. (1984). Changing interpretive schemes and organizational restructuring. *Administrative Science Quarterly, 29,* 355-372.

Bielby, W. T., & Baron, J. N. (1986). Men and women at work: Sex segregation and statistical discrimination. *American Journal of Sociology, 91,* 759-799.

Carroll, G. R. (1985). Concentration and specialization: Dynamics of niche width in populations of organizations. *American Journal of Sociology, 90,* 1262-1283.

Editors' Note: Some nominations included books and journal articles published prior to 1980. They are not included here.

Connolly, T., & Wholey, D. R. (1988). Information mispurchase in judgment tasks: A task-driven causal mechanism. *Organizational Behavior and Human Decision Making Processes, 42*, 75-87.

Dougherty, T. W., Ebert, R. J., & Callender, J. C. (1986). Policy capturing in the employment interview. *Journal of Applied Psychology, 71*, 9-15.

Eisenhardt, K. M., & Bourgeois, L. J. (1988). Politics of strategic decision making in high-velocity environments: Toward a midrange theory. *Academy of Management Journal, 31*, 737-770.

Freeman, J., Carroll, G. R., & Hannan, M. T. (1983). Age dependence in organizational death rates. *American Sociological Review, 48*, 692-710.

Gersick, C. J. G. (1988). Time and transition in work teams: Toward a new model of group development. *Academy of Management Journal, 31*, 9-41.

Greenwood, R., & Hinings, R. (1988). Organizational design, types, tracks and the dynamics of strategic change. *Organizational Studies, 9*, 293-316.

Gronn, P. C. (1983). Talk as the work. *Administrative Science Quarterly, 28*, 1-21.

Harris, S. G., & Sutton, R. I. (1983). Functions of parting ceremonies in dying organizations. *Academy of Management Journal, 29*, 5-30.

Harvey, R. J., Billings, R. S., & Nilan, K. J. (1985). Confirmatory factor analysis of the job diagnostic survey: Good news and bad news. *Journal of Applied Psychology, 70*, 461-468.

Hirsch, P. M. (1986). From ambushes to golden parachutes: Corporate takeovers as an instance of cultural framing and institutional integration. *American Journal of Sociology, 91*, 800-837.

Hulin, C. L., Drasgow, F., & Komocar, J. (1982). Applications of item response theory to analysis of attitude scale translations. *Journal of Applied Psychology, 67*, 818-825.

Isenberg, D. J. (1986). Thinking and managing: A verbal protocol analysis of managerial problem solving. *Academy of Management Journal, 29*, 775-788.

Jermier, J. M. (1985). "When the sleeper wakes": A short story extending themes in radical organization theory. *Journal of Management, 2*, 67-80.

Latham, G. P., Erez, M., & Locke, E. A. (1988). Resolving scientific disputes by the joint design of crucial experiments by the antagonists: Application to the Erez-Latham dispute regarding participation in goal setting. *Journal of Applied Psychology, 73*, 753-772.

Luthans, F., Paul, R., & Baker, D. (1981). An experimental analysis of the impact of contingent reinforcement on salespersons' performance behavior. *Journal of Applied Psychology, 66,* 314-323.

March, J., & Feldman, M. S. (1981). Information in organizations as sign and symbol. *Administrative Science Quarterly, 26,* 171-186.

Martin, J., Brickman, P., & Murray, A. (1984). Moral outrage and pragmatism: Explanations for collective behavior. *Journal of Experimental Social Psychology, 20,* 484-496.

Martin, J., Feldman, M. S., Hatch, M. J., & Sitkin, S. B. (1983). The uniqueness paradox in organizational stories. *Administrative Science Quarterly, 28,* 438-453.

McPherson, M. (1983). An ecology of affiliation. *American Sociological Review, 48,* 519-532.

Meyer, A. D. (1982). Adapting to environmental jolts. *Administrative Science Quarterly, 27,* 515-537.

Miller, K. I., & Monge, P. R. (1987). The development and test of a system of organizational participation and allocation. In M. McLaughlin (Ed.), *Communication yearbook 10* (pp. 431-455). Newbury Park, CA: Sage.

Mintzberg, H., & Waters, J. A. (1982). Tracking strategy in an entrepreneurial firm. *Academy of Management, 3,* 465-499.

Mumby, D. (1987). The political function of narrative in organizations. *Communication Monographs, 54,* 113-127.

Pasmore, W., & Friedlander, F. (1982). An action-research program for increasing employee involvement in problem solving. *American Sociological Quarterly, 27,* 343-362.

Pearlman, K., Schmidt, F. L., & Hunter, J. E. (1980). Validity generalization results for tests used to predict job proficiency and training success in clerical occupations. *Journal of Applied Psychology, 65,* 373-406.

Pierce, J. L., Gardner, D. G., Cummings, L. L., & Dunham, R. D. (1989). Organization-based self-esteem: Construct definition, operationalization and validation. *Academy of Management Journal, 32,* 622-648.

Ross, J., & Staw, B. M. (1986). Expo 86: An escalation prototype. *American Sociological Quarterly, 31,* 274-297.

Schall, M. (1983). A communication-rules approach to organizational culture. *Administrative Science Quarterly, 28,* 557-581.

Smith, K. K., & Simmons, V. M. (1983). A Rumpelstiltskin organization. *Administrative Science Quarterly, 28,* 377-392.

Sutton, R. I., & Rafaeli, A. (1988). Untangling the relationship between displayed emotions and organizational sales: The case of convenience stores. *Academy of Management Journal, 31,* 461-487.

Swindler, A. (1986). Culture in action: Symbols and strategies. *American Sociological Review, 51,* 273-286.

Tetrick, L. E., & LaRocco, J. M. (1987). Understanding, prediction, and control as moderators of the relationship between perceived stress, satisfaction, and psychological well-being. *Journal of Applied Psychology, 72,* 538-543.

Tolbert, P. S. (1985). Resource dependence and institutional environments: Sources of administrative structure in institutions of higher education. *Administrative Science Quarterly, 30,* 1-13.

Tolbert, P. S., & Zucker, L. G. (1983). Institutional sources of change in the formal structure of organizations: The diffusion of civil service reform, 1880-1935. *American Sociological Quarterly, 28,* 22-39.

Weick, K. (1990). The vulnerable system: An analysis of the Tenerife air disaster. *Journal of Management, 16,* 571-593. (Note: This was nominated as an article accepted for publication in 1989.)

References

Academy of Management. (1990). The Academy of Management Code of Ethical Conduct. *Academy of Management Journal, 33*, 901-908.

Adorno, T. W. (1973). *Negative dialectics.* New York: Seabury. (Original work published 1966)

Alderfer, C. P. (1977). Group and intergroup relations. In J. R. Hackman & J. L. Suttle (Eds.), *Improving life at work* (pp. 227-296). Santa Monica, CA: Goodyear.

American Anthropological Association. (1971). *Principles of professional responsibility.* Washington, DC: Author.

American Psychological Association. (1973). *Code of ethics of the American Psychological Association.* Washington, DC: Author.

American Psychological Association, Committee for the Protection of Human Participants in Research. (1982). *Ethical principles.* Washington, DC: Author.

American Sociological Association. (1982). *Code of ethics.* Washington, DC: Author.

Ash, M. K. (1984). *Mary Kay on people management.* New York: Warner.

Ashby, W. R. (1960). *Design for a brain.* London: Chapman & Hall.

Astley, W. G., & Van de Ven, A. H. (1983). Central perspectives and debates in organization theory. *Administrative Science Quarterly, 28*, 245-273.

Baker, E. L. (1980). Managing organizational culture. *Management Review, 69*, 8-13.

Bandura, A. (1977). *Social learning theory.* Englewood Cliffs, NJ: Prentice-Hall.

Baritz, L. (1960). *The servants of power.* Minneapolis: Greenwood.

Barley, S. R., Meyer, G. W., & Gash, D. C. (1988). Cultures of culture: Academics, practitioners and the pragmatics of normative control. *Administrative Science Quarterly, 33*, 24-60.

Baron, J. N., & Bielby, W. T. (1980). Bringing the firm back in: Stratification, segmentation, and the organization of work. *American Sociological Review, 45*, 737-765.

Baron, J. N., Dobbin, F. R., & Jennings, P. D. (1986). War and peace: The evolution of modern personnel administration in U.S. industry. *American Journal of Sociology, 92*, 350-383.

Baron, J. N., Dobbin, F. R., & Jennings, P. D. (1988). Rome wasn't built in a day: Reply to Denk. *American Journal of Sociology, 93*, 1231-1234.

Baron, J. N., Jennings, P. D., & Dobbin, F. R. (1988). Mission control? The development of personnel systems in U.S. industry. *American Sociological Review, 53*, 497-514.

Baron, J. N., Mittman, B., & Newman, A. (1991). Targets of opportunity: Organizational and environmental determinants of gender integration within the California civil service, 1979-1985. *American Journal of Sociology, 96*, 1362-1401.

Baron, J. N., & Newman, A. (1990). For what it's worth: Differences across organizations, occupations, and the value of work done by women and nonwhites. *American Sociological Review, 55,* 155-175.

Bass, B. M. (1982). *Stogdill's handbook of leadership.* New York: Free Press.

Bass, B. M. (1985). *Leadership and performance beyond expectations.* New York: Free Press.

Becker, H. (1986). *Writing for social scientists.* Chicago: University of Chicago Press.

Bell, E. L. (1989). Racial and ethnic diversity: The void in organizational behavior courses. *Organizational Behavior Teaching Review, 13*(4), 56-67.

Ben-David, J., & Sullivan, T. A. (1975). Sociology of science. *Annual Review of Sociology, 1,* 203-222.

Benson, J. K. (1977). Organizations: A dialectical view. *Administrative Science Quarterly, 22,* 1-21.

Berg, D. N., & Smith, K. K. (Eds.). (1988). *The self in social inquiry.* Newbury Park, CA: Sage.

Berger, P., & Pullman, S. (1965). Reification and the sociological critique of consciousness. *History and Theory, 4,* 195-208.

Beyer, J. M. (1981). Ideologies, values and decision making in organizations. In P. C. Nystrom & W. H. Starbuck (Eds.), *Handbook of organizational design* (Vol. 2, pp. 166-202). New York: Oxford University Press.

Beyer, J. M. (1982). Introduction. In J. M. Beyer (Ed.), The utilization of organizational research [Special issue]. *Administrative Science Quarterly, 27,* 588-590.

Beyer, J. M. (1985). From the editor. *Academy of Management Journal, 28,* 5-8.

Beyer, J. M., & Trice, H. M. (1982). The utilization process: A conceptual framework and synthesis of empirical findings. In J. M. Beyer (Ed.), The utilization of organizational research [Special issue]. *Administrative Science Quarterly, 27,* 591-622.

Bielby, W., & Baron, J. (1986). Men and women at work: Sex segregation and statistical discrimination. *American Journal of Sociology, 91,* 759-799.

Billings, R. S., Milburn, T. W., & Schaalman, M. L. (1980). A model of crisis perception: A theoretical and empirical analysis. *Administrative Science Quarterly, 25,* 300-316.

Blau, P. M. (1970). A formal theory of differentiation in organizations. *American Sociological Review, 35,* 201-218.

Blau, P. M., & Schoenherr, R. A. (1971). *The structure of organizations.* New York: Basic Books.

Bodenheimer, T. (1975). The malpractice blow-up. *Health Policy Advisory Center Bulletin, 64,* 12-15.

Boudon, R. (1979). *The logic of social action.* London: Routledge & Kegan Paul.

Bramel, D., & Friend, R. (1981). Hawthorne, the myth of the docile worker, and the class bias in psychology. *American Psychologist, 36,* 867-878.

Brandes, S. D. (1976). *American welfare capitalism, 1880-1940* (2nd ed.). Chicago: University of Chicago Press.

Braverman, H. (1974). *Labor and monopoly capital.* New York: Monthly Review Press.

Brecher, J., et al. (1983, August 22). Taking drugs on the job. *Newsweek.*

Bronner, S. E., & Kellner, D. M. (Eds.). (1989). *Critical theory and society.* New York: Routledge.

Brown, R. H. (1977). *A poetic for sociology.* Boston: Cambridge University Press.

Burrell, G., & Morgan, G. (1979). *Sociological paradigms and organizational analysis.* London: Gower.

Business Week. (1980, October 27). Corporate cultures: The hard-to-change values that spell success or failure. Pp. 148-160.

Calas, M. B., & Smircich, L. (1988). Reading leadership as a form of cultural analysis. In J. G. Hunt, B. R. Baliga, H. P. Dachler, & C. A. Schriesheim (Eds.), *Emerging leadership vistas* (pp. 201-228). Lexington, MA: Lexington.

Campbell, D. J., & Gingrich, K. F. (1986). The interactive effects of task complexity and participation on task performance: A field experiment. *Organizational Behavior and Human Decision Process, 38,* 162-180.

Campbell, D. T. (1979). Reforms as experiments. *American Psychologist, 24,* 409-429.

Campbell, J. P., Campbell, R. J., & Associates. (1988). *Productivity in organizations.* San Francisco: Jossey-Bass.

Campbell, J. P., Daft, R., & Hulin, C. (1982). *What to study: Generating and developing research questions.* Beverly Hills, CA: Sage.

Campbell, J. P., Dunnette, M. D., Lawler, E. E., & Weick, K. E. (1970). *Managerial behavior, performance, and effectiveness.* New York: McGraw-Hill.

Carlsmith, J. M., Collins, B. E., & Helmreich, R. L. (1966). Studies in forced compliance: 1. The effect of pressure for compliance on attitude change produced by face-to-face role playing and anonymous essay writing. *Journal of Personality and Social Psychology, 4,* 1-13.

Cherns, A. B. (1972). Models for the use of research. *Human Relations, 25,* 25-33.

Clark, B. R. (1972). The organizational saga in higher education. *Administrative Science Quarterly, 17,* 178-184.

Clawson, D. (1980). *Bureaucracy and the labor process.* New York: Monthly Review Press.

Clegg, S., & Dunkerley, D. (1980). *Organisation, class, and control.* London: Routledge & Kegan Paul.

Clifford, J., & Marcus, G. E. (Eds.). (1986). *Writing culture: The poetics and politics of ethnography.* Berkeley: University of California Press.

Cook, K. S., & Hegtvedt, K. (1983). Distributive justice, equity, and equality. *Annual Review of Sociology, 9,* 217-241.

Cook, T. D., & Campbell, D. T. (1979). *Quasi-experimentation: Design and analysis issues for field settings.* Chicago: Rand McNally.

Cooper, L. (1987). Louis Agassiz as a teacher. In R. C. Christiansen (Ed.), *Teaching and the case method: Text, cases and readings* (pp. 79-82). Boston: Harvard Business School.

Cooper, R., & Burrell, G. (1988). Modernism, postmodernism and organizational analysis: An introduction. *Organization Studies, 9,* 91-112.

Corwin, R. G., & Louis, K. S. (1982). Organizational barriers to the utilization of research. In J. M. Beyer (Ed.), The utilization of organizational research [Special issue]. *Administrative Science Quarterly, 27,* 623-640.

Crandall, R. (1986). Editorial: A new journal with real differences. *Journal of Social Behavior and Personality, 1,* 1-2.

Cronbach, L. J., & Meehl, P. E. (1955). Construct validity in psychological tests. *Psychological Bulletin, 52,* 281-302.

Crosby, F. J. (1976). A model of egoistical relative deprivation. *Psychological Review, 83,* 85-113.

Cummings, L. L., & Frost, P. J. (Eds.). (1985). *Publishing in the organizational sciences.* Homewood, IL: Irwin.

Cyert, R. M., & March, J. G. (1963). *A behavioral theory of the firm.* Englewood Cliffs, NJ: Prentice-Hall.

Czepiel, J. A., Solomon, M. R., & Surprenant, C. F. (Eds.). (1985). *The service encounter.* Lexington, MA: Lexington.

Daft, R. L. (1983). Learning the craft of organizational research. *Academy of Management Review, 8,* 539-546.

Davis, M. S. (1971). That's interesting! Towards a phenomenology of sociology and a sociology of phenomenology. *Philosophy of Social Science, 1,* 301-344.

Davis, R. C. (Ed.). (1986). *Contemporary literary criticism.* New York: Longman.

Deal, T. E., & Kennedy, A. A. (1982). *Corporate cultures.* Reading, MA: Addison-Wesley.

Denk, C. (1988). Many roads lead to Rome: Implications of heterogeneous diffusion for institutionalization and "internal imperatives." *American Journal of Sociology, 93,* 1224-1231.

Denzin, N. (1970). *The research act: A theoretical introduction to sociological methods.* Chicago: Aldine.

DiMaggio, P. J., & Powell, W. W. (1991). Introduction. In W. W. Powell & P. J. DiMaggio (Eds.), *The new institutionalism in organizational analysis.* Chicago: University of Chicago Press.

Dobbin, F. (1988). *The privatization of American social insurance: Organizations, fringe benefits and the state, 1920-1950.* Paper presented at the annual meetings of the American Sociological Association, Atlanta, GA.

Doeringer, P. B., & Piore, M. J. (1971). *Internal labor markets and manpower analysis.* Lexington, MA: D. C. Heath.

Donnellon, A., Gray, B., & Bougon, M. (1986). Communication, meaning, and organized action. *Administrative Science Quarterly, 31,* 43-55.

Dossett, D. L., Latham, G. P., & Mitchell, T. R. (1979). The effects of assigned versus participatively set goals, KR, and individual differences when goal difficulty is held constant. *Journal of Applied Psychology, 64,* 291-298.

Dunbar, R. L. M. (1983). Toward an applied administrative science. *Administrative Science Quarterly, 28,* 129-144.

Duncan, W. J. (1974). Transferring management theory to practice. *Academy of Management Journal, 17,* 724-738.

Eagleton, T. (1976). *Marxism and literary criticism.* Berkeley: University of California Press.

Edwards, M., Miller, J. D., & Schumacher, R. (1972). Classification of community hospitals by scope of services: Four indexes. *Health Services Research, 7,* 301-312.

Edwards, R. (1979). *Contested terrain: The transformation of the workplace in the twentieth century.* New York: Basic Books.

Ekman, P. (1980). Biological and cultural contributions to body and facial movement in the expression of emotion. In A. O. Rorty (Ed.), *Explaining emotions* (pp. 73-102). Berkeley: University of California Press.

Elbaum, B. (1984). The making and shaping of job and pay structures in the iron and steel industry. In P. Osterman (Ed.), *Internal labor markets* (pp. 71-108). Cambridge: MIT Press.

Eldredge, N., & Gould, S. J. (1972). Punctuated equilibria: An alternative to phyletic gradualism. In T. J. Schopf (Ed.), *Models in paleobiology* (pp. 82-115). San Francisco: Freeman, Cooper.

Erez, M. (1977). Feedback, a necessary condition for the goal setting-performance relationship. *Journal of Applied Psychology, 62,* 624-627.

Erez, M., & Arad, A. (1986). Participative goals setting: Social, motivational and cognitive factors. *Journal of Applied Psychology, 71,* 591-592.

Erez, M., & Earley, P. C. (1987). Comparative analysis of goal-setting strategies across culture. *Journal of Applied Psychology, 72,* 658-665.

Erez, M., Earley, P. C., & Hulin, C. L. (1985). The impact of participation on goal acceptance and performance: A two-step model. *Academy of Management Journal, 28*, 50-66.

Erez, M., & Kanfer, F. H. (1983). The role of goal acceptance in goal setting and task performance. *Academy of Management Review, 8*, 454-463.

Erez, M., & Zidon, I. (1984). Effect of goal acceptance on the relationship of goal difficulty to performance. *Journal of Applied Psychology, 69*, 69-78.

Evered, R., & Louis, M. R. (1981). Alternative perspectives in the organizational sciences: "Inquiry from the inside" and "inquiry from the outside." *Academy of Management Review, 5*, 385-395.

Farnham, A. (1989, December). The trust gap. *Torture*, pp. 56-78.

French, J. R. P., Kay, E., & Meyer, H. H. (1966). Participation and the appraisal system. *Human Relations, 19*, 3-20.

Frost, P. (1980). Toward a radical framework for practicing organization science. *Academy of Management Review, 5*, 501-507.

Geertz, C. (1980). Blurred genres: The refiguration of social thought. *American Scholar, 49*, 165-179.

Geertz, C. (1988). *Works and lives: The anthropologist as author.* Stanford, CA: Stanford University Press.

Gersick, C. J. G. (1988). Time and transition in work teams: Toward a new model of group development. *Academy of Management Journal, 31*, 9-41.

Gersick, C. J. G. (1989). Marking time: Predictable transitions in task groups. *Academy of Management Journal, 32*, 274-309.

Gersick, C. J. G. (1991). Revolutionary change theories: A multilevel exploration of the punctuated equilibrium paradigm. *Academy of Management Review, 16*, 10-36.

Gladstein, D. (1984). Groups in context: A model of task group effectiveness. *Administrative Science Quarterly, 29*, 499-517.

Goffman, E. (1959). *The presentation of self in everyday life.* Garden City, NY: Doubleday.

Goffman, E. (1969). *Strategic interaction.* Philadelphia: University of Pennsylvania Press.

Goldman, P. (1985). *Mainstream and critical perspectives on organizations: Shared and conflicting domains.* Unpublished manuscript, University of Oregon, Eugene, Department of Sociology.

Goldman, P., & Van Houten, D. R. (1977). Managerial strategies and the worker: A Marxist analysis of bureaucracy. *Sociological Quarterly, 18*, 108-115.

Goodstein, L. D., & Dovico, M. (1979). The decline and fall of the small group. *Journal of Applied Behavioral Science, 15*, 320-328.

Gordon, D. M., Edwards, R., & Reich, M. (1982). *Segmented work, divided workers.* London: Cambridge University Press.

Gould, S. J. (1980). *The panda's thumb.* New York: W. W. Norton.

Gould, S. J. (1989). *Wonderful life.* New York: W. W. Norton.

Gouldner, A. W. (1970). *The coming crisis of Western sociology.* New York: Basic Books.

Gouldner, A. W. (1979). *The future of intellectuals and the rise of the new class.* Oxford: Oxford University Press.

Graham, J. W., & Stablein, R. E. (1985). Newcomer's perspective on publishing in the organizational sciences. In L. L. Cummings & P. J. Frost (Eds.), *Publishing in the organizational sciences* (pp. 138-154). Homewood, IL: Irwin.

Gramsci, A. (1971). *Selections from the prison notebooks.* New York: International Publishers.

Gray, R. D. (1943). *Systematic wage administration in the Southern California aircraft industry* (Industrial Relations Monograph No. 7). New York: Industrial Relations Counselors.

Habermas, J. (1971). *Knowledge and human interests*. Boston: Beacon.

Hackman, J. R., & Oldham, G. R. (1980). *Work redesign*. Reading, MA: Addison-Wesley.

Hage, J., & Dewar, R. (1973). Elite values versus organizational structure in predicting innovation. *Administrative Science Quarterly, 18*, 279-290.

Hall, R. I. (1976). A system pathology of an organization: The rise and fall of the old *Saturday Evening Post. Administrative Science Quarterly, 21*, 185-210.

Hammond, P. E. (Ed.). (1964). *Sociologists at work*. New York: Basic Books.

Hannan, M. T., & Freeman, J. H. (1977). The population ecology of organizations. *American Journal of Sociology, 82*, 929-964.

Hannan, M. T., & Freeman, J. H. (1978). The population ecology of organizations. In Marshal W. Meyer & Associates (Eds.), *Environments and organizations* (pp. 131-172). San Francisco: Jossey-Bass.

Hannan, M. T., & Freeman, J. H. (1984). Structural inertia and organizational change. *American Sociological Review, 49*, 149-164.

Harris, S., & Sutton, R. I. (1986). Functions of parting ceremonies in dying organizations. *Academy of Management Journal, 29*, 5-30.

Hartman, E. M. (1988). *Conceptual foundations of organizational theory*. Cambridge, MA: Ballinger.

Hassard, J., & Pym, D. (Eds.). (1990). *The theory and philosophy of organizations*. London: Routledge.

Hedberg, B. (1981). How organizations learn and unlearn. In P. C. Nystrom & W. H. Starbuck (Eds.), *Handbook of organizational design* (Vol. 1, pp. 3-27). New York: Oxford University Press.

Heimer, C. A. (1985). Allocating information costs in a negotiated information order: Interorganizational constraints on decision making in Norwegian oil insurance. *Administrative Science Quarterly, 30*, 395-417.

Hirsch, P. (1987). *Pack your own parachute*. Reading, MA: Addison-Wesley.

Hochschild, A. R. (1979). Emotion work, feeling rules and social structure. *American Journal of Sociology, 85*, 551-575.

Hochschild, A. R. (1983). *The managed heart*. Berkeley: University of California Press.

Hofstede, G. (1980). *Culture's consequences*. Beverly Hills, CA: Sage.

Homans, G. (1961). *Social behavior: Its elementary forms*. New York: Harcourt, Brace & World.

Horkheimer, M. (1972). Traditional and critical theory. In M. Horkheimer, *Critical theory: Selected essays* (pp. 253-272). New York: Seabury. (Original work published 1937)

Horkheimer, M. (1974). *Eclipse of reason*. New York: Continuum. (Original work published 1947)

Horkheimer, M., & Adorno, T. W. (1972). *Dialectic of enlightenment*. New York: Seabury. (Original work published 1944)

Huber, G. P., & Daft, R. L. (1987). The information environments of organizations. In F. M. Jablin, L. L. Putnam, K. H. Roberts, & L. W. Porter (Eds.), *Handbook of organizational communication* (pp. 130-164). Newbury Park, CA: Sage.

Huse, E., & Cummings, T. (1985). *Organization development and change* (3rd ed.). Saint Paul, MN: West.

Inkson, K. (1988). Challenging hegemony in organizational behavior. *Organizational Behavior Teaching Review, 13*(1), 1-9.

Isaac, L. W., & Griffin, L. J. (1989). A historicism in time-series analyses of historical process: Critique, redirection, and illustrations from U.S. labor history. *American Sociological Review, 54*, 873-890.

Iser, W. (1978). *The act of reading*. Baltimore: Johns Hopkins University Press.

Israel, J. (1975). Alienation and reification. *Social Praxis, 3*, 40-57.

Jacoby, R. (1975). *Social amnesia.* Boston: Beacon.

Jacoby, S. M. (1983). Industrial labor mobility in historical perspective. *Industrial Relations, 22*, 261-281.

Jacoby, S. M. (1984). The development of internal labor markets in American manufacturing. In P. Osterman (Ed.), *Internal labor markets* (pp. 23-70). Cambridge: MIT Press.

Jacoby, S. M. (1985). *Employing bureaucracy: Managers, unions, and the transformation of work in American industry, 1900-1945.* New York: Columbia University Press.

Jaeger, G., & Selznick, P. (1964). A normative theory of culture. *American Sociological Review, 29*, 653-669.

Jauch, L. R., & Wall, J. L. (1989). What they do when they get your manuscript: A survey of Academy of Management reviewer practices. *Academy of Management Journal, 32*, 157-173.

Jennings, P. D., & Moore, L. (1990). *Does professionalizing HR pay? The importance of recognition for managerial earnings.* Paper submitted for presentation at the annual meetings of the Academy of Management.

Jermier, J. M. (1982). Infusion of critical social theory into organizational analysis: Implications for studies of work adjustment. In D. Dunkerley & G. Salaman (Eds.), *The international yearbook of organization studies 1981* (pp. 195-211). London: Routledge & Kegan Paul.

Jermier, J. M. (1985). "When the sleeper wakes": A short story extending themes in radical organization theory. *Journal of Management, 11*(2), 67-80.

Jick, T. D. (1979). Mixing qualitative and quantitative methods: Triangulation in action. *Administrative Science Quarterly, 24*, 602-611.

Jung, C. G. (1970). *Psychological reflections: A new anthology of his writings, 1905-1961.* Princeton, NJ: Princeton University Press.

Kahn, L. M. (1976). Internal labor markets: San Francisco longshoremen. *Industrial Relations, 15*, 333-337.

Kahn, R. L. (1981). *Work and health.* New York: John Wiley.

Kanfer, F. H. (1980). Self-management methods. In F. H. Kanfer & A. P. Goldstein (Eds.), *Helping people manage* (2nd ed., pp. 334-389). New York: Pergamon.

Kanter, R. M. (1977). *Men and women of the corporation.* New York: Basic Books.

Kidder, L. H. (1981). *Research methods in social relations* (4th ed.). New York: Holt, Rinehart & Winston.

King, N. (1970). Clarification and evaluation of the two factor theory of job satisfaction. *Psychological Bulletin, 74*, 18-31.

Kochan, T. A., & Capelli, P. (1984). The transformation of the industrial relations and personnel function. In P. Osterman (Ed.), *Internal labor markets* (pp. 133-162). Cambridge: MIT Press.

Krieger, S. (1979). Research and the construction of text. In N. Denzin (Ed.), *Studies in symbolic interactionism* (Vol. 2). Greenwich, CT: JAI.

Kroeber, A. L., & Parsons, T. (1958). The concepts of culture and of social system. *American Sociological Review, 23*, 582-583.

Kübler-Ross, E. (1970). *On death and dying.* New York: Macmillan.

Kuhn, T. S. (1962). *The structure of scientific revolutions.* Princeton, NJ: Princeton University Press.

Kuhn, T. S. (1970). *The structure of scientific revolutions* (2nd ed.). Chicago: University of Chicago Press.

Kunda, G. (1991). *Engineering culture: Control and commitment in a high tech corporation.* Philadelphia: Temple University Press.

Kunda, G., & Barley, S. R. (1988). *Designing devotion: Corporate culture and ideologies of workplace control.* Paper presented at the 83rd Annual Meeting of the American Sociological Association, Washington, DC.

Labov, W., & Fanshel, D. (1977). *Therapeutic discourse.* New York: Academic Press.

Laing, R. D. (1965). *The divided self.* Middlesex, England: Penguin.

Lakatos, I. (1970). Falsification and the methodology of scientific research programmes. In I. Lakatos & A. Musgrave (Eds.), *Criticism and the growth of knowledge* (pp. 91-196). Cambridge: Cambridge University Press.

Lakoff, G., & Johnson, M. (1980). *Metaphors we live by.* Chicago: University of Chicago Press.

Landsberger, H. A. (1958). *Hawthorne revisited: Management and the worker, its critics and developments in human relations in industry.* Ithaca: New York State School of Industrial and Labor Relations.

Latham, G. P., Erez, M., & Locke, E. A. (1988). Resolving scientific disputes by the joint design of crucial experiments by the antagonists: Application to the Erez-Latham dispute regarding participation in goal setting. *Journal of Applied Psychology, 73,* 753-772.

Latham, G. P., & Kinne, S. B., III. (1974). Improving job performance through training in goal setting. *Journal of Applied Psychology, 59,* 187-191.

Latham, G. P., Mitchell, T. R., & Dossett, D. L. (1978). Importance of participative goal setting and anticipated rewards on goal difficulty and job performance. *Journal of Applied Psychology, 63,* 163-171.

Latham, G. P., & Saari, L. M. (1979a). The effects of holding goal difficulty constant on assigned and participatively set goals. *Academy of Management Journal, 22,* 163-168.

Latham, G. P., & Saari, L. M. (1979b). Importance of supportive relationships in goal setting. *Journal of Applied Psychology, 64,* 151-156.

Latham, G. P., & Steele, T. P. (1983). The motivational effects of participation versus goal setting on performance. *Academy of Management Journal, 26,* 406-417.

Latham, G. P., Steele, T. P., & Saari, L. M. (1982). The effects of participation and goal difficulty on performance. *Personnel Psychology, 35,* 677-686.

Latham, G. P., & Yukl, G. A. (1975). Assigned versus participative goal setting with educated and uneducated woods workers. *Journal of Applied Psychology, 60,* 299-302.

Latham, G. P., & Yukl, G. A. (1976). Effects of assigned and participative goal setting on performance and job satisfaction. *Journal of Applied Psychology, 61,* 166-171.

Latour, B., & Woolgar, S. (1979). *Laboratory life: The social construction of scientific facts.* Beverly Hills, CA: Sage.

Lawler, E. E., III. (1981). *Pay and organization development.* Reading, MA: Addison-Wesley.

Lawrence, P. (1984). *The history of human resource management in American industry.* Paper presented at the annual meeting of the Academy of Management, Boston.

Lefebvre, H. (1970). *The explosion.* New York: Monthly Review Press.

Levinson, D. J. (1978). *The seasons of a man's life.* New York: Alfred A. Knopf.

Levinson, D. J. (1986). A conception of adult development. *American Psychologist, 41,* 3-14.

Lewin, K. (1943). Forces behind food habits and methods of change. *Bulletin of the National Resource Council, 108,* 36-65.

Lewin, K. (1951). *Field theory in social science.* New York: Harper & Row.

Likert, R. (1967). *The human organization: Its management and values.* New York: McGraw-Hill.

Locke, E. A. (1968). Toward a theory of task motivation and incentives. *Organizational Behavior and Human Performance, 3,* 157-189.

Locke, E. A., & Latham, G. P. (1990). *A theory of goal setting and task motivation.* Englewood Cliffs, NJ: Prentice-Hall.

Locke, E. A., & Schweiger, D. M. (1979). Participation in decision-making: One more look. In L. L. Cummings & B. M. Staw (Ed.), *Research in organizational behavior* (Vol. 1, pp. 265-339). Greenwich, CT: JAI.

Lofland, J., & Lofland, L. H. (1984). *Analyzing social settings* (2nd ed.). Belmont, CA: Wadsworth.

Louis, M. R. (1983). Organizations as culture-bearing milieux. In L. R. Pondy, P. J. Frost, G. Morgan, & T. C. Dandridge (Eds.), *Organizational symbolism* (pp. 39-54). Greenwich, CT: JAI.

Lukács, G. (1971a). *History and class consciousness.* Cambridge: MIT Press. (Original work published 1923)

Lukács, G. (1971b). *The theory of the novel.* Cambridge: MIT Press. (Original work published 1962)

Lynd, R. S. (1939). *Knowledge for what?* Princeton, NJ: Princeton University Press.

Lyotard, J. F. (1984). *The postmodern condition.* Minneapolis: University of Minnesota Press.

Mann, M. (1973). *Consciousness and action among the Western working class.* London: Macmillan.

Manning, P. K. (1979). Metaphors of the field: Varieties of organizational discourse. *Administrative Science Quarterly, 24,* 660-671.

March, J. G. (1976). The technology of foolishness. In J. G. March & J. P. Olsen, *Ambiguity and choice in organizations* (pp. 69-81). Bergen, Norway: Universitetsforlaget.

Marcus, G. E., & Fischer, M. M. J. (1986). *Anthropology as cultural critique.* Chicago: University of Chicago Press.

Mars, G., & Nicod, M. (1984). *The world of waiters.* London: George Allen & Unwin.

Martin, J. (1981). Relative deprivation: A theory of distributive justice for an era of shrinking resources. In L. L. Cummings & B. M. Staw (Eds.), *Research in organizational behavior* (Vol. 3). Greenwich, CT: JAI.

Marx, K. (1964). *The economic and philosophical manuscripts of 1844.* New York: International. (Original work published 1932)

Matza, D., & Wellman, D. (1980). The ordeal of consciousness. *Theory and Society, 9,* 1-28.

McCall, M. W., Jr., & Lombardo, M. M. (1978). *Leadership: Where else can we go?* Durham, NC: Duke University Press.

McGrath, J. E. (1986). Studying groups at work: Ten critical needs for theory and practice. In P. S. Goodman & Associates (Eds.), *Designing effective work groups* (pp. 363-392). San Francisco: Jossey-Bass.

McGuire, W. J. (1980). The development of theory in social psychology. In R. Gilmour & S. Duck (Eds.), *The development of social psychology.* New York: Academic Press.

McGuire, W. J. (1983). A contextualist theory of knowledge: Its implications for innovation and reform in psychological research. In L. Berkowitz (Ed.), *Advances in experimental social psychology* (Vol. 16). New York: Academic Press.

Meyer, A. D. (1977). *Hospital strategy, structure and process: The role of managerial perception and choice.* Unpublished doctoral dissertation, University of California, Berkeley.

Meyer, A. D. (1982). Adapting to environmental jolts. *Administrative Science Quarterly, 27,* 515-537.

Meyer, J. W., & Rowan, B. (1977). Institutionalized organizations: Formal structure as myth and ceremony. *American Journal of Sociology, 83,* 340-363.

Miles, M. B. (1979). Qualitative data as an attractive nuisance: The problem of analysis. *Administrative Science Quarterly, 24,* 590-601.

Mills, C. W. (1959). *The sociological imagination.* Oxford: Oxford University Press.

Mirvis, P., & Berg, P. (1977). *Failures in organizational development.* New York: John Wiley.

Morgan, G. (Ed.). (1983). *Beyond method.* Beverly Hills, CA: Sage.

Morgan, G. (1984). Opportunities arising from paradigm diversity. *Administration and Society, 16,* 306-327.

Morgan, G., & Smircich, L. (1980). The case for qualitative research. *Academy of Management Review, 5,* 491-500.

Myrdal, G. (1969). *Objectivity in social research.* New York: Pantheon.

National Industrial Conference Board. (1947). *Personnel practices in factory and office* (Studies in Personnel Policy, No. 86). New York: Author.

Nord, W. (1977). A Marxist critique of humanistic psychology. *Journal of Humanistic Psychology, 17,* 75-83.

Normann, R. (1971). Organizational innovativeness: Product variation and reorientation. *Administrative Science Quarterly, 16,* 203-215.

Ouchi, W. G. (1981). *Theory Z.* Reading, MA: Addison-Wesley.

Parasuraman, A., Zeithamal, V. A., & Berry, L. L. (1985). A conceptual model of service quality and its implications for future research. *Journal of Marketing, 49,* 41-50.

Parks, D. S. (1936). 1936 personnel trends. *Factory Management and Maintenance, 12,* 39.

Parsons, T. (1951). *The social system.* New York: Free Press.

Perrow, C. (1985). Journaling careers. In L. L. Cummings & P. J. Frost (Eds.), *Publishing in the organizational sciences.* Homewood, IL: Irwin.

Peters, T. J., & Austin, N. (1985). *A passion for excellence.* New York: Random House.

Peters, T. J., & Waterman, R. H., Jr. (1982). *In search of excellence.* New York: Harper & Row.

Pettigrew, A. M. (1979). On studying organizational cultures. *Administrative Science Quarterly, 24,* 570-581.

Pettigrew, A. M. (1985). *The awakening giant: Continuity and change in ICI.* Oxford: Basil Blackwell.

Pfeffer, J. (1981). Management as symbolic action: The creation and maintenance of organizational paradigms. In L. L. Cummings & B. M. Staw (Eds.), *Research in organizational behavior* (Vol. 3, pp. 1-52). Greenwich, CT: JAI.

Pfeffer, J., & Baron, J. N. (1988). Taking the workers back out: Recent trends in the structuring of employment. In B. M. Staw & L. L. Cummings (Eds.), *Research in organizational behavior* (Vol. 10, pp. 257-303). Greenwich, CT: JAI.

Pfeffer, J., & Cohen, Y. (1984). Determinants of internal labor markets in organizations. *Administrative Science Quarterly, 29,* 550-573.

Pfeffer, J., & Salancik, G. (1978). *The external control of organizations.* New York: Harper & Row.

Pierce School of Business Administration. (1935). *Current personnel practices.* Philadelphia: Author.

Podsakoff, P. M., & Dalton, D. R. (1987). Research methodology in organizational studies. *Journal of Management, 13,* 419-441.

Pondy, L. R., & Boje, D. (1975, August). *Bringing mind back in: Paradigm development as a frontier problem in organization theory.* Paper presented at the annual meeting of the American Sociological Association, San Francisco.

Pondy, L. R., & Mitroff, I. I. (1979). Open system models of organization. In L. L. Cummings & B. M. Staw (Eds.), *Research in organizational behavior* (Vol. 1, pp. 3-39). Greenwich, CT: JAI.

Poole, M. S. (1981). Decision development in small groups I: A comparison of two models. *Communication Monographs, 48,* 1-24.

Poole, R. (1972). *Towards deep subjectivity.* New York: Harper Torchbooks.

Porter, L., & McKibben, L. (1988). *Management education and development: Drift or thrust into the 21st century.* New York: McGraw-Hill.

Pugh, D. S., Hickson, D. J., Hinings, C., & Turner, C. (1968). Dimensions of organization structure. *Administrative Science Quarterly, 13,* 33-47.

Rafaeli, A. (1989). The customers' role in service employees role set: An analysis of the role of supermarket cashiers. *Academy of Management Journal, 34,* 245-273.

Rafaeli, A., & Sutton, R. I. (1987). The expression of emotion as part of the work role. *Academy of Management Review, 12,* 23-37.

Rafaeli, A., & Sutton, R. I. (1989). The expression of emotion in organizational life. In L. L. Cummings & B. M. Staw (Eds.), *Research in organizational behavior* (Vol. 11, pp. 1-42). Greenwich, CT: JAI.

Richman, T. (1984). A tale of two companies. *Inc., 6*(7), 38-43.

Ronan, W. W., Latham, G. P., & Kinne, S. B. (1973). Effects of goal setting and supervision on worker behavior in an industrial situation. *Journal of Applied Psychology, 58,* 302-307.

Rosen, M. (1985). Breakfast at Spiro's: Dramaturgy and dominance. *Journal of Management, 11*(2), 31-48.

Rubery, J. (1978). Structured labor markets, worker organization and low pay. *Cambridge Journal of Economics, 2,* 17-36.

Runciman, W. G. (1966). *Relative deprivation and social justice: A study of attitudes to social inequality in twentieth century England.* Berkeley: University of California Press.

Salaman, G. (1979). *Work organizations: Resistance and control.* London: Longman.

Salancik, G. R. (1979). Field stimulations for organizational behavior research. *Administrative Science Quarterly, 24,* 638-649.

Sartre, J. P. (1966). *What is literature?* New York: Washington Square. (Original work published 1949)

Sartre, J. P. (1974). *Between existentialism and Marxism.* New York: Pantheon. (Original work published 1972)

Schein, E. (1981). Does Japanese management style have a message for American managers? *Sloan Management Review, 22,* 42-52.

Schmidt, F. L., Hunter, J. E., Pearlman, K., & Hirsh, H. R. (1985). Forty questions about validity generalization and meta analysis (with commentary by P. R. Sackett, N. Schmitt, M. L. Tenopyr, J. Kehoe, & S. Zedeck). *Personnel Psychology, 38,* 697-798.

Schneider, B. (1985). Some propositions about getting research published. In L. L. Cummings & P. J. Frost (Eds.), *Publishing in the organizational sciences.* Homewood, IL: Irwin.

Scholte, B. (1987). The literary turn in contemporary anthropology. *Critique of Anthropology, 7,* 33-47.

Schwab, D. (1980). Construct validity in organizational behavior. In L. L. Cummings & B. M. Staw (Eds.), *Research in organizational behavior* (Vol. 2, pp. 3-43). Greenwich, CT: JAI.

Sechrest, L., & Phillips, M. (1979). Unobtrusive measures: An overview. In L. Sechrest (Ed.), *New directions for methodology of behavioral science.* San Francisco: Jossey-Bass.

Seeger, J. A. (1983). No innate phases in group problem solving. *Academy of Management Review, 8*, 683-689.

Simon, H. A. (1969). The architecture of complexity. In H. A. Simon (Ed.), *The sciences of the artificial* (pp. 84-118). Cambridge: MIT Press.

Sims, N. (Ed.). (1984). *The literary journalists.* New York: Ballantine.

Sjoberg, G. (Ed.). (1989). Autobiography, social research, and the organizational context [Special issue]. *Journal of Applied Behavioral Science, 25*(4).

Skinner, B. F. (1953). *Science and human behavior.* New York: Macmillan.

Slichter, S. (1919). *The turnover of factory labor.* New York: Appleton.

Smircich, L. (1983). Concepts of culture and organizational analysis. *Administrative Science Quarterly, 28*, 339-358.

Smircich, L., & Calás, M. B. (1987). Organizational culture: A critical assessment. In F. M. Jablin, L. L. Putnam, K. H. Roberts, & L. W. Porter (Eds.), *Handbook of organizational communication* (pp. 228-263). Newbury Park, CA: Sage.

Spencer, N. J., Harnett, J., & Mahoney, J. (1986). Problems with reviews in the standard editorial practice. *Journal of Social Behavior and Personality, 1*, 21-36.

Spradley, J. P. (1980). *Participant observation.* New York: Holt, Rinehart & Winston.

Steiber, J. (1959). *The steel industry wage structure.* Cambridge, MA: Harvard University Press.

Starbuck, W. H. (1976). Organizations and their environments. In M. D. Dunnette (Ed.), *Handbook of industrial and organizational psychology* (pp. 1069-1123). Chicago: Rand McNally.

Starbuck, W. H. (1982). Congealing oil: Inventing ideologies to justify acting ideologies out. *Journal of Management Studies, 18*, 3-27.

Starbuck, W. H., Greve, A., & Hedberg, B. L. T. (1978). Responding to crises. *Journal of Business Administration, 9*, 111-137.

Starbuck, W. H., & Nystrom, P. C. (1981). Designing and understanding organizations. In P. C. Nystrom & W. H. Starbuck (Eds.), *Handbook of organizational design* (Vol. 1, pp. ix-xxii). New York: Oxford University Press.

Staw, B. M. (1981). The escalation of commitment to a course of action. *Academy of Management Review, 30*, 431-450.

Staw, B. M., & Boettger, R. D. (1990). Task revision: A neglected form of work performance. *Academy of Management Journal, 33*, 534-559.

Staw, B. M., Sandelands, L. E., & Dutton, J. E. (1981). Threat-rigidity effects in organizational behavior: A multilevel analysis. *Administrative Science Quarterly, 26*, 501-524.

Stinchcombe, A. (1965). Social structure and organizations. In J. G. March (Ed.), *Handbook of organizations* (pp. 142-193). Chicago: Rand McNally.

Stone, K. (1974). The origins of job structures in the steel industry. *Review of Radical Political Economy, 6*, 61-97.

Strang, D., & Baron, J. N. (1990). Categorical imperatives: The structure of job titles in California state agencies. *American Sociological Review, 55*, 479-495.

Susman, G. I., & Evered, R. D. (1978). An assessment of the scientific merits of action research. *Administrative Science Quarterly, 23*, 582-602.

Sutton, R. I., & Rafaeli, A. (1988). Untangling the relationship between displayed emotions and organizational sales: The case of convenience stores. *Academy of Management Journal, 31*, 461-487.

Taylor, F. (1911). *Principles of scientific management.* New York: W. W. Norton.

Thomas, K. W., & Tymon, W. G., Jr. (1980, August). *Recent criticisms of organizational science research: A shift in the dialectic between practice and science?* Paper presented at the annual meetings of the Academy of Management, Detroit.

Thompson, J. D. (1956). On building an administrative science. *Administrative Science Quarterly, 1,* 102-111.

Thompson, J. D. (1967). *Organizations in action.* New York: McGraw-Hill.

Thompson, J. D., & McEwen, W. (1958). Organizational goals and environment: Goal-setting as an interaction process. *American Sociological Review, 23,* 23-31.

Timmons, B. F. (1931). *Personnel practices among Ohio industries.* Columbus: Ohio State University Press.

Tolbert, P. S., & Zucker, L. G. (1983). Institutional sources of change in the formal structure of organizations: The diffusion of civil service reform, 1880-1935. *Administrative Science Quarterly, 28,* 22-39.

Tompkins, J. (Ed.). (1980). *Reader-response criticism.* Baltimore: Johns Hopkins University Press.

Tuckman, B. (1965). Developmental sequence in small groups. *Psychological Bulletin, 63,* 384-399.

Tuckman, B., & Jensen, M. (1977). Stages of small-group development. *Group and Organization Studies, 2,* 419-427.

Tuma, N. (Ed.). (1989). *Feminism and science.* Bloomington: Indiana University Press.

Tyler, S., & Nathan, J. (1985). *In search of excellence* [film]. New York: Public Broadcasting System.

U.S. Bureau of the Census. (1975). *Historical statistics of the United States: Colonial times to 1970.* Washington, DC: Government Printing Office.

U.S. Bureau of Labor Statistics. (1940-1945, 1947). *Monthly labor review.* Washington, DC: Government Printing Office.

U.S. Bureau of Labor Statistics. (1949). *Occupational outlook handbook* (Bulletin No. 940). Washington, DC: Government Printing Office.

Van Maanen, J. (1975). Police socialization. *Administrative Science Quarterly, 20,* 207-228.

Van Maanen, J. (1979a). The fact of fiction in organizational ethnography. *Administrative Science Quarterly, 24,* 539-550.

Van Maanen, J. (Ed.). (1979b). Qualitative methodology [Special issue]. *Administrative Science Quarterly, 24.*

Van Maanen, J. (1988). *Tales of the field: On writing ethnography.* Chicago: University of Chicago Press.

Van Maanen, J., & Kunda, G. (1989). "Real feelings": Emotional expression and organizational culture. In L. L. Cummings & B. M. Staw (Eds.), *Research in organizational behavior* (Vol. 11, pp. 43-104). Greenwich, CT: JAI.

Vroom, V. H., & Yetton, P. W. (1973). *Leadership and decision-making.* Pittsburgh, PA: University of Pittsburgh Press.

Waldo, D. (1968). *The novelist on organization and administration: An inquiry into the relationship between two worlds.* Berkeley, CA: Institute of Governmental Studies.

Walster, E., Walster, G. W., & Berscheid, E. (1978). *Equity: Theory and research.* Boston: Allyn & Bacon.

Walters, J. E. (1945). What war industries have learned about personnel administration. *Personnel Administration, 7*(6), 9-12.

Wassenberg, A. (1977). The powerlessness of organisation theory. In S. Clegg & D. Dunkerley (Eds.), *Critical issues in organisations* (pp. 86-98). London: Routledge & Kegan Paul.

Watson, A. (1980). *Sociology, work, and industry.* London: Routledge & Kegan Paul.

Webb, E. J., Campbell, D. T., Schwartz, D. S., Sechrest, L., & Grove, G. B. (1981). *Nonreactive measures in the social sciences.* Boston: Houghton Mifflin.

Weber, M. (1946). *Essays in sociology.* New York: Oxford University Press.

Webster, J., & Starbuck, W. H. (1988). Theory building in industrial and organizational psychology. In C. L. Cooper & I. Robertson (Eds.), *International review of industrial and organizational psychology*. New York: Wiley.

Weick, K. E. (1969). *The social psychology of organizing*. Reading, MA: Addison-Wesley.

Weick, K. E. (1976). Educational organizations as loosely coupled systems. *Administrative Science Quarterly, 21*, 1-19.

Weick, K. E. (1977). Enactment processes in organizations. In B. M. Staw & G. R. Salancik (Eds.), *New directions in organizational behavior* (pp. 267-300). Chicago: St. Clair.

Weick, K. E. (1979). *The social psychology of organizing* (2nd ed.). Reading, MA: Addison-Wesley.

Weick, K. E. (1984). Small wins. *American Psychologist, 39*, 40-49.

Weick, K. E. (1985). Systematic observational methods. In G. Lindzey & E. Aronson (Eds.), *Handbook of social psychology* (Vol. 1, 3rd ed., pp. 567-634). Reading, MA: Addison-Wesley.

Weick, K. E. (1989). Theory construction as disciplined imagination. *Academy of Management Review, 14*, 516-531.

Weiss, R. S. (1968). Issues in holistic research. In H. S. Becker, B. Greer, D. Riesman, & R. Weiss (Eds.), *Institutions and the person* (pp. 342-350). Chicago: Aldine.

Wildavsky, A. (1989). *Craftways: On the organization of scholarly work*. New Brunswick, NJ: Transaction.

Williams, R. (1977). *Marxism and literature*. Oxford: Oxford University Press.

Williamson, O. E. (1975). *Markets and hierarchies: Analysis and antitrust implications*. New York: Free Press.

Woodward, J. (1964). *Industrial organisation, theory and practice*. London: Oxford University Press.

Yukl, G. P., & Latham, G. P. (1978). Interrelationships among employee participation, individual differences, goal difficulty, goal acceptance, goal instrumentality, and performance. *Personnel Psychology, 31*, 305-324.

Zald, M. N. (1988). *Sociology as a discipline: Quasi-science and quasi-humanities*. CSST Working Paper No. 12/CRSO Working Paper No. 369, University of Michigan, Department of Sociology.

Zald, M. N. (1989). *Organizational studies as a scientific and humanistic enterprise: Notes on the reconceptualization of the foundation of the field*. CRSO Working Paper No. 406.

About the Authors

Stephen R. Barley is an Associate Professor of Organizational Behavior at Cornell University's School of Industrial and Labor Relations. He received his Ph.D. in organization studies from the Massachusetts Institute of Technology in 1984. His research has focused on the implications of microelectronic technologies for the social organization of work, the commercialization of biotechnology in the United States, and organizational culture. His papers have appeared in the *Administrative Science Quarterly, Organization Science,* and a number of other journals and edited books. With Pamela Tolbert, he has recently edited a special volume of *Research in the Sociology of Organizations* on professions and organizations.

James N. Baron is Professor of Organizational Behavior and Business School Trust Faculty Fellow for 1990-1991 in the Graduate School of Business and Professor of Sociology at Stanford University. He is currently conducting research in the areas of complex organization, economic sociology, and socioeconomic inequality.

Janice M. Beyer is Rebecca L. Gale Regents Professor in Business at the University of Texas in Austin. She is currently President of the Academy of Management and President-Elect of the International Federation of Scholarly Associations in Management. She has also served as Editor of the *Academy of Management Journal,* as a member of the Board of Governors of the Eastern Academy of Management, as a member of the Executive Council of the Society for the Advancement of Socio-Economics, and on the editorial boards of the *Administrative Science Quarterly* and the *Journal of Socio-Economics.* Her recent research has focused on ideologies, the cultures of organizations, work-family issues, and professional issues in the study of management and organizations.

John P. Campbell is Professor of Psychology and Industrial Relations and Director of the Industrial and Organizational Psychology Graduate Program at the University of Minnesota. He was Associate Editor and Editor of the *Journal of Applied Psychology* from 1973 to 1982 and served as President of the Division of Industrial and Organizational Psychology of the American Psychological Association in 1977-1978. His research has covered a broad spectrum of issues in training, personnel selection, and performance assessment. In 1991 he received the Distinguished Scientific Contribution Award from the Society of Industrial and Organizational Psychology.

Larry L. Cummings is the Carlson Professor of Strategic Management and Organization at the Carlson School of Management, University of Minnesota. He is the author or coauthor of more than 100 articles and author of 13 books. He has served as Editor of the *Academy of Management Journal* and as President of the Academy of Management. He is a Fellow of the American Psychological Association and the Institute of Decision Sciences, and currently serves as Dean of the Fellows of the Academy of Management.

Frank R. Dobbin is Assistant Professor of Sociology at Princeton. His work focuses on the historical rise of organizational practices and of government strategies for industrial growth. He is currently finishing a book on the development of American, French, and British public policies for promoting railways. His other projects include an analysis of the effects of state policy on foundings and failures among early American railroads, and a collaborative study of public policy and postwar changes in organizational personnel practices.

P. Christopher Earley is an Associate Professor of Strategic Management and Organization in the Carlson School of Management at the University of Minnesota. His Ph.D. in social and organizational psychology is from the University of Illinois. He has published more than 25 articles in the best scholarly journals in his field. He is a member of the Society of Organizational Behavior and recently completed a year as a Fulbright Research Scholar in Israel.

Cathy A. Enz, Ph.D. (Ohio State University), is an Associate Professor of Management, Cornell University School of Hotel Administration. She is the author of *Power and Shared Values in the Corporate Culture* and numerous articles and book chapters on value sharing, organizational culture, and influence. She is currently on the editorial review boards of the *Journal of Managerial Issues, International Journal of Value-Based Management,* and the *Journal of Management Education.* She has served on the Board of Directors of the Organizational Behavior Teaching Society and the Executive Committee of the Midwest Academy of Management.

Miriam Erez is an Associate Professor and Head of the Area of Behavioral Sciences, Faculty of Industrial Engineering and Management, Technion—Israel Institute of Technology. She is a Fellow of the American Psychological Association and serves on the editorial boards of the *Journal of Applied Psychology, Organizational Behavior and Human Decision Processes,* and *Applied Psychology: An International Review.* Her main research and applied work is in the field of work motivation. She has published numerous studies on the motivational effects of feedback, goals, commitment, and participation in goal setting. Recently, she has expanded her research interest to the area of the moderating effect of culture on the effectiveness of motivational techniques.

Peter J. Frost holds the Edgar F. Kaiser, Jr., Chair in Organizational Behavior at the University of British Columbia. He has published several books in collaboration with other scholars. His recent publications include *Reframing Organizational Culture* (Sage, 1991), with Larry Moore, Meryl Louis, Craig Lundberg, and Joanne Martin; *Management Live: The Video Book* (Prentice-Hall, 1991), with Bob Marx and Todd Jick; and a fourth edition of *Organizational Reality: Reports from the Firing Line* (Harper Collins, in press), with Vance Mitchell and Walter Nord. His current research interests and publications focus on innovation and organizational politics, shamanism, and environmental issues. He received his Ph.D. from the University of Minnesota in 1973. He is an editor of *Organizational Science* and Executive Director of the Organizational Behavior Teaching Society. He is an avid movie fan and an enthusiastic birder.

Debra C. Gash received her M.S. and Ph.D. degrees in organizational behavior from the New York State School of Industrial Relations at Cornell University. From 1987 through 1990 she was on the faculty of the School of Labor and Industrial Relations at Michigan State University. Her research has focused on issues of shared cognitions in organizations, perceptions of time, and a variety of topics around information technology in organizations, including end-user training, changing roles and skills of information systems professionals, and implementation and organization change. She is currently consulting on large-scale organizational change and information technology projects in the federal sector, through the Volpe National Transportation Systems Center in Cambridge, Massachusetts.

Connie J. G. Gersick is Assistant Professor at the Graduate School of Management at the University of California, Los Angeles. She has been interested in social change since high school, and was Director of Yale's Office on the Education of Women before earning her Ph.D. in organizational behavior there. "Time and Transition in Work Teams," her first publication, won the 1988 award for outstanding contribution to organizational behavior from the OB Division of the Academy of Management. Her subsequent laboratory study of project groups was named Best Paper of 1989 in the *Academy of Management Journal*. She has continued exploring change in human systems through research on theories of punctuated equilibrium, start-up companies, and athletic teams.

J. Richard Hackman is the Cahners-Rabb Professor of Social and Organizational Psychology at Harvard University. He received his undergraduate degree in mathematics from MacMurray College in 1962, and his doctorate in social psychology from the University of Illinois in 1966. He taught at Yale until 1986, when he moved to Harvard. He conducts research on a variety of topics in social psychology and organizational behavior, including the performance of work teams, social influences on individual behavior, and the design and leadership of self-managing units in organizations. He is the author or editor of six books and more than 50 chapters and articles. His most recent book is *Groups That Work* (Jossey-Bass, 1989).

P. Devereaux Jennings is now an Assistant Professor of Organizational Behavior at the University of British Columbia, a job that he loves. At UBC he has been able to continue his research on the evolution of personnel and a very separate line of study focusing on the impact of ownership and control on corporate behavior. Some of this work is still being done with former coauthors, but he has found new intellectual companions in Canada. He finds his students especially to be a great source of stimulation and challenge. Through all, his approach has remained the same: Political processes precede and drive institutionalization.

John M. Jermier is Professor of Organizational Behavior in the College of Business, University of South Florida. Much of his work has been focused on the development of a critical science of organizations, with a particular interest in research philosophy and methodology.

Gary P. Latham is the Secretary of State Professor of Organization Effectiveness at the University of Toronto. In addition, he is a Fellow in the American Psychological Association, the Canadian Psychological Association, and the Academy of Management. For a quarter of a century, he has been actively engaged in field and laboratory experiments on the motivational effects of goal setting. This work has been summarized in a recent book he coauthored with Ed Locke, *A Theory of Goal Setting and Task Performance* (Prentice-Hall, 1990). In 1989 his research with Drs. Miriam Erez and Edwin Locke, discussed in the present book, received an award as the most outstanding paper from the Organization Behavior Division of the Academy of Management. He consults widely in industry and teaches in executive programs in North America and abroad.

Edwin A. Locke is Chairman of the Faculty of Management and Organization at the University of Maryland, College Park. He is a Fellow of the American Psychological Association, the American Psychological Society, and the Academy of Management. He is internationally known for his research on work motivation and goal setting. He has published widely in professional journals and is the author of numerous books, including *A Theory of Goal Setting and Task Performance*, with W. G. Latham (Prentice-Hall, 1990).

Joanne Martin is Professor of Organizational Behavior in the Graduate School of Business, and (by courtesy) in the Sociology Department at Stanford University. She has published extensively in two fields of interest: economic injustice and organizational culture. More recently, she has begun to examine the dynamics of sexism and racism in organizational theory.

Alan D. Meyer is Associate Professor of Management at the University of Oregon. His research interests lie in the areas of organization design, strategy, innovation, and change. He likes using multiple methods and collecting data by talking with informants in their own language, on their own turf. Currently, he is interviewing CEOs in a longitudinal study of organizations' responses to quantum changes in the structure and boundaries of their industries. He received his B.A. in economics from the University of Washington, and his doctorate in organizational behavior and industrial relations from the University of California,

Berkeley. He serves as an Editorial Board Member of *Administrative Science Quarterly*, and as Consulting Editor of the *Academy of Management Journal*.

Gordon W. Meyer is an Assistant Professor of Management at Bucknell University in Lewisburg, Pennsylvania. His professional experiences include employment both as a teacher/scholar and as an internal quality of work life consultant. His published works include critical pieces on organizational development interventions and the work described in this volume. His current research interests include the application of social network analysis to the study of organizational structure and culture, experiential approaches to management education at the undergraduate level, metaphors for alternative organizational change approaches, and ethnographic approaches to understanding the use of measures in organizations. He holds graduate degrees from Brigham Young and Cornell universities.

Richard T. Mowday is the Gerald B. Bashaw Professor of Management at the University of Oregon. Active within the Academy of Management, he has served as Editor of the *Academy of Management Journal*, as Chairperson of the Organizational Behavior Division, and as a member of the Board of Governors. His primary research interests have been in the areas of employee commitment to organizations and employee turnover, particularly during the early employment period.

Walter W. Powell is Professor of Sociology at the University of Arizona. He has also been a member of the faculty at MIT and at Yale University. He received his Ph.D. (1978) in sociology from the State University of New York at Stony Brook. He is coeditor of *The New Institutionalism in Organizational Analysis*, editor of and contributor to *The Non-Profit Sector: A Research Handbook* (1967), author of *Getting into Print: The Decision Making Process in Scholarly Publishing* (1985), and coauthor of *Books: The Culture and Commerce of Publishing*, with L. A. Coser and C. Kadushin (1982).

Linda L. Putnam is Professor in the Department of Communication at Purdue University. She is the past Chair of the Organizational Communication Divisions of the Speech Communication Association and the International Communication Association. She is currently Chair of the Power, Negotiation and Conflict Management Interest Group of the Academy of Management Association. She has been involved in field research on teachers' negotiations and on the use of symbols in organizational communication. She has a particular interest in the use of rituals, narratives, and paradoxes in forms of organizational communication. She has edited several volumes in the areas of interpretive approaches to organizational communication, organizational theory, and negotiation.

Anat Rafaeli received her Ph.D in industrial and organizational psychology from the Ohio State University in 1984. She is an Associate Professor at the School of Business Administration at the Hebrew University of Jerusalem. Her primary conceptual interests are in the expression of emotion in organizational life, social influence, the meanings and messages conveyed through organizational dress, and the special dynamics of service occupations. Her primary methodological interest is in developing quantitative and qualitative approaches for making firsthand observations of organizational behavior. Her recent articles include "Emotional Contrast Strategies as Means of Social Influence: Lessons from Criminal Interrogators and Bill Collectors," with Robert I. Sutton (*Academy of Management Journal*, 1991) and "When Cashiers Meet Customers: An Analysis of the Role of Supermarket Cashiers" (*Academy of Management Journal*, 1989).

Linda Smircich received a B.A. in social science from the State University of New York at Oswego, and an M.B.A. and Ph.D. from the School of Management at Syracuse University. She was previously a faculty member at Penn State University and is now a faculty member at the University of Massachusetts at Amherst. In her research and teaching and life she has been exploring the connections among culture, feminism, poststructuralism, postmodernism, and organization and management theory.

Ralph E. Stablein is Senior Lecturer in Organization Theory in the Department of Management of the University of Otago in Dunedin, New Zealand. He received a B.A. in economics and psychology from Illinois Benedictine College, an M.A. in economics from Western Illinois University, and a Ph.D. in organization behavior from Northwestern University. He has published sparingly in social psychology and organizational outlets. He is on the Editorial Board of *Asia Pacific HRM*. His current research involves the theory and practice of organizational research. He is particularly interested in developing the legitimacy of critical studies within the community of organizational scholars.

Barry M. Staw holds the Mitchell Chair in Leadership and Communication at the University of California, Berkeley. He is also the Chairperson of the Organizational and Industrial Relations Group at the Berkeley Business School. He has taught previously at Northwestern University, the University of Illinois, and the University of Iowa. He is coeditor of *Research in Organizational Behavior: An Annual Series of Analytical Essays and Critical Reviews,* and has served on the editorial boards of most of the field's journals, including *Administrative Science Quarterly, Organizational Behavior and Human Performance, Journal of Applied Psychology,* and the *Academy of Management Journal.* Currently, his research focuses on the issues of escalating commitment, job attitudes, and work innovation.

Robert I. Sutton received his Ph.D. degree in organizational psychology from the University of Michigan in 1984. He is Associate Professor of Organizational Behavior in the Department of Industrial Engineering and Engineering Management at Stanford University. He is currently serving as Associate Editor of the *Administrative Science Quarterly.* His primary research interests include organizational decline and death and the role of emotion in organizational life. His other interests include impression management, institutional theory, and job stress. He uses a blend of quantitative and qualitative methods to study these topics. He has published in *Academy of Management Journal, Academy of Management Review, Administrative Science Quarterly, Human Relations,* and *Research in Organizational Behavior.*

Pamela S. Tolbert is an Associate Professor in the School of Industrial Relations at Cornell University. She received her Ph.D. in sociology from the University of California at Los Angeles, where she began her research on the institutional sources of formal organizational structure. She is currently pursuing this interest in a longitudinal study of the effects of selection and adaption on curriculum change among institutions of higher education. Her other research interests include studying the role of organizations in producing social stratification, and the relationship between occupations and organizations as institutions of control.

Karl E. Weick is the Rensis Likert Collegiate Professor of Organizational Behavior and Psychology at the University of Michigan, and also former Editor of *Administrative Science Quarterly.* He studies such topics as how people make sense of confusing events, the effects of stress on thinking and imagination, the consequences of indeterminacy in social systems, and high-reliability organizations.

Mayer N. Zald is Professor of Sociology, Social Work and Business Administration at the University of Michigan. He has published widely on complex organizations, social welfare, and political sociology. Recently he coedited *Social Movements in an Organizational Society: Collected Essays*, with John D. McCarthy (Transaction). Aside from essays on social movements, he is currently engaged in studies of the intersection of sociology as science and humanities. In 1986-1987 he was Vice President of the American Sociological Association. Currently, he serves as Chair of the Department of Sociology.